NetWare 4:
Planning and Implementation

Sunil Padiyar

Michael Day

Michael Koontz

Dan Marshall

NRP
NEW RIDERS
PUBLISHING

New Riders Publishing, Carmel, Indiana

NetWare 4: Planning and Implementation

By Sunil Padiyar, et al

Published by:
New Riders Publishing
11711 N. College Ave., Suite 140
Carmel, IN 46032 USA

Printed in the United States of America 1 2 3 4 5 6 7 8 9 0

Library of Congress Cataloging-in-Publication Data .

```
NetWare 4: Planning and Implementation /Sunil Padiyar...[et al.].
    p. cm.
Includes index.
ISBN 1-56205-159-8
1. Operating systems (Computers) 2. NetWare (Computer file) I. Padiyar,
Sunil, 1960-
QA76.76.063N458   1993                                    93-19563
005.7'1369—dc20                                               CIP
```

Publisher
Lloyd J. Short

Associate Publisher
Tim Huddleston

Acquisitions Manager
Cheri Robinson

Acquisitions Editor
Rob Tidrow

Managing Editor
Matthew Morrill

Marketing Manager
Brad Koch

Product Director
Drew Heywood

Production Editor
Nancy Sixsmith

Editors
Geneil Breeze
Steve Weiss

Book Design and Production
Jodie Cantwell
Christine Cook
Lisa Daugherty
Brook Farling
Dennis Clay Hager
Roger Morgan
Juli Pavey
Amy Peppler-Adams
Angela M. Pozdol
Michelle Self
Alyssa Yesh

Proofreaders
Terri Edwards
Mitzi Gianakos
Howard Jones
Sean Medlock
Donna Winter

Indexed by
Joy Dean Lee
Suzanne Snyder

Acquisitions Coordinator
Stacey Beheler

Editorial Secretary
Karen Opal

Publishing Assistant
Melissa Keegan

About the Authors

Sunil Padiyar is Vice-President of Engineering at Artisoft, Inc., in Tucson, Arizona. He worked at Novell, Inc. (Provo, Utah) until March, 1993. As Director of Software Engineering, Padiyar oversaw the development of the NetWare 4.0 operating system and other state-of-the-art fault-tolerance technologies (such as SFT III). He has been involved with NetWare 4.0 from the very beginning, and has worked with Drew Major, Kyle Powell, and other engineers to define and manage several key technologies of NetWare 4.0.

Michael Day is a documentation engineer for the NetWare 386 development program at Novell, Inc. He works as a programmer and as a technical writer, specializing in network operating systems and network programming. Day has written books on NetWare workstation troubleshooting and LAN Manager troubleshooting, and has published more than 150 articles on networking subjects. He is the former chief technical editor for *LAN Times*.

Michael Koontz is a technical writer for Novell, Inc., specializing in documentation for NetWare 3.x and 4.x. For the past three years, he has been involved in documenting the use of NetWare core OS. Koontz also co-authored a book on NetWare Loadable Module (NLM) programming. He received B.A and M.A. degrees from Brigham Young University.

Daniel Marshall worked as a business applications programmer for five years before joining Novell, Inc. as a programming instructor. He developed and taught NetWare courses for six years before becoming a technical writer. Marshall has co-authored a book on NetWare Loadable Module (NLM) programming. He attended Brigham Young University and the University of Utah, and is a Certified NetWare Engineer (CNE) and a Certified NetWare Instructor (CNI).

Dedication

This book is dedicated to the two most beautiful and wonderful people I know: my wife, Linda, and my daughter, Amita.

Acknowledgments

I offer my thanks to the following:

Drew Heywood, of New Riders Publishing, on whose recommendation I wrote this book. His consistent support and encouragement contributed significantly.

Raymond J. Noorda, CEO of Novell, Inc. I credit him with building the network-computing industry. I am grateful for the experience I gained under his leadership.

Drew Major, genius extraordinaire! Simplicity, performance, and elegance are the hallmarks of NetWare, and he has been a key contributor to this philosophy.

Kyle Powell and Dale Niebaur, members of the superset—the creators of NetWare. Thanks for your continuing efforts to make NetWare a top-notch product.

Kevin Kingdon, the architect of NetWare Directory Services (NDS). Thanks also to Dale Olds, Mark Muhlstein, Layne Izatt, Ranjan Prasad, DeeAnne Higley, Mark Hinckley, and Greg Hundley for taking Kevin's architecture and turning it into a quality commercial product.

Jim Nicolet and Kirk Matheson, who often performed beyond the call of duty to make critical deadlines.

James P. McNeil, Vice-President of Cheyenne Software and my good friend, for his incredible support and faith in me.

Chris Sontag, for his key role in defining and coordinating the development of NetWare 4.0. My good friends, Ty Mattingly and Adam Au, who helped me develop a good operating system. Thanks also to Jared Blazer and Kevin Auger, for providing leadership to the NetWare 4.0 effort.

The following exceptional people who helped throughout the development process of NetWare 4.0: Charles Hatch, Mike Colemere, Steve Jackson, Neil Taylor, Dana Henrikson, Joe Carter, Craig Teerlink, Steve Holbrook, Darren Major, Mike Christensen, Roland Whatcott, Bob Lewis, Jonathan Richey,

Rey Furner, Stuart Newton, Neal Christensen, Doug Hale, Brian Jarvis, Bob Larson, Bart Wise, Del Robins, Phil Karren, Jeff Hawkins, Kirk Kimball, Kent Erickson, and Joyce Gardner.

My wife, Linda, and my daughter, Amita, who stood by my side through the challenge of producing NetWare 4.0 and writing this book at the same time.

Contributing authors Michael Day, Mike Koontz, and Dan Marshall. Their terrific work helped make this book great.

New Riders Publishing also expresses thanks to the following people for their contributions to this book:

Drew Heywood, for developing the project.

Tim Huddleston and Matthew Morrill, for their serenity in the face of adversity.

Nancy Sixsmith, for managing the project and steering it through production.

Editors Geneil Breeze and Steve Weiss, for their careful editing and cheerful demeanors.

Cheri Robinson, Rob Tidrow, and Stacey Beheler, for keeping everyone on-track.

Karen Opal, for editorial assistance whenever needed.

As always, the production staff of PHCP, for working their miracles.

Trademark Acknowledgments

Warning and Disclaimer

Contents at a Glance

Table of Contents

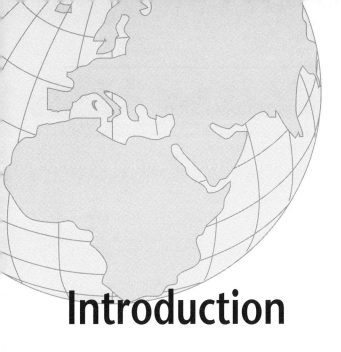

Introduction

Because NetWare met its customers' needs when it was introduced, it literally sold itself. As NetWare conquers new frontiers, however, there is a need for a book such as *NetWare 4: Planning and Implementation* to put NetWare in current perspective.

This book gives you, the reader, a basic understanding of the NetWare 4.0 technology. It also discusses reasons for choosing NetWare and Novell to solve the corporate computing problems of your business, large or small.

Who Should Read This Book?

The topics covered in *NetWare 4: Planning and Implementation* make it appropriate for corporate executives and MIS managers who are evaluating NetWare 4.0 as a platform for their computing needs.

This book answers questions both in terms of business and technology, and has sufficient technical depth for any reader who wants to gain an understanding of the NetWare 4.0 technology.

How This Book Is Organized

Netware 4: Planning and Implementation is divided into four parts. The following is an overview of the book's organization.

Part One: NetWare 4.0 and Corporate Computing

Chapter One, "The Business Perspective," begins the book by giving you a good business perspective on Novell and NetWare.

Chapter Two, "The Evolution of NetWare," is an overview and history of the topic.

Chapter Three, "Understanding NetWare," discusses NetWare, both as a product and as a computing environment.

Part Two: Features of NetWare 4.0

Chapter Four, "NetWare 4.0 Product Features," describes all the features of the NetWare 4.0 operating system. This chapter is a microscopic view of what is covered in this book.

Chapter Five, "Understanding NetWare 4.0 Services in Detail," discusses some key services offered by the NetWare 4.0 operating system, including print and backup services.

Part Three: NetWare 4.0 in Depth

Chapter Six, "NetWare Directory Services," gives an architectural overview of the NetWare 4.0 Directory (NDS) technology.

Chapter Seven, "NetWare 4.0 Security," explains all the security features provided by NetWare 4.0, and describes in particular the security features offered by NDS and those of the NetWare 4.0 file system.

Chapter Eight, "File Systems and Media Management," describes the NetWare 4.0 file system and many of the new features offered, including background file compression and block suballocation. Also discussed is the new media-management feature of NetWare 4.0.

Chapter Nine, "Security Auditing," explains the new auditing technology that is part of NetWare 4.0. The scope and depth of the auditing features are covered, and the chapter draws attention to global auditing that is enabled through NetWare Directory Services.

Chapter Ten, "Global Time Synchronization," discusses in depth the time-synchronization technology offered by NetWare 4.0 that keeps all clocks of all computers in a NetWare network close to the correct network time.

Chapter Eleven, "Communication Services," gives you a detailed overview of the communication technologies under NetWare 4.0, and covers IPX and SPX in detail.

Part Four: Upgrading to NetWare 4.0

Chapter Twelve, "Planning the NetWare 4.0 Network," is perhaps the most important chapter in this book. Planning a network under NetWare 4.0 requires thorough top-down planning, and this chapter gives you important guidelines and suggestions.

Chapter Thirteen, "Installing and Upgrading to NetWare 4.0," walks you through the installation process of NetWare 4.0, and gives concrete suggestions on upgrade considerations from all previous versions of NetWare.

Chapter Fourteen, "Managing NetWare 4.0 for NetWare Administrators," discusses the new utilities provided by NetWare 4.0 under DOS and Windows environments.

Conventions Used in This Book

As you work through this book, you will notice special typeface conventions that show you, at a glance, what actions to take.

❖ All NetWare commands, names of files and directories, and screen messages appear in this `special typeface`.

❖ Information that you type appears in this **`bold, special typeface`**.

❖ All variable elements appear in this *italic typeface*.

This book also uses special icons to help you identify certain parts of the text.

TIP

A **tip** gives you "extra" information that can boost productivity , or provides a shortcut for your tasks.

WARNING

A **warning** serves as a caution to help prevent you from losing data or work.

SOAPBOX

A **soapbox** is a story from the author. It gives you glimpses of the people who built NetWare and visions of the future of the network-computing industry.

New Riders Publishing

The staff of New Riders Publishing is committed to bringing you the very best in computer reference material. Each New Riders book is the result of months of work by authors and staff, who research and refine the information contained within its covers.

As part of this commitment to you, the NRP reader, New Riders invites your input. Please let us know if you enjoy this book, if you have trouble with the information and examples presented, or if you have a suggestion for the next edition.

Please note, however, that the New Riders staff cannot serve as a technical resource for NetWare/NetWare-related questions, including hardware- or software-related problems. Refer to the Novell documentation for help with specific problems.

If you have a question or comment about any New Riders book, please write to NRP at the following address. We will respond to as many readers as we can. Your name, address, or phone number will never become part of a mailing list or be used for any other purpose than to help us continue to bring you the best books possible.

> New Riders Publishing
> Paramount Publishing
> Attn: Associate Publisher
> 11711 N. College Avenue
> Carmel, IN 46032

If you prefer, you can send a FAX to New Riders Publishing at the following number:

> (317) 571-3484

We welcome your electronic mail to our CompuServe ID:

> 70031,2231

Thank you for selecting *NetWare 4: Planning and Implementation*!

NetWare 4.0 and Corporate Computing

The Business Perspective

The Evolution of NetWare

Understanding NetWare

The Business Perspective

Not long ago, computer users looked to mainframe and minicomputers to run business applications. The customer need at that time (as well as today) was for reliable platforms to run mission-critical applications that had high-volume data-storage needs and transaction output.

Other requirements were that the platform be easy to manage and provide a comfortable level of security. Mainframes and minicomputers were clearly the answer for that era, and many large computer companies, such as IBM and DEC, made their fortunes selling high-cost, proprietary computer systems to the user community.

Companies had to structure themselves in an appropriate organizational fashion to accommodate their computing needs. They needed experts in white coats to run their computers. This gave way to the creation of the *MIS (Management Information Systems)* function in the organization. The charter given to the MIS was to provide both for the organization's current computing needs and for those in the future. Because mainframes and minis were built to be managed centrally, the MIS department, which administered these "dinosaurs," came to be the sole provider of any computing need of the user community.

Understanding Today's Computing Needs

Much has changed since the days of mainframes and minis. Today, the choices for computing range from super-fast PCs to high-end RISC (Reduced Instruction Set Computing) workstations and servers that are capable of hosting almost any kind of mission-critical application. These small machines have enough bandwidth to provide almost unlimited data-storage capacity and high transaction output.

Most important, these machines are affordable, and they provide such robust application development tools that hundreds of thousands of off-the-shelf applications are available to run on them. These factors make these computers an irresistible choice for any organization's computing needs.

The market for these low-cost computers is twofold. First is the workstation market (occupied by Sun, Hewlett-Packard, and others), which provides high-end computing workstations based on the RISC architecture. This segment of the market caters to the scientific community and to the business needs of many Fortune 1000 organizations.

The second segment of the market is the PC market, which specializes in computers built with Intel microprocessors. Intel produces popular micro-processors, such as the 80386, that operate on an instruction set architecture called *CISC (Complex Instruction Set Computing)*.

TIP

Because a CISC instruction takes longer to execute than a RISC instruction does, a RISC computer actually can execute faster than a CISC computer for many activities.

Personal Computer Market

The explosive growth of the PC market can be attributed to one factor: the availability of similar hardware from many vendors. Intense competition in this market has driven prices down so that PCs are affordable to the smallest businesses and homes.

Hundreds of thousands of software packages are available that provide services ranging from filing an income tax return to performing sophisti-cated business-inventory management. In this segment of the market, some of the world's largest computer software companies operate (for example, Microsoft, Novell, Lotus, and Borland). Each company gained fame and fortune by capitalizing on the vast availability and affordability of these computers and by providing superior services to users through state-of-the-art software solutions.

Of these companies, Microsoft may be the most dominant. It provides operating systems, development tools, applications, and miscellaneous software services. Novell provides the networking software that links these computers together. In other words, Microsoft dominates the "desktop" marketplace by providing superior application services: Novell dominates the "server" marketplace, in which these applications are hosted and administered by system administrators. These two companies now are fighting intense battles to capture a piece of the other's market.

TIP

This book is written in the context of the server segment of the market. Although the server segment appears to be a small piece of the overall pie, it is, in reality, a large market.

In the last few years, the behemoth computer companies of the 1960s and 1970s have fallen. For example, IBM's market value has fallen by more than half, while Microsoft's market value more than doubled. At the time of this printing, Microsoft is worth nearly $30 billion; Novell is worth $10 billion. At this rate, Microsoft may soon outdo IBM in terms of market value.

Software and other services provided by Microsoft and Novell are no longer relegated to the back seat as they were when PCs were considered a nuisance, and mainframes and minis were dominant. The limitations of the PC in the areas of their networkability, manageability, capacity for high-volume data storage and transaction throughput, and fault tolerance are now being addressed.

High-speed networks (*LANs*, or *local area networks*) of PCs that host mission-critical applications and provide for the needs of the largest companies are a clear possibility. As a matter of fact, many medium to large businesses use PCs connected in LANS to provide all computing needs for their companies.

Advantages of NetWare 4.0

With the advent of Novell's NetWare 4.0, a new era has dawned in network computing. This product promises to reduce the cost of computing, improve capacity, and provide high-volume data storage and retrieval. It offers high-transaction throughput, fault tolerance to run mission-critical applications, better application development tools, better user interfaces and connectivity methods, direct responses to end-user demands, smooth administration of large and complicated networks, and more easily managed applications. NetWare 4.0's scope is so vast that it almost seems unrealistic. Almost every convenience that is available with a mainframe or minicomputer is provided by NetWare 4.0, along with a host of other features that users and administrators have come to love about PC networks.

This book helps you understand both the business and technology implications of NetWare 4.0, and provides helpful suggestions and guidelines for using NetWare 4.0 accounting for migration, coexistence, upgrade, and backward-compatibility. You get insight about why some things are the way they are in NetWare 4.0, and you learn what Novell can do in the future to improve its NetWare technology.

The rest of this chapter discusses Novell and NetWare. It introduces you to Raymond J. Noorda, the father of the network computing industry, who built a multibillion dollar industry and a multibillion dollar company from scratch.

Understanding the Client/Server Paradigm

With the advent of low-cost PCs, the need arose to network them so that they could share each other's resources, such as hard disks and printers. Although users had to share files and print files out on a printer, system administrators needed to consolidate all applications on one PC and make them available to all. This process made it easy to put applications on the hard disk, to upgrade them, and to maintain and enhance them when necessary.

The need for security on this "server" PC that serviced so many other "clients" arose so that access was granted only to authorized users. This security prevented misuse and provided access to sensitive information only to those users who should have that privilege. Thus was born the *client/server paradigm*, which made it easy to conceptualize the existence of small LANs of PCs in which one server and many PCs were housed. This definition was later broadened to include many such LANs—with many servers and many clients all connected together through a variety of connections.

Summary

This chapter introduced you to the business perspective of computing. Today's PC and networking markets are explosive, and Microsoft and Novell have emerged as leaders. The client/server paradigm enables LANs and PCs to function together with great efficiency.

The next chapter discusses ways that NetWare is evolving into a true enterprise network-computing product.

2

The Evolution of NetWare

Novell's NetWare was the best way to connect PCs together into small LANs. NetWare was not an operating system—it was the "glue" that held PCs together into LANs, and it provided filing, printing, and security. When Drew Major created NetWare, he was essentially writing a file and print server. Drew Major and the superset of NetWare creators (Kyle Powell, Dale Neibaur, and Mark Hearst) made a high-performance file and print server that was simple and elegant, and met the filing and printing needs of their customers.

Understanding the File and Print Market

The man who actually "productized" Drew's technology vision was none other than Raymond J. Noorda. Called upon to rescue a company in distress, Ray Noorda provided the necessary focus and direction to Novell, and laid the foundation for Novell's vast distribution empire. Like putting up gas stations all across the country, Ray made the availability of NetWare a key objective. His grand mission to popularize NetWare and to provide it in more outlets than there are convenience stores proved to be very successful (his theme was "NetWare Everywhere"). NetWare has emerged as the predominant file and print product of choice all over the world.

The reseller channel that Noorda created also paid handsome dividends. *VARs (Value Add Resellers)* used NetWare as their foundation, and placed all kinds of end-use applications on it. Thousands of small businesses bought NetWare without even knowing it; they were buying applications that had NetWare bundled in.

SOAPBOX

It is interesting to compare Ray Noorda's strategy with that of William H. Gates, the head of Microsoft Corporation. Ray believed that customer needs had to be met in an evolutionary way; Bill Gates tried the revolutionary approach. Although Ray and Drew were building the fastest and best file and print server, Microsoft set out to build the ultimate networking software that could do it all. Some people at Novell referred to Microsoft's strategy as the "battle of the tick marks."

In a comparison sheet, Microsoft needed to have more tick marks for its LAN Manager product than NetWare ever did. The first release of Microsoft's LAN Manager was a dud. Because it carried excess baggage, it did not hold its own in filing and printing against Drew's war horse, NetWare. Eventually, LAN Manager emerged as a superior product, but by then it was too late—NetWare was too firmly entrenched in the marketplace. The battle for the file and print market had been won by Ray Noorda.

Understanding the Workgroup Market

As NetWare became the dominant file and print server, users started using NetWare for more than just filing and printing. After all, Drew had provided the capability to write *VAPs (Value Added Processes)* that run on the NetWare 286 product. VAPs, the most primitive of applications, were application programs that ran as extensions of the NetWare operating system.

Some argue that writing applications under DOS is easier than writing VAPs under NetWare. No good development tools were provided, and documentation was poor. Microsoft meanwhile was advocating "safe" applications that did not run as extensions of the operating systems, and that had sophisticated application-development tools under LAN Manager. Drew did not want to sacrifice NetWare's performance so that safe applications could be written.

To make applications safe has a cost, so Drew did some "plug and play." He provided VAPs that could plug in and run with the operating system as fast as the operating system itself. Given that NetWare was built for speed, a third-party vendor conceivably could write a VAP that was as fast, and some vendors did write VAPs that ran very fast.

TIP

The true advent for application developers came with the introduction of NetWare 386 (later renamed NetWare 3.11) in the form of *NLMs (NetWare Loadable Modules)*. NLMs provided a more robust way of writing applications on NetWare. With NetWare 4.0, Novell provides system administrators a safe way to run applications. This way is optional so that system administrators can still operate these applications without the safety net, and they can realize high performance.

Meanwhile, customers using NetWare in departmental LANs became increasingly frustrated with the lack of good *wide area network (WAN)* connectivity options. In late 1989, Novell acquired Excelan, which, coupled with the introduction of NetWare 3.11 in early 1990, gave Novell the ammunition to go after the workgroup segment of the market.

Workgroups represent departmental LANs of PCs that provide filing; printing; and a variety of other applications, such as databases, communication services, and so on. In a typical Fortune 1000 organization, many departments operate in this workgroup fashion.

Excelan (later named to the Interoperability Systems Group, headed by Kanwal Rekhi) provided the connectivity options that these workgroups needed to "plug in" to other dissimilar, yet mainstream computer networks that the rest of the organization used.

The MIS departments were perturbed by this encroachment at first, but soon overlooked these incursions on their turf after they saw how well these workgroups were self-managed. (Of course, the day came when entire organizations ran as a bunch of workgroup LANs connected together through various WAN links.)

Exploring the Enterprise Market

Organizations began asking whether their entire networks could rely on these super-fast, super-efficient, low-cost PC LANs. Some big obstacles stood in the way.

The first obstacle was that these workgroups were simply not manageable as a whole. NetWare did not provide global administration; each server had to be administered, one at a time. For small businesses, this worked fine because they did not have many servers to administer.

For bigger businesses that had hundreds (and in some cases, thousands) of NetWare servers, however, this was a big headache. Each server maintained its own database of user accounts and other objects of interest, and had to be updated every time something changed. If user Joe went from the payroll department to the human resources department, someone had to delete his account from the payroll server and re-create it at the human resources server. In addition, Joe's whole environment had to be set up again—where he had files, how he used his applications, and so on. Imagine the situation if the payroll department had 50 NetWare servers, and Joe had access to all of them! Someone had to administer each server and remove Joe's entry from each server's database.

TIP

To solve this problem, Novell created a product called *NetWare Name Service (NNS)* that was not very successful. NNS had limitations that made it only partially useful in large organizations. For more information on NNS, refer to Chapter 6.

The answer is a global directory service that maintains one logical database for the entire network. If every server in the network operates off of one database that holds user accounts and information, changes can be made only once and take place immediately. At the time of NetWare 3.11's introduction, Novell was working on such a directory service.

The second obstacle was that mission-critical applications could not run on these platforms. NetWare, with all of its robustness and high performance, could not guarantee that the server never went down. Fault tolerance was a key issue. Of course, Novell provided disk mirroring and duplexing for fault tolerance at the data storage level. You could be certain that your data was replicated continuously someplace else as an insurance against failure, but you could not trust that the application you were running always stayed up. Some kind of memory failure or a misbehaving application could bring the server down and the application along with it.

What users needed was memory replication as well as disk replication—*SFT III (Server Fault Tolerance III)*. Levels I and II provided disk duplexing and mirroring, and were available in NetWare 3.11, Novell's dominant workgroup operating system. SFT III finally became a reality, and started shipping commercially in early 1993.

TIP

Novell promises a version that runs on NetWare 4.0 shortly after the introduction of NetWare 4.0 in March, 1993. If things work as stated in the SFT III brochure, the corporate customer will finally have a platform on which to run mission-critical applications on PC LANs.

The final roadblock for an enterprise NetWare was its capacity to handle massive transaction volume. The capability to sustain high-transaction volume is the lifeblood of many businesses. An airline company, for instance, needs to process millions of transactions per day. Massive disk storage was needed, and NetWare servers needed to handle many more transactions-per-second (TPS) to become viable in this market.

Fortunately, some of the advances that were necessary to satisfy this requirement were handled by the hardware industry. The FDDI LAN standard promised to open up LAN bandwidth to as much as 100 mbits-per-second. Given that current Ethernet LANs run at about 10 mbits-per-second, that was a tenfold improvement.

Massive disk-array products also were being built with storage capacities stretching into several gigabytes. Costs on these devices also were dropping fast.

On the microprocessor front, Intel was readying the Pentium microprocessor, which promised to give more CPU power to operating systems. The most promising advancement, however, came from DEC, which had the Alpha microprocessor running at stunning speeds.

Novell teamed up with DEC, HP, and Sun to provide NetWare on their RISC platforms. On a DEC Alpha, the HP PA-RISC, and the Sun SPARC microprocessors, enough power was available to process many transactions-per-second. Some preliminary numbers placed a DEC Alpha delivering at about three times the number of transactions-per-second as the fastest Intel microprocessor. If this is true, the third big obstacle also can be overcome. Slated to be released in late 1994, the versions of NetWare 4.0 that run on these platforms can unleash massive CPU horsepower.

Mastering the Art of Leveraging

Novell's mission statement states that it will increase the network computing industry and stay two years ahead of the competition. Ray Noorda always has seen alliances with key players as a way to increase the market and Novell's share of it. At key junctures in Novell's growth into the world's premier networking company, you can see many alliances that Ray Noorda has made to propel Novell into newer markets and to "leverage" someone else's technology onto NetWare.

With NetWare 4.0, Novell's alliances with HP, Sun, and DEC are examples of such leveraging deals. A customer is guaranteed that NetWare 4.0 is present and available on many hardware platforms, offering many vendor choices.

Defining "Co-opetition"

Unlike Microsoft, which has run into trouble with the FTC with its alleged uncompetitive, monopolizing practices, Novell always has maintained that it is the "networking" company, and it does not step into the turf of many others who work with Novell to develop applications on NetWare. Ray Noorda calls it "co-opetition," and it is music to the ears of many software development companies such as Lotus, Borland, and others. The goodwill that Novell has cultivated might be the key to the success of NetWare 4.0. From the first announcement, NetWare 4.0 has received outpourings of support from almost all software-development companies in the world. This guarantees that many industry-popular applications will be available on NetWare 4.0 that will use its advanced features to the customers' benefit.

Fitting the MIS Model

As the rest of this book illustrates, NetWare 4.0 requires top-down planning and bottoms-up implementation. In other words, a global directory tree infrastructure needs to be defined and in place before each department can build its own LAN. This is a big paradigm shift from the way things were done before.

If each department were to build its own NetWare 4.0 directory tree, no provisions would be available to plug all these departmental trees into one. Things would be the same as before, if not worse, because NetWare 4.0 networks do not interoperate as well because of high-security procedures for user authentications and logins. This means that the central MIS departments must play a lead role in the planning and roll-out of NetWare 4.0 in their organizations.

This requirement, imposed by NetWare 4.0 on central MIS departments, may fit the current operating mold in many Fortune 1000 companies. After the ground rules are set for a corporate-wide network, the central MIS department steps back and allows each department to manage its own LAN. Because of the global nature of the directory, users who are transferred or need access to other parts of the networks can be given that authority easily. This enables organizations to realize the benefits of centralized administration and management flexibility provided by mainframes, while realizing productivity and cost gains that stand-alone PC LANs traditionally provide.

Summary

Novell's evolutionary growth of NetWare to meet customer needs provides handsome dividends for both Novell and its customers. Novell provides the best file and print server, the best workgroup server, and now, with NetWare 4.0, appears poised to provide the best enterprise server product as well.

Many of the technology alliances that Novell has created with leading computer companies such as HP, DEC, Sun, Apple, and IBM mean that NetWare can interoperate and coexist with a variety of different computer hardware and software architectures currently on the market.

Understanding NetWare

This chapter discusses NetWare, both as a product and as a computing environment. Chapters 1 and 2 discussed the way that the corporate computing scene is rapidly changing. Businesses are moving away from mainframes and minicomputers, and are increasingly making use of LANs and networking technology.

Specific topics covered in this chapter include the characteristics and features of NetWare that make it suitable to be the corporate computing environment, both today and in the future; the services offered by NetWare; and NetWare's overall design.

This chapter positions NetWare as a "glue" technology—a technology that bonds together disparate computing resources throughout an enterprise, and then integrates them into a cohesive whole.

Building the Consummate Network Operating System

As the role of network operating systems has expanded from workgroup-oriented file- and printer-sharing to enterprise-wide networking, so has the scope and robustness of NetWare. However, certain characteristics have remained constant throughout NetWare's history. These include a strict focus on network services, an integrative (rather than comprehensive) approach to features, and an accomodation for future technologies.

Focusing on Network Services

As an operating system, NetWare focuses directly on providing services and resources over a network. Perhaps the most immediate example of this specialized focus is the NetWare file system, which is designed specifically to meet the rigorous demands of network file service.

The File-System Analogy

NetWare file-system features, such as disk mirroring and duplexing, concurrency control, and transaction control, have been part of NetWare for years. NetWare 4.0 further enhances the already rich file system. These features were designed into NetWare to preserve the integrity of server-based data in the face of conflicting and concurrent requests for access to that data. In other words, they were designed into NetWare to meet the unique requirements of file access over a LAN. The NetWare file system cache, which was unique when first implemented, was designed specifically to provide high-performance file access for LAN workstations.

TIP
The NetWare file system is designed for the unique requirements of LANs. Applying the NetWare file system to a workstation operating system such as DOS or OS/2 is like using a 175mm howitzer to kill a rat. However, when placed within NetWare's focused context—providing file service over a network—the NetWare file system is appropriately designed. The same analysis can be applied to NetWare's device-driver interface, its communications-protocol environment, the NLM environment, and other components of NetWare.

The NetWare file system can be used as an analogy for the way that NetWare's architects designed services into the NetWare operating system. Every feature of NetWare focuses on providing services over a network. Certainly, most of NetWare's architectural designs would be inappropriate if applied to traditional operating systems. Within the context of NetWare's tight focus, however, NetWare's architecture makes good sense. NetWare's focused design enables it to do things that other general-purpose operating systems can't do—or can't do as well.

The Role of Workstation Operating Systems

Conversely, NetWare's focus on providing services over a LAN makes it inappropriate for NetWare to assume the functions of workstation-based operating systems. NetWare lacks features that many expect in workstation-based operating systems, such as virtual memory and preemptive multitasking.

These omissions in NetWare's design are not weaknesses. Rather, they reflect NetWare's specialized nature. NetWare was not designed to run interactive graphical productivity applications, which frequently require virtual memory and preemptive multitasking. Rather, it was designed to complement workstation operating systems by providing services to them—services such as files, communication links, and server-based "back-end" applications.

Under this arrangement, NetWare does what it can do best (provide resources over a LAN), although workstation-based operating systems such as UNIX, Windows NT, OS/2, and DOS do what they do best (run interactive user applications). For this arrangement to work effectively, NetWare must provide support for different workstation operating systems and communications protocols, which it does.

A Specialized Operating System

NetWare's tight focus on providing services over a LAN means that NetWare should be viewed as a specialized operating system—its specialty is being a network server. As businesses migrate their legacy applications to the client/server model, NetWare stands ready to host the server-based components of these applications.

TIP

Businesses that are downsizing from mainframe and minicomputers to NetWare-based LANs find that NetWare's client/server focus serves their migration plans very well. Servers are the most secure, reliable, and high-performance machines—machines which provide needed network services to disparate and diverse workstations and users. In other words, servers are required to serve many workstations and users concurrently. LAN workstations, on the other hand, place all of their resources behind satisfying a single user very well. Workstation operating systems must provide a good user interface, preemptive multitasking, and other features required to run interactive user-oriented software.

NetWare's focus on providing services over a LAN is what ultimately has made NetWare 4.0 possible. NetWare 4.0 extends NetWare's traditional role into the realm of the enterprise, enabling NetWare to integrate and consolidate all the computing resources of the enterprise. This focus on the enterprise is a logical step in NetWare's evolution. Having provided robust "file and print" service as an entry-level network operating system, NetWare has graduated to being a solid workgroup computing platform and, with version 4.0, it has become an enterprise computing platform.

Integrating Network Resources

NetWare has traditionally taken an integrative, rather than comprehensive approach. That is to say, NetWare *integrates* (accommodates) existing computer technologies instead of providing a monolithic replacement for those technologies. The integrative approach first appeared with NetWare 2.0a, when NetWare integrated support for the DOS file system on the server platform instead of replacing the DOS file system. Users who ran off-the-shelf DOS applications were able to gain access to server-based files without sacrificing access to files that resided on local DOS drives. DOS applications could read and write server-based files without knowing that they were doing so.

TIP

Another example of NetWare's integrative approach was its early support for third-party network interface cards. Instead of requiring users to purchase and install Novell-supplied network interface cards, NetWare integrated existing third-party interface cards—whether they were ARCnet, Ethernet, or Token Ring cards.

Over the years, NetWare's integrative approach has persisted, and it has influenced every aspect of the NetWare operating system. The integrative approach has been applied to communications protocols (NetWare supports IPX/SPX, TCP/IP, AppleTalk, and OSI); file systems (NetWare supports DOS, OS/2 HPFS, UNIX and NFS, and AFP); network management (NetWare supports SAA, SNMP, and DCA); routing; and so on. Novell is currently developing a hardware-independent operating system that can run on popular non-Intel computers.

Novell has designed NetWare to work with the technologies that people are already using, rather than dictating specific technologies to which the user must migrate. NetWare's goal has always been to do more than just work with existing technologies: NetWare has been moving toward the point at which it can bind the computing resources of an entire enterprise into a cohesive whole that is manageable from a single point and usable from any location or workstation.

NetWare 4.0, with the NetWare Directory Services (NDS), is the logical result of NetWare's integrative approach. It comes close to meeting NetWare's ultimate goal of binding an enterprise's computing resources together into a cohesive whole. Using NetWare 4.0, an enterprise can enhance its existing technology without replacing that technology.

Ray Noorda is determined to make NetWare a commodity technology. He wants his operating system to run on anything and everything: from Intel to HP PA RISC to Sun SPARC. Ray also believes in leveraging other people's technology. Look at all the investment that Sun, Hewlett-Packard, and Intel have made in their microprocessors. For the nominal cost it takes to make NetWare run on its hardware, Novell leverages millions, if not billions, of dollars worth of research and development.

Throughout Novell's history, Ray Noorda has stewarded Novell into providing a value-based product and retaining a distinctive edge in its product offerings over its competitors. As soon as a software technology attained a "commodity" status, Ray threw that technology to the marketplace to maintain, and commanded his engineers to build the next highest level of services that Novell's customers desired. Getting out of the businesses of writing drivers and developing hardware were two such steps.

With the hardware-independent NetWare that Novell is building to run on Intel, Sun, and HP microprocessors, Ray has taken the steps to make NetWare machine-independent and to provide interfaces so that machine manufacturers can provide the modules that NetWare needs to run on their machines. Expect NetWare to run on virtually any machine in the future—maybe even your toaster!

When implementing new technology, the enterprise is free to select hardware and software based on their merits alone because NetWare's integrative approach ensures that new technology can be successfully bound in to the enterprise's existing resource base.

Looking to the Future

When extending the capabilities of NetWare, the focus has been on making NetWare more modular, so that it is easily adaptable to future technologies. Two examples illustrate this point: NetWare's protocol support and file-system support.

Open-Ended Protocol Architecture

When support was added in NetWare for the AppleTalk and TCP/IP communications protocols, these protocols were not just dumped into the operating system. First, Novell and Apple jointly developed the Open

Datalink Interface (ODI), which allows an unlimited number of protocol suites to be loaded and unloaded dynamically by the NetWare operating system. After adding the ODI interface to the NetWare operating system, Novell developed the actual AppleTalk and TCP/IP protocol suites for NetWare. In addition, Novell ported the native IPX/SPX protocol suite to the ODI interface, bringing all of NetWare's protocol suites under the same architecture.

Later, when Novell developed the OSI TP0-TP4 protocols, it was easier to integrate those protocols with NetWare because the original ODI architecture was designed to accommodate multiple protocol suites in an open-ended fashion. In the future, when new protocol suites are developed, Novell can add those suites to NetWare in a modular and non-disruptive fashion. Novell even designed ODI to allow third parties to develop protocol suites for NetWare, although none have yet done so.

TIP

The result of ODI is that NetWare's communications protocol architecture is modular and open-ended. Accommodations for future protocol suites are already present in the NetWare operating system. If the time comes when a new protocol suite needs to be added to a NetWare installation, an adminstrator can do so without disruption (the server does not need to be downed) and without worries over backward compatibility.

Open-Ended File System Architecture

NetWare's support of multiple file formats (DOS, Macintosh, UNIX, OS/2, and so on) is similar to the protocol suite example. Before adding support for Macintosh and UNIX file formats to NetWare, Novell engineers designed the Name Space mechanism, which adds support for multiple file formats to a NetWare server in a modular and efficient fashion. Novell designed the Name Space mechanism to use abstract data types, which means that any future file format can be supported by NetWare. As in ODI protocol suites, third parties can develop file formats for NetWare by using the Name Space mechanism.

NetWare 4.0 and the Future

NetWare 4.0 is by far the most open-ended operating system Novell has ever developed. The same philosophy that Novell engineers applied to protocol-suite and file-format support in previous versions of NetWare has been extended throughout the operating system. NetWare's routing functions, NetWare Core Protocol processing, network management, storage-media interface, and more have been modularized and opened so that third parties can plug their own extensions into these services.

Understanding the NetWare Architecture

To understand the NetWare architecture, think of the operating system as a collection of services. *Services* make computing resources (storage, communications links, printers, and so on) available to other computers over the network. Some services organize these resources, for example, the NetWare scheduler, which controls the execution of programs running on the server. Other services, such as security, control access to the server. Further services provide information (such as network management) about the hardware, operating system, and network.

In technical terms, the overriding themes of the present NetWare architecture are modularity and dynamic operation. *Modularity* means that services can be added to the operating system without disrupting NetWare (forcing major code changes). Modularity also means that new services can be added to the NetWare operating system (or existing services replaced) in the future, such as NetWare Directory Services (new with version 4.0).

Dynamic operation means that a network administrator can activate or deactivate services, and then tune them and configure them on an ad-hoc basis without affecting the normal operation of the server. A good example of dynamic operation is the NetWare device-driver interface, which enables the loading and unloading of device drivers while the server is running. Thus, storage devices and network segments can be added and removed without taking down the server.

Understanding NetWare Service Layers

Figure 3.1 shows—in generalized terms—the layered service architecture of NetWare.

In figure 3.1, NetWare is shown as a collection of layered services. There is a rough correspondence between NetWare services and the OSI network model. The figure represents server-based applications as triangles, and depicts the central NetWare services as being in the presentation layer. These central services include File, Print, Name, Security, and others.

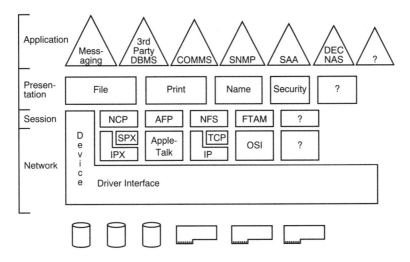

Figure 3.1:

NetWare, viewed as a collection of layered, modular services.

Notice the question marks along the right side of figure 3.1. These represent protocols, services, and applications that can be supported by NetWare in the future. The question marks illustrate that NetWare has the infrastructure to support such technologies in the future.

NetWare 4.0 fills in some of the question marks, so to speak. For example, it includes special image-related extensions to the standard file service. Novell and AT&T are jointly developing telephony applications, which, when available, will show up as a triangle at the application level in figure 3.1. New filing protocols will be supported by NetWare when they gain market presence, and so on.

NetWare 4.0 also demonstrates the feasibility of replacing central services in a modular fashion. For example, the traditional NetWare naming service (the bindery) has been replaced in NetWare 4.0 by NetWare Directory Services.

TIP

The central services—File, Print, Name, Security, and others—use protocol stacks and device drivers while they present resources to application-level services. Thus, they are in the center, so to speak, of the layered-service model.

Understanding the Protocol Environment

The NetWare communications-protocol environment is based on the Open Datalink Interface (ODI). ODI enables the following capabilities:

❖ Multiprotocol support is available within the operating system.

❖ A single network card can send and receive packets.

❖ Protocol suites can be added to and and subtracted from the operating system dynamically while the operating system is running.

❖ Network interface card device drivers can be loaded and unloaded dynamically while the operating system is running.

❖ Network segments can be brought up and down dynamically while the operating system is running.

The Link-Support Layer

The key to the design of the ODI is the *Link-Support Layer*, or *LSL*. The function of the LSL is to bind specific network interface card device drivers with specific protocol suites. The act of binding a network device to a protocol stack is the key event for creating a network segment or, if a segment already exists, for making the NetWare server active on that segment.

Figure 3.2 shows the role of the LSL in binding network interface card drivers to protocol stacks.

For example, to bind the NE2-32 Ethernet card to the IPX protocol stack and create IPX network number 00001234, LOAD the NE2-32 driver, and then BIND the NE2-32 to the IPX protocol stack, assigning the network number 00001234 to the "binding." Figure 3.3 shows the configuration of the LSL after the binding is performed.

To bind the same NE2-32 Ethernet card to TCP/IP, LOAD (re-entrantly) the NE2-32 driver once more. *Re-entrant loading* means that the operating system has activated another instance of the driver, although it is still working with the same physical NE2-32 card. Then BIND this second instance of the NE2-32 driver with the IP protocol stack. Figure 3.4 shows the configuration of the LSL after these tasks are performed.

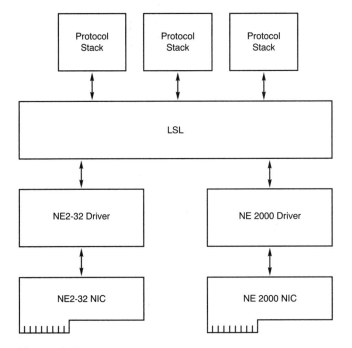

Figure 3.2:

The role of the LSL in binding network interface card drivers to protocol stacks.

As figure 3.4 illustrates, the LSL enables a single network interface card to service more than one protocol stack. Implicitly, this means also that the LSL is the key to NetWare's multiprotocol support. The LSL maintains bindings between protocol stacks and network interface card drivers. These bindings enable the LSL to channel data sent back and forth between network interface cards and the correct protocol stacks.

The possible combinations of protocol stacks and network interface cards allowed by the LSL are completely open-ended. The server can be configured so that it has several network interface cards servicing IPX, while one of those cards is also servicing AppleTalk, and two of those cards are also servicing IP. Or, each network interface card in the server can be dedicated to the service of a single protocol stack (or any combination).

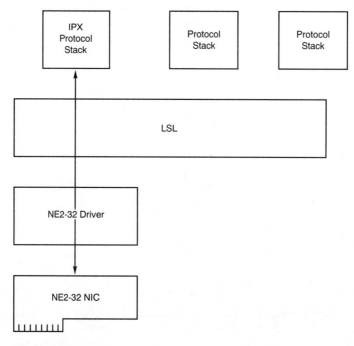

Figure 3.3:
The configuration of NE2-32/IPX protocol stack after binding.

Protocol Stacks

Under NetWare, protocol stacks are NLMs, which means they can be loaded and unloaded dynamically. (The only exception is the IPX/SPX protocol stack, which is loaded automatically during server initialization, and cannot be unloaded.) New protocol stacks can be added to the NetWare server in the future as those protocol stacks become available. (As user demand for other protocol suites increases, third parties will have the tools to provide such services on NetWare.)

Routing

Routing is the process of directing network packets across an internetwork so that packets arrive at their correct destinations. Routing is necessary in an environment with more than one network segment, and it is essential in one with more than one protocol suite. Routing is a requirement for NetWare sites with more than one server. Many NetWare sites have multiple NetWare servers, plus other types of computers, such as UNIX hosts and IBM mainframes. In these types of environments, routing is essential.

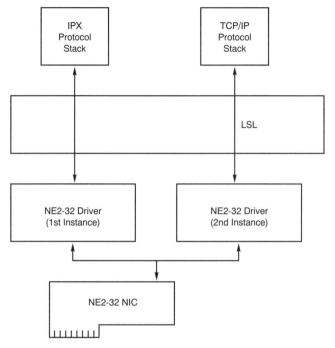

Figure 3.4:

The LSL enables one physical network interface card to service multiple protocol stacks.

TIP

Novell has adhered to the philosophy that protocol stacks that are active on the server should also perform routing. IPX routing was built into NetWare very early in the operating system's evolution. As NetWare has come to support multiple protocol stacks, Novell has ensured that those protocol stacks—including TCP/IP, AppleTalk, and OSI—perform routing functions.

Under NetWare, routing functions are tightly integrated with the various protocol stacks themselves. Routing functions also rely heavily on the LSL to direct network traffic in the right direction.

NetWare 4.0 extends NetWare's routing architecture to include *replaceable routers*. That is, built-in routing functions of one or more protocol stacks can be replaced by loading a specialized router written to NetWare 4.0's replaceable router interface.

Furthermore, NetWare has always supported *stand-alone routers* (those that are not tied to the NetWare operating system). Use of stand-alone routers has become increasingly popular as NetWare sites have grown to include hundreds of servers. The use of a stand-alone router is strictly a performance enhancement, however, and does not add functionality to a NetWare installation.

The Multiprocotol Operation

A crucial aspect of NetWare's communications protocol environment is that it was designed specifically for *multiprotocol operation*. When multiple protocol stacks are made active on a NetWare server, each protocol stack gains equal access to operating system resources, network interface device drivers, and hardware resources. The protocol stacks are not, as some have suggested, layered on top of one another. Rather, they are peers to each other, and each relies on the operation of the LSL to the same degree.

Novell has added sophisticated mechanisms to the LSL to ensure that NetWare continues to operate efficiently, even when many protocol stacks are active on the server. These scaling enhancements include the capability for the LSL to "pre-scan" packets that are delivered from network interface card drivers, thus speeding the delivery of the packet to the correct protocol stack.

NetWare's efficiency as a multiprotocol environment is due to all the mechanisms discussed thus far in this chapter, including the device-driver interface, the ODI specification, the LSL, and the NLM environment. (Protocol stacks are NLMs.)

Understanding File Services

Fast and robust file service has been the hallmark of NetWare since the beginning. In fact, the excellent reputation that NetWare has earned for file service has at times overshadowed other equally important aspects of NetWare. NetWare has been labelled by its competition as having great file service, with the implication that file service, along with print service, is all that NetWare offers. In fact, one editor of an industry publication recently characterized NetWare as being "nothing more than a glorified disk cache and print buffer."

Clearly, characterizing NetWare as offering primarily file service is misleading. Yet, it begs the question of why Novell has for so long placed such a high priority on providing the best file service on the market. The answer is rather complicated, but it is important to note that file service is the most heavily used of all NetWare services, even under NetWare 4.0. Moreover, studies have shown that file service alone accounts for up to 70 percent of the traffic on a network. In addition, most NetWare services, including printing, naming, security, and others, are either built on NetWare's file service, or use it heavily to perform their own functions.

Novell's longtime goal of making NetWare the best platform for enterprise legacy applications requires a prodigious and robust file service. Virtually all legacy applications are, at their core, database management systems. And good database management systems demand an excellent file service.

Presently, the capacity of the NetWare file system is as follows:

❖ It can contain up to four terabytes of on-line storage

❖ It can contain up to 100,000 concurrently open files

❖ It can contain up to 100,000 concurrent record or file locks

❖ It can contain up to 100,000 concurrently active transactions

❖ A volume can consist of up to 32 physical media devices

❖ A single file can be up to four gigabytes in size

❖ A single server can have up to 64 volumes

❖ Each physical media device can be mirrored to as many as 15 redundant devices

File-Service Design Goals

The design goals of NetWare's file service are as follows:

❖ Preserve the integrity of data

❖ Offer excellent performance

❖ Support multiple file formats

❖ Enable easy file-system management

These goals are discussed in the sections that follow.

Preserving the Integrity of Data

The NetWare file system has several mechanisms for preserving data integrity. These are collectively referred to as *System Fault Tolerance*, or *SFT*.

Features of SFT include the capability to install redundant storage-media devices and controllers (*disk mirroring and duplexing*), the capability to roll back groups of file updates (*transaction tracking*), the capability to map out and replace bad media sectors (*hot fix*), and the capability to verify data written to physical media (*read-after-write verification*).

In addition to the SFT-related aspects of NetWare's file service, there are extensive concurrency controls built into the NetWare file system, plus the file-cache management features that preserve the integrity of data.

NetWare's concurrency controls are designed to prevent data corruption in the face of concurrent and conflicting requests to read or write file-system data. NetWare enables workstations and server-based applications to have files open for reading and writing concurrently. At the same time, however, NetWare offers extensive file- and record-locking mechanisms. These mechanisms offer different levels of atomicity, and are designed specifically for high-end database management systems.

NetWare's concurrency controls and Transaction Tracking System (TTS) are both integrated within the core of the NetWare file system. This tight integration of the file system, concurrency controls, and transaction controls is a rare and innovative aspect of NetWare's file-service architecture that is frequently overlooked by the industry. However, integration of these mechanisms in the core of the file system offers both increased robustness and increased performance over other design options.

Increasing Performance

NetWare's file service includes a massive file-system cache for increasing system performance. During server operation, all memory that is not in use by the operating system itself or by loaded NLMs is, by default, assigned to the file-system cache. In the typical server, this resolves to around 80 percent of all memory installed in the server machine.

The file-system cache memory is divided between volume data structures and file data. Caching of volume data structures enables the file system to traverse these data structures, which are necessary for opening files, without issuing any read requests to the physical storage media.

Caching of file data enables the file system to perform read and write operations without issuing read or write requests to the physical media. In the case of writing requests, the NetWare file system first writes the new data to the file-system cache. After a short interval, the NetWare file system "flushes" the cache memory by writing its data to the physical media. However, NetWare can choose the best time for flushing cache buffers, which is typically when there is no other critical work for the operating system to perform.

The use of file-system cache memory speeds up file read and write operations many hundreds of times over their speed without the cache system. NetWare manages its file-cache memory on a *Least-Recently Used (LRU)* basis, meaning that the most recently accessed files are always cached.

The use of file-cache memory has implications for preserving the integrity of file-system data. What happens, for instance, if power to the server goes down after a file write operation, yet before NetWare flushes the data from cache? To protect against this possibility, the administrator can set the maximum interval that updated file data will be allowed to reside in cache before NetWare flushes that data. Or, the administrator can force immediate updates for specific files, which means that the updated data goes directly from the file system to the physical media device, bypassing the cache memory altogether.

Like concurrency control and transaction control, the file-cache system is tightly integrated with all of NetWare's low-level file read and write routines. In other words, the file-cache system is, in the strictest sense, part of the NetWare file system. Again, this architecture is somewhat unprecedented but entirely appropriate, given NetWare's specialized focus.

The NetWare file system has many unspectacular, yet highly effective mechanisms designed to increase performance. One of these is the *disk elevator*, which is a special algorithm that executes underneath the file system but above the NetWare device driver interface. The disk elevator reorganizes physical read and write requests into the most efficient order before issuing those requests to the actual media device drivers. The disk elevator minimizes movement of the media device's heads, which increases media device performance. The disk elevator, despite its name, works equally well for streaming tape devices, hard disks, and other storage media.

TIP
Although there are unavoidable conflicts between file-system performance and data integrity, the tightly integrated architecture of the NetWare file system minimizes these conflicts, and provides tuning and configuration options for the special cases that inevitably arise.

Supporting Multiple File Formats

To act as an integrating platform, NetWare must support different file formats, including DOS, UNIX, Macintosh, OS/2, and others. Each of these file formats introduces peculiarities that are inherent in the various workstation operating systems. NetWare's primary mechanism for supporting multiple file formats is called name spaces.

Name spaces are like lenses that provide different views of the same NetWare file to different types of workstation operating systems supported by NetWare. For example, the Macintosh name space is like a lens that makes NetWare files appear as if they were Macintosh files. The organization of the actual NetWare file remains constant, yet it appears differently—depending on the lense through which the user views it.

Technically, name spaces are special directory entries—one for each NetWare file—that contain information specific to the workstation operating system that they support. The *directory entry* in the Macintosh name space contains the long Macintosh name of the file, Macintosh finder information, and a pointer to the file's Macintosh resource fork. The primary directory entry, Macintosh directory entry, and UNIX directory entry point to the same file. Each directory entry contains unique information. This unique information provides the "lens" through which different workstation operating systems view the file.

The name-space mechanism uses abstract data types to ensure that radically new file systems will be supported by NetWare in the future. The advantages and disadvantages of the name space mechanism are as follows:

Advantages:

❖ There is open-ended support for multiple file formats

❖ There is no significant impact on file-system performance

❖ Actual files are stored only once while available in multiple formats

❖ NetWare provides for future file formats

Disadvantages:

❖ Each file consumes more directory space

❖ Each name space consumes slightly more server memory

❖ NetWare must track internally which name space it is using to gain access to a file

To compensate for these disadvantages, NetWare enables name-space support to be added on a per-format and per-volume basis. That is, support can be added to a specific volume for only UNIX or only Macintosh name spaces. Or a volume can be configured to support all possible name spaces, while only the primary name space is active on other volumes.

Overall, the name-space mechanism is an efficient and elegant method of supporting multiple file formats within a single operating system. New efficiencies in the NetWare 4.0 file system, including compression and suballocation, more than compensate for the disadvantages of activating additional name spaces.

Managing the NetWare File System

The tightly integrated design of the NetWare file system makes it relatively easy to manage (especially when compared to relatively static file-system designs such as UNIX). Some of the management and tuning operations that can be performed while the server is running include the following:

- ❖ Extend on-line storage by adding media devices to a volume

- ❖ Activate or deactivate media device mirroring or duplexing

- ❖ Load and unload media device drivers

- ❖ Perform destructive or non-destructive surface tests of physical media devices

- ❖ Increase or decrease the amount of memory dedicated to the file-cache system

- ❖ Shorten or lengthen the time interval between a write operation and the flushing of that data from cache to media device

- ❖ Increase or decrease the maximum number of concurrently open files, concurrent record or file locks, or concurrently active transactions

- ❖ Mount or dismount volumes

- ❖ Activate or deactivate name spaces for specific volumes

While the NetWare operating system is running, it is continually adjusting its internal tuning parameters to reflect the demands being placed on it by external forces, including client workstations. Most of the tuning required for NetWare involves setting upper and lower limits for the various heuristic tuning algorithms internal to the operating system.

File-Service Protocols

File-service protocols are special communications subprotocols that are designed to provide file service remotely over a network. Examples of file-service protocols include the NetWare Core Protocol (NCP), the AppleTalk Filing Protocol, and the UNIX NetWare File System (NFS). NetWare currently supports NCP, AFP, NFS, and the OSI FTAM file-service protocols.

File-service protocols are necessary for a network server to provide workstations with remote access to its file system. Because of the role played by file-service protocols, they must be tailored to both a file system and a lower-level communications protocol suite. Even if NetWare supported multiple file formats, it couldn't truly support multiple workstation operating systems unless it supported the file-service protocols used by those workstations.

In figure 3.1, the various file-service protocols supported by NetWare reside just below the central services (File, Print, Security, and so on) and just above the commuinications protocols (IPX, AppleTalk, IP). The job of file-service protocols is to bridge the gap between the network and the server file system.

Just as protocol stacks are NLMs, file-service protocols are also NLMs. They can be loaded and unloaded dynamically while the server is operating. Novell placed "hooks" in both the LSL and the NetWare file system to support modularly designed file-service protocols. As in every other aspect of NetWare, Novell engineers have made accommodations for future file-service protocols.

TIP

NetWare itself uses file-service protocols to provide server-to-server file-system access. This is what makes possible the distributed design of NetWare Directory Services (described in later chapters).

Understanding Print Services

Many NetWare users first installed NetWare in order to share expensive laser printers. NetWare's printing services have been a key selling point since the system's early days. By now, however, as LANs have evolved workgroup systems to the point at which these systems are poised to become the central computing platform of worldwide enterprises, the printing needs of users have also evolved.

NetWare's printing services enable the following configurations:

❖ Sharing of printers across the enterprise

❖ Total freedom regarding the physical location of printers

❖ Support for all printer types, and page description languages and control protocols

❖ Security and configuration management of printers

❖ Cross-platform printing

❖ Customization of printer configuration on a per-user basis

In earlier versions of NetWare, printing services were built into the NetWare operating system, and printing hardware was attached directly to the NetWare server. (This was referred to as *core printing* by many users).

Today, however, core printing has been replaced with a more modular and flexible printing-service architecture that is consistent with the overall design of NetWare. Printing services under NetWare consist of the following modules:

❖ Print server

❖ Printer queues

❖ Printing device

❖ Configuration, administration, and management software

These modules are discussed in the following sections.

Print servers under NetWare are software modules that advertise their presence over the network, thus providing a way for users to identify them and send printing jobs to them. Each print server is associated with one or more actual printers and one or more printer queues.

Printer queues are special files that hold printer jobs, and spool those jobs to printers. When a NetWare user prints a job, the print server writes that job to the print queue, along with management and configuration information (such as the identity of the user who submitted the print job), and formatting information for the print job. As soon as the print job is written to the printer queue, the user who submitted it is free to continue performing other work.

Printer queues can hold many specific print jobs at any one time. The print server "spools" each job to an available printer, based on that job's order in the queue, the priority of that job, and other information.

NetWare enables specific print jobs to be preceded by control codes for a specific printer type, thus enabling re-initialization or reconfiguration of the actual printer that produces the hard copy output. In addition, NetWare enables post-printing initialization and configuration.

Each print job in a NetWare print queue contains information that enables the print server to notify a user when the print job is complete, notify an adminstrator that the printer is suffering an error, or notify a user when the printer needs more paper, toner, and so on.

Print servers, print queues, and actual printers are subject to NetWare security, which means that there can be limits on the users who can submit jobs to a printer, print queue, or print server. Limits can also be placed on which users are allowed to configure and manage printers, queues, and print servers.

Associating Printers, Print Servers, and Print Queues

With the exception of print queues, which always reside on a NetWare server, the administrator is free to locate any component of NetWare's print services anywhere on the network. Print servers can be running on workstations attached to the network or to NetWare servers, or they can be embedded as firmware into actual printers.

Actual printers can be attached directly to the network, attached to a network workstation, or attached to a NetWare server. A single print server can manage multiple printers. A single printer can service multiple print queues, and a single print queue can spool jobs to multiple servers.

Understanding Print-Service Protocols

Just as file-service protocols enable workstations to receive file service remotely over a network, print-service protocols enable workstations to print remotely over a network. NetWare has always had its own propri-etary print-service protocol, which is a subset of the NCP protocols. Other platforms, such as UNIX and Macintosh, also have well-developed and widely used print-service protocols.

TIP

NetWare supports the inclusion, in a modular fashion, of alternative print-service protocols. Presently, support for Macintosh print-service protocols can be added by purchasing the NetWare for Macintosh product, and support for UNIX print-service protocols can be added by purchasing NetWare NFS.

When support for alternative print-service protocols, such as Macintosh and UNIX, is added, NetWare integrates those protocols into its overall print-service architecture, which enables cross-platform printing. For example, Macintosh users can submit print jobs to a NetWare print server, DOS or Windows users can submit print jobs to a Macintosh print server, and UNIX clients can submit print jobs to a NetWare print server. Users of NetWare print services, therefore, do not even need to be aware of NetWare's existence. Print services—like many of NetWare's services—use the NetWare file system and file-service protocols heavily.

NetWare 4.0 Print Services

Although the basic print-service architecture remains the same under NetWare 4.0, the presentation of print services to the user and administrator is dramatically different. By taking advantage of NetWare Directory Services, the information available to users regarding printers, print servers, and printer queues is more useful and relevent. It is easier under NetWare 4.0 to configure and manage components of NetWare's print services, and its configuration and management options available are also more extensive.

Future Enhancements to Print Services

A *naming service* has two basic functions: it determines the way users view and gain access to network resources; it is also a repository of information that the operating system uses to manage, process, and update the status of network resources and users.

For example, users query the NetWare naming service to discover the existence of network applications, printers, file systems, or communications links. When a user issues a request to gain access to one of these resources, the operating system uses the information stored in the naming service to grant or deny that user the access he requested.

Naming services can be very simple (as in the NetWare bindery) or very complex (as in NetWare Directory Services). However, regardless of the complexity or simplicity of a particular naming service, a network cannot function without one.

NetWare Bindery

Up until NetWare 4.0, naming services for NetWare have been supplied by a flat-file database called the bindery. The *bindery* is a per-server, unique-key, variable-length database that contains information about all resources associated with a specific server and information about network-based resources known to that server.

In the bindery, all objects have a unique key, which is also the offset within the bindery file of that object's record. Each object has a variable number of properties, which are contained in 128-byte segments of raw information associated with their object.

For example, registered users of a NetWare server have a corresponding bindery object and ID number. The ID number of a user is also the user object's unique bindery key, which is also the offset of the user object's record within the bindery database. Each user object in the bindery has a password property, a security property, and other properties that combine to form a user identity. Print servers, groups, server-based applications, and other network resources may also have objects (and hence properties) in a NetWare server's bindery.

TIP

Some bindery objects are static—for example, users and groups. *Static* objects persist after the server has been downed and restarted, and remain until they are explicitly deleted. Other objects, such as network-based print servers, are *dynamic*, which means that they persist only as long as the object they represent is running on the network.

Advantages of the Bindery

The bindery has served NetWare well over the years for the following reasons:

❖ It is simple and very robust

❖ It offers excellent performance

❖ Dynamic objects are easy to add and delete

❖ It is easy to customize, but only by adding objects of a simple data type

Disadvantages of the Bindery

When NetWare servers were used primarily in workgroup settings, the bindery provided a robust and efficient naming service that was appropriate for the tasks required. As NetWare became more popular in large multiserver installations, however, the shortcomings of the bindery became evident. These shortcomings include the following:

❖ The bindery is local (server) in scope

❖ Information stored in the bindery must be interpreted by the creator of that data: it is not in human-readable format

❖ Most object properties consume far fewer than 128 bytes; therefore, space is wasted because the smallest segment of the bindery is 128 bytes

❖ The bindery is inappropriate for the storage of complex data types

The most telling disadvantage of the bindery is its *local scope*. That is, every server on an internetwork contains its own bindery, and there is no coordination of objects among binderies. Administrators must add users to each server, one user at a time. Because each bindery stores information about network-based resources (such as print servers), this information is duplicated throughout a multiserver network. (The information is stored once on every server, although only one instance of the information suffices.)

The other disadvantages of the bindery are a result of the algorithms used to store and retrieve bindery information. Information stored in the bindery was designed primarily for use by the NetWare operating system, not for consumption by users. Therefore, the meaning of bindery-based information is not obvious to users. Clever programmers have devised methods for "hiding" the format of bindery-based data, and presenting this data in a more "human-friendly" format, but these methods only serve to mask some of the bindery's shortcomings, not fix them.

Unhooking Naming Services

One of the biggest challenges of creating NetWare 4.0 was to unhook the bindery from the NetWare operating system. In other words, developers made name services modular in NetWare, rather than hard wired. This was the first big step toward enabling of NetWare Directory Services in NetWare 4.0.

Now that naming services are modular in NetWare, users can swap in the bindery or NetWare Directory Services, or both. This capability is necessary for the success of NetWare Directory Services because many NetWare sites will choose to install 4.0 servers on internetworks that have existing v2.x and v3.x bindery-based NetWare servers.

In fact, the default for NetWare 4.0 is to use NetWare Directory Services as the primary naming service, but also to support the bindery. This makes integration of 4.0 servers into an existing network easier than it otherwise would be. It also allows users to migrate from bindery-based utilities to NDS-based utilities at their own pace.

The decision to make naming services modular in NetWare also makes NetWare more open to the future. It also raises interesting possibilities for third party developers. NetWare Directory Services represents a great leap forward in naming-service architecture. NDS is discussed further later in this book.

Understanding Security

Network security is important for all sites, both large and small. Users want their data to be private, and enterprises want absolute assurance that corporate databases are both secure from corruption and are private. On a network, security is a more complex issue than on other types of systems. This is true primarily because over-the-network sessions may be forged, which is a concern only for networked systems. The traditional security concerns are also addressed by NetWare, including user authentication and user-privilege levels.

Components of NetWare Security

NetWare imposes security in three primary areas:

- ❖ User authentication
- ❖ User-privilege enforcement
- ❖ Session authentication

These components are discussed in the following sections.

User authentication means that the operating system verifies that a given user is projecting a legitimate identity. For example, John is not allowed to log in to the network, claiming that he is actually Larry.

User-privilege enforcement means that specific users are granted access to network resources according to their privilege levels (and never exceeding their privilege levels). For example, user John is not allowed to view files in the ACCOUNTING directory, but he can view files in his own personal directory. User Julie is not allowed to submit print jobs to the ENGINEER-ING print server, but she can submit print jobs to the ACCOUNTING print server.

Privilege enforcement under NetWare also extends to the number of times that a user is allowed to log in, the workstations from which a user is allowed to log in, and (through the Accounting System) the cumulative levels of resources that a user is allowed to consume.

Session authentication means that hackers or snoops cannot forge an ongoing network session. NetWare establishes a session for each user who successfully logs in to the server. (User authentication occurs during the login procedure.) If a hacker is able to forge an ongoing session, he assumes the identity of the user whose session he forged.

User Authentication

Under NetWare 3.11, *user authentication* occurs during the login process. A user issues a login request to the NetWare server, and the login request arrives at the server in the form of an encrypted password image. The password encryption serves two purposes: encryption makes it impossible to capture a clear-text passwords by using a protocol analyzer, and encryption makes it nearly impossible to log in by using unauthorized NetWare client software.

NetWare enables the user to log in to the server if the password has been correctly encrypted. Otherwise, NetWare fails the login request. Once a user successfully logs in to a NetWare 3.11 server, that user is considered to be *authenticated* by the operating system. The user is then free to consume server resources, subject to the privilege levels established for that user by the network administrator.

TIP
NetWare 4.0 extends the scope of user authentication from being a per-server authentication to a network-wide authentication. Moreover, NetWare 4.0 uses a more secure form of authentication that is based on RSA public-key encryption algorithms. Authentication is therefore an ongoing background process that precedes the user wherever he or she goes on the enterprise network.

User authentication is the most important area of security on a network. Establishing a rigorous and comprehensive system of user-privilege levels is pointless if users can assume bogus network identities.

User-Privilege Enforcement

Privilege enforcement under NetWare is extensive—it permeates the naming service, the file system, communications links, database management systems, and other services running on the NetWare server.

Each resource on a NetWare server has a trustee list and a rights mask. The *trustee list* is a collection of user ID numbers; the *rights mask* is a per-user list that enumerates the privileges allowed to that user for each specific resource. For each ID number in the trustee list, there is a corresponding rights mask. The combination of the trustee list and the rights mask determines which users gain access to a specific server resource, and which operations each user is allowed to perform on that resource.

Specific privileges that can be granted to users in the file system include reading a file, writing to a file, viewing a file's directory entry, creating a file, deleting a file, executing a file, and more. Other services have similar allowable privileges. For example, the adminstrator can grant users the ability to submit jobs to a print server, to change the format of printing jobs, to grant privileges for the print server to other users, and so on.

NetWare's privilege-enforcement system allows literally thousands of combinations of privilege levels for each type of server resource. NetWare is the only network operating system that allows the establishment of privilege levels for individual files (rather than only for directories).

Session Authentication

NetWare is the only networking product that provides session authentication. A *session* is an ongoing exchange of service protocol packets between a network server and a client. Without session authentication, talented hackers can forge a service protocol packet and open a crack in the server's security system. This method of cracking a network system's security is not always reliable, but it is becoming more prevalent. All networked systems—not just NetWare—face this threat to security.

NetWare closes the door on session forging by authenticating each packet of an ongoing service-protocol session. An adminstrator can choose the level of session authentication he wants (including none at all), and he can also choose the specific authentication algorithm desired. Forgery of a service protocol packet is impossible when session authentication is active.

Auxiliary Security Features

NetWare has a collection of utilities and commands that audit the server's security system and close security "holes." For example, the SECURITY utility verifies the consistency of the server's user-privilege settings. The server console can be locked, the NetWare internal debugger deactivated, the console TIME command deactivated, access to the server's floppy drives blocked, and more.

Passwords can be forced to be a certain minimum length, and NetWare's intruder detection can lock user accounts after a series of unsuccessful login attempts. NetWare passwords are stored in an encrypted format in a secure area of the server's naming database.

The NetWare 4.0 auditing system adds a lot of muscle to NetWare's extensive security system. Using auditing, the auditor can track inappropriate uses of server resources, which may or may not be actual violations of the security system you have established for the server. This adds an entirely new dimension to security for NetWare, but it also opens the possibility for abuse by overbearing managers.

Understanding NetWare Application Services

As discussed in the first part of this chapter, NetWare is able to run server-based applications. These applications (represented in figure 3.1 as triangles) include Messaging, Communications, SAA links, SNMP agents, Database Management Systems, and more.

NetWare is able to support such a wide array of server-based applications because it provides a stable and comprehensive environment for applications. This environment consists of modules throughout the NetWare operating system, and is located within all layers of the layered service model depicted in figure 3.1. Collectively, the modules that comprise the NetWare applications environment are called *application services*, and they include the following:

- ❖ Kernel-level scheduling, which provides 32-bit, multithreaded, multitasking execution

- ❖ Dynamic memory allocation

- ❖ Load-time linking, which allows shared code libraries

- ❖ Programming interfaces to all NetWare services and service layers

- ❖ A device-driver interface, which allows loadable device drivers

Understanding NetWare Loadable Modules

Server-based applications that are written for NetWare are called NetWare Loadable Modules (NLMs). The NLM format is so-named because of the load-time linking performed by the NetWare operating system. This means that applications can share loaded-code libraries, which makes the operating system a more efficient platform for server-based applications.

Novell engineers developed a very powerful NLM programming interface. Using this interface, third-party developers gain access to all services and service levels of the NetWare operating system. The NLM programming interface enables server-based applications to become extensions of the operating system itself, rather than lower-priority execution threads. This provides greater performance and efficiency to server-based applications than is offered by other operating systems such as UNIX and OS/2.

The number of third-party NLMs currently on the market is a validation of the NLM platform. Products such as network management agents, communications servers, and database management systems have proven the effectiveness and robustness of the NLM platform.

The most important point to remember about NLMs is that, when loaded, they are integrated into the NetWare layered-service model, just as core operating-system services are. NLMs, then, are "linked" into the operating system as a standard, modular service. Not only does this make NetWare an excellent platform for server-based applications today, but it makes NetWare completely open to the future.

TIP

A great example of this is the advent of telephony applications currently being developed jointly by Novell and AT&T. These applications will be NLMs, and, when loaded on the server, actually extend the operating system to support telephony services.

New Application Services

NetWare 4.0 represents a major extension of NetWare application services. Hundreds of new programming interfaces are featured in NetWare 4.0, and developers have unprecedented access to internal operating system data structures and routines.

Moreover, NetWare 4.0 features a more robust scheduler, which makes it easier for developers to create efficient multithreaded NLMs. The addition of optional memory protection enables developers to eliminate memory-oriented programming errors very early in the development process, and provides users of NetWare with a way to protect the operating system from renegade NLMs.

Novell is working aggressively to provide several object-oriented programming interfaces and toolkits to NLM developers. These toolkits and interfaces make it easier to develop client-server applications, and to pave the way for the enterprise's in-house programmers to develop sophisticated client-server MIS applications.

Understanding Network Management

Network management is as critical to NetWare's success as an enterprise platform as NetWare Directory Services is. Rather than build a single comprehensive network-management service into NetWare, Novell elected instead to provide full support for existing network-management protocols, including SNMP, IBM's NetView, and others. (Network-management services are depicted as a triangle (application layer) in figure 3.1.)

To support multiple network-management protocols and information bases, Novell provided hooks in the core operating system that provide network-management information. This information is made available in a generic format to application-layer network management agents and consoles.

NetWare can be integrated within an enterprise's existing network management architecture, regardless of what that network management architecture is. This is another indication of NetWare's integrative (rather than comprehensive) approach to providing services.

One of the best examples of network management-related hooks in the operating system is the device-driver interface. Every device driver written for NetWare is required to maintain a comprehensive table of statistics and counters. NLMs may query device drivers for a copy of their statistics and counters. Driver statistics and counters can therefore be used by any network-management application or agent that is loaded on a NetWare server or workstation. Similar hooks are included in all areas of the operating system, including the file system, the security system, and others.

Because the NetWare operating system is so open to network-management applications, and because of the management-related information maintained by the operating system, several vendors of network media (hubs, concentrators, and interface cards) have chosen to base their network-management systems on a run-time version of the NetWare operating system.

NetWare as a Proactive Management Platform

Network-management applications that are based on NetWare can do more than passively collect and maintain information about NetWare itself. For example, NetWare for SAA enables an administrator to perform management functions on IBM mainframes by using the NetWare server as the management console.

Network-Management Information in NDS

NetWare Directory Services is designed to be friendly to network management systems and protocols. In fact, NDS is probably the best source of management-related information in NetWare 4.0. The base schema of NDS maintains a large body of management-related information, and has an excellent programming interface by which NLMs may obtain this information.

The real exploitation of NDS as a network-management tool will come in the future, when third-party developers extend the base schema of NDS to include customized management-related information. This is a rich area of potential for NDS that will provide many benefits to NetWare users.

Supporting Wide-Area Networks (WANs)

NetWare has historically been weak in its support of wide-area networks. This is true, not for any technical limitations of NetWare, but rather due to the historically-patterned priorities of NetWare's customers. However, if NetWare is to be a successful enterprise platform, it must provide robust support for wide-area networks.

Novell engineers have been improving NetWare's support of wide-area networks gradually over the years. Some of the most important developments were introduced with NetWare 3.11, including the following:

❖ IP tunnelling, which allows two NetWare servers to be connected via an IP WAN link

❖ Internal changes to the IPX routing protocol to allow for WAN links

❖ Packet-burst NCP, which improves file-service efficiency over WAN links

❖ Large Internet Packets (LIP), which increase the maximum packet size across internetwork routers

❖ The NetWare Communications Server, which integrates NetWare-to-host links and WAN links into a single service

NetWare 4.0 WAN Support

With NetWare 4.0, NetWare WAN support really comes of age. NetWare 4.0 features incremental improvements to all of the elements of WAN support listed previously. In addition, NetWare 4.0 introduces some powerful new mechanisms for WAN support. These mechanisms include the following:

❖ A replaceable router interface, which allows customized WAN routers to run on a NetWare server

❖ Support for Point-To-Point (PTP) WAN protocols

❖ Phasing out of the Service Advertising Protocol (SAP)

❖ New WAN-friendly versions of protocol stacks, including IPX/SPX and IP

NetWare 4.0's WAN features, together with the incremental improvements made to NetWare 3.11, eliminate the historical weaknesses of NetWare as a WAN platform.

Understanding Messaging Services

Traditionally, electronic mail has been the most popular application in networked environments. There are currently many different e-mail systems and protocols, and new requirements of e-mail systems are emerging, such as workflow automation and messages that contain alternative data types such as sound and imagery.

The current messaging service for NetWare is provided by a set of NLMs called *NetWare Global Messaging*. These NLMs enable an enterprise to integrate the different e-mail systems it uses, allowing administration and management of corporate e-mail from a single point. Global Messaging also enables the integration of the different message transmission methods currently in use, including modems, satellites, network media, and leased-lines.

The real importance of NetWare Global Messaging is that it allows e-mail to serve a more prominent role in corporate information processing. Global messaging allows for implicit document-format conversions, and contains many "automation hooks" that provide a foundation for automated workflow systems based upon messaging.

Summary

This chapter introduced NetWare as a computing environment. As such, NetWare's primary focus is to provide services to other computers over a network.

Architecturally, NetWare is a collection of network-related services. These services are all modular and extendible, and are linked together by the operating-system kernel. NetWare is designed to allow for the alteration and replacement of existing services, as well as for the introduction of new services in the future.

In the context of the enterprise, NetWare should be viewed as a *glue* technology. In other words, NetWare provides the glue with which to bind all the computing resources of the enterprise into a cohesive whole. Just as the NetWare kernel binds together modular services, forming a robust and unified operating system, NetWare as an environment can bind together the computing resources of the entire enterprise, regardless of the types of hardware or software currently in use.

PART 2

Features of NetWare 4.0

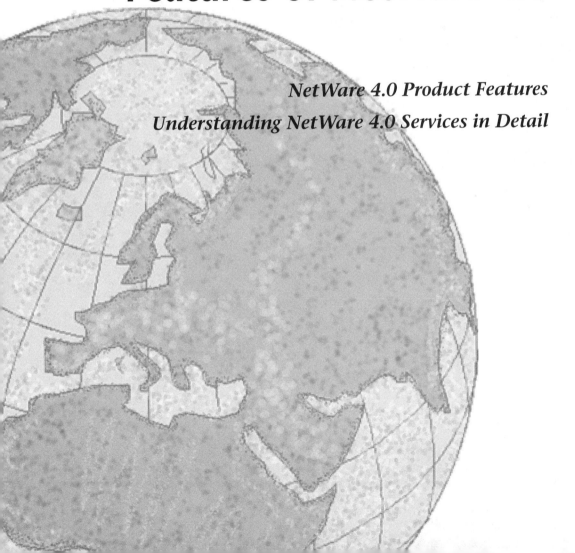

NetWare 4.0 Product Features

Understanding NetWare 4.0 Services in Detail

NetWare 4.0 Product Features

NetWare 4.0 is a significant step forward for Novell, in that it extends NetWare's reach to serve enterprise-wide network environments. This chapter discusses the important features of NetWare 4.0, and illustrates the enterprise-wide focus of those features where applicable.

Becoming a Foundation for the Enterprise Network

NetWare 4.0 was designed to bring an organization's computing resources under one umbrella, from both an administrative and user perspective. This "umbrella" is the NetWare 4.0 global directory services tree. A properly designed NetWare 4.0 network not only makes huge networks of computers easily manageable, but also makes all the resources in the network (file volumes, printers, application programs, and so on) available to the user in a transparent and user-friendly manner. Users are no longer limited to using resources of those NetWare servers on which they have accounts and authorization rights.

System administrators also now have more flexibility for managing the whole network (centralized) or sharing responsibilities with other system administrators (decentralized). The global directory tree makes all this possible by enabling system administrators to define their network in a logical manner that resembles their organizational structure, and by providing mechanisms to implement access control, also based on the same logical view.

Scaling NetWare from the Workgroup to the Enterprise

In addition to the global directory that builds the backbone for an enterprise network, NetWare 4.0 offers high-security support for a wide variety of storage-management devices. It also offers an enhanced file system, internationalization capabilities, graphical utilities that are supported on multiple client platforms, an easy-to-use printing service, host-connectivity options, and sophisticated network-management capabilities.

TIP

With the exception of the global directory service and a few other features, NetWare 4.0 is based on NetWare 3.11 (in terms of program source code); it derives its filing, printing, and LAN and WAN capabilities from this version. NetWare 4.0 is thus the platform of choice for workgroup computing because NetWare 3.11 has the lion's share of the market. Because of the global directory, NetWare 4.0 ensures that the network operating system of a business will provide the scalability necessary for a smooth transition from workgroup computing to enterprise computing.

Extending Fault Tolerance

Novell pioneered system reliability and fault tolerance through various levels of *Server Fault Tolerance (SFT)* technology. SFT level I, introduced with an early version of NetWare, provided two mechanisms that protect against data loss and data corruption.

The first mechanism is *read-after-write verification*. By reading back and verifying that every piece of data written to the disk is written accurately, this level of protection guarantees against data corruption.

The next mechanism, called the *hot fix*, handles bad blocks by redirecting writes to another area. The hot fix mechanism ensures that bad blocks are not used. Other procedures that SFT level I uses for fault tolerance and reliability include duplicating volume directories and file allocation tables (FATs), and using the duplicate copy in case the originals become corrupted.

SFT level II provides for mirroring disk drives or a complete disk channel. In *disk mirroring*, all data written to one disk is duplicated on the other. The duplicate data is used transparently by the server if any error happens while retrieving the original data. Disk channel mirroring, or *duplexing*, is an extension of disk mirroring, but it duplicates the entire disk channel.

SFT level III, which was under development by Novell for years, has finally ushered in the ultimate in server fault tolerance and reliability: both the memory and disk images from one server (the *primary* server) are duplicated onto another server (the *secondary* server). If the primary server fails, users are switched automatically to the secondary server, and continue operating as if nothing happened (see fig. 4.1).

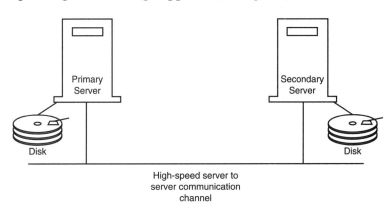

Figure 4.1:

NetWare SFT level III fault tolerance.

When the primary server comes back up, it resynchronizes its memory and disk image with that of the secondary server (which has now become the primary server), and assumes the role of the secondary server for continued fault tolerant operation.

TIP

SFT level III technology recently saw the light of day in a product release from Novell as a part of NetWare 3.11. Novell is now working on providing this technology on NetWare 4.0 (to be shipped a few months after NetWare 4.0 ships). This technology will enable organizations to use NetWare to run mission-critical applications without fear of downtime.

SOAPBOX

As I have elaborated in Chapters 1 and 2, Novell started out by filling the need for a "file and print server" product in the LAN marketplace. Ray Noorda (CEO, President, and Chairman of Novell, Inc.) believed in expanding Novell and its products in an "evolutionary" rather than a "revolutionary" way. While Microsoft and IBM were falling over themselves trying to build revolutionary products that customers needed tomorrow, Noorda set out to build "evolutionary" products that filled the top few needs of today's customers—he delayed advanced features until the customers were really ready to use them.

This delaying strategy worked well: Novell captured the huge *file-and-print* segment of the market, and worked up to slowly capture what it now calls the *workgroup-computing* market. This file-and-print market consisted primarily of small businesses that used NetWare in small LANs, mostly for printing and filing. VARs (Value Added Resellers) infiltrated this market by selling value-added applications, with NetWare "bundled" as the primary NOS. This process made NetWare a bigger presence in this market. Customers thought they were buying an application; they had no knowledge of NetWare or any other technology.

I remember walking into a dental office in Salt Lake City, Utah to find NetWare running on a server, and yet the people who worked there had no idea that they had NetWare. All they knew was that a VAR had sold them a dental business application.

The workgroup-computing segment of the market that Novell had grown into consisted primarily of departmental LANs that had started out with NetWare in small LANs, and had gradually diversified into bigger and bigger LANs connected through various WAN links. To satisfy an increasing customer need for better WAN connectivity, Noorda acquired Excelan, which offered connectivity solutions for WAN needs.

This acquisition, coupled with the introduction of NetWare 386 (now known as the NetWare 3.x product line), placed Novell in the position to win over the next market segment—the *enterprise* customer. Noorda's evolutionary strategy worked, and was providing handsome dividends.

During 1989 and 1990, Noorda set in motion plans to make a big thrust into what he defined as the enterprise market, and set his engineering resources to build the next generation of NetWare NOS. Having taken well over three years to build and undergo a name change from 3.2 to 4.0, Novell's engineers built an enterprise NOS with the features that were traditionally demanded by the enterprise customer. The engineers also worked to retain the simplicity, elegance, and performance that had made NetWare dear to many hearts in the file-and-print and workgroup-computing segments of the marketplace.

The NetWare Directory Services (NDS)

NetWare Directory Services (NDS) maintains a globally distributed and replicated database that contains all information about the computer network. In other words, the information database is broken into many logical pieces and is carried by many servers in the network (for easier maintenance). The information also can be replicated so that it can be available in all the parts of the network where users need it. This database is referred to as the *Directory Information Base (DIB)*. Information is quantified around objects that make up the network such as users, computers, servers, printers, modems, and so on. The user's access to this information and the resources defined in the DIB are transparent.

Another primary intent of building NDS was to migrate the user from using a server, and the resources on it, to a network with resources in it (see fig. 4.2). Instead of attaching to a server and finding resources on it (as under the previous versions of NetWare), the user accesses the directory database to find all resources in the network.

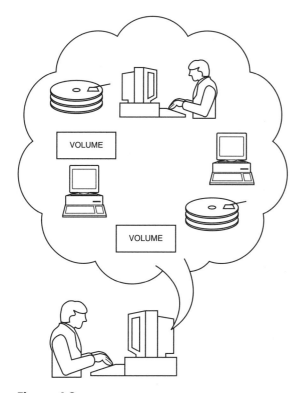

Figure 4.2:
Dealing with the network.

NDS was a feature that almost didn't make it into NetWare 4.0 because developing it was too ambitious a task, and the real development work did not begin on it until the third year of the project.

Kevin Kingdon, a brilliant computer software architect, was on a relentless quest to explore all of the work ever done on building a global directory by all past and present computer companies. He also was receiving mixed signals from many of Novell's leaders about which existing directory technology he should study for adopting into NetWare. For a few months, it was AT&T and its global directory technology; then, it was Sun Microsystems' technology. For a long time, it seemed to Kevin that life was full of meetings, and he would be lucky if he ever got any work done. When I came on board, the current fancy was the X.500 directory services definition standard, and Kevin had done some incredible work on it.

Admittedly having little knowledge of name services or X.500, I set my foot down, built a project plan and a firm set of deliverables, and commandeered my rather small programmer army (five engineers—one of them a documentor) to build a X.500-based name service. A few months down the road (early 1991), I realized that what Kevin had undertaken to do was one mammoth "mother" of a project. No one in the industry had ever built anything similar to this beast, and we had to accomplish this by the end of 1991.

Having been caught in the expectations trap that I set up for myself, I paid a mighty penalty to keep the project alive, get the necessary staffing and commitment, keep from being fired or relocated to Siberia, and take a year longer to build and deliver on my commitment. In the end, I went through hell and high water to deliver my baby, but my reputation was a bit tarnished for being late.

With the shipping of NetWare 4.0, I feel a tremendous amount of satisfaction for a task well done: a global, replicated, distributed, hierarchical, enterprise-wide naming service with strong authentication and rich access control. Even Microsoft, with its massive R&D budget, an army of programmers, and industry gurus such as Dave Cutler and Jim Allchin, was at least two years behind. Ray Noorda had met the commitment to the industry to keep Novell "two years ahead, and gaining" on its competitors.

Due to the read/write replication of data, NetWare 4.0 has no single point of failure. That is, access to required information always can be granted, even if the server holding that information is down, because the requested information is made available from another replicated copy somewhere else in the network.

Figure 4.3 illustrates that user Fred still can access information about a resource, even though the server he accesses for this information is down. In this example, Fred tries to get information about object FAX1 from SERVER1. SERVER1 is down. NDS software on the client workstation automatically locates and obtains this information from SERVER2.

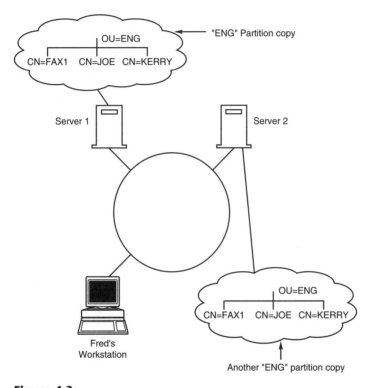

Figure 4.3:

NDS fault-tolerant access to data.

Note that this directory database partition has an organizational unit (OU) called ENG, under which are the FAX1 object and two other user objects, Joe and Kerry. CN refers to the Common Name property, which is a way of naming leaf objects under the directory.

TIP

See Chapter 6 for more information on leaf objects and NetWare Directory Services.

The directory database provides a logical framework for defining the objects in the network. This logical framework can and should resemble the organizational structure. Thus, the network can look the same as the user's own organization. For example, all servers, users, printers, and other resources are presented to the user in the same logical fashion as they are in real life.

As figure 4.4 illustrates, user Fred looks up a laser printer belonging to his department (engineering) under an organizational unit called Engineering in the global NDS tree. It is easy for Fred to look up any resource in the network simply by going to that part of the NDS tree in which he expects that resource to belong.

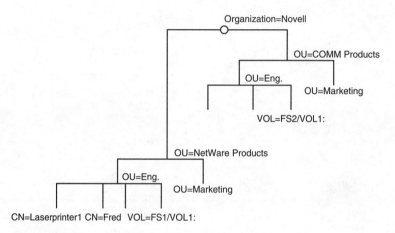

Figure 4.4:

NDS logical tree.

The *network view* that NDS provides needs to be reflected in many of today's popular desktop applications. Novell is actively working with many of these application vendors to enable them to provide this NDS view. For example, with previous versions of NetWare, if user Fred uses the WordPerfect word processing application and wants to print a document, he must do the following:

❖ Print to a print queue that is specifically located on a given server and serviced by a specific print server that then prints to a specific printer. For this printing to happen flawlessly, user Fred must configure his WordPerfect application to print to specific print queues, and he must have access to these specific print queues given to him by a system administrator. Fred also must be aware of which print queues map to which printer devices, and where the printers are located in the building.

If WordPerfect is "NDS-aware," user Fred only has to do the following:

❖ Query WordPerfect to present to him all available printers in his department. He can specify a search criteria that includes the desired characteristics of the printer, whether it must be a Postscript printer, be capable of printing nine pages-per-minute, or be located in a certain part of the building. WordPerfect then performs a search of the NDS database for the given department to find all printers that match the search criteria, and presents them to user Fred in, perhaps, a list box. Fred then selects the printer of his choice and performs his printing.

NDS makes all this possible by holding information about all relevant network objects and providing different ways to access this information (read, search-through critera, and so on). Organizations can extend the information about these network objects to make them customizable for their user community, as well as store their own objects' definitions.

TIP

Several chapters of this book deal with the architecture of NDS, and the process involved in proper planning and the use of the NDS tree. Specifically, refer to Chapter 6 and Chapter 12.

High-Performance Network Operating System

NetWare is a high-performance network operating system that was designed to handle thousands of interrupts, as well as thousands of client workstation requests-per-second. NetWare is also a *non-preemptive* operating system—tasks run to completion, and do not yield the CPU until they are done with their job. Applications can use NetWare's non-preemptive nature to their advantage by providing maximum performance and throughput to users. This is especially true for task-oriented applications, in which throughput can be maximized if the application can complete the task at hand—uninterrupted—before the CPU is given to some other application. NetWare has highly efficient process arbitration and process-execution algorithms.

In addition to the features that characterize NetWare releases to date, NetWare 4.0 also employs a new process-management concept that speeds network-packet processing and, therefore, increases overall throughput. In addition, NetWare 4.0 gives network administrators the capability to internally "handicap" network applications that may be slowing down the overall operation of the server.

The new Work-To-Do algorithms replace the low priority polling process that characterized previous versions of NetWare. The polling process provides the vehicle whereby hardware devices attached to the server present packets to the operating system. Although not obsolete, the polling process wastes CPU cycles by running through packets in a mechanical, predictable way.

The Work-To-Do algorithm still uses polling to get information from device drivers that do not use hardware interrupts, but the flow of execution is much more dynamic, depending on the current workload of the server. The polling process handled one packet per server process; the Work-To-Do algorithms enable server processes to handle many packets, according to the length of the Work-To-Do queue.

Memory Management

NetWare 4.0 has a simplified, highly optimized memory-management scheme that is adaptable to servers supporting hundreds of users at any given time.

NetWare 4.0 has only one memory allocation pool (instead of the five or more memory pools managed by previous versions of NetWare). This enables an efficient allocation/deallocation scheme, and fewer operations are required for an application to access and use memory.

Performance was one of the main reasons for the overhaul of memory management under NetWare 4.0. NetWare now uses an Intel-based paging mechanism to allocate and manage the system's memory resources. Memory allocation will be easier for application NLM (NetWare Loadable Module) developers because only one global allocation pool exists. Figure 4.5 illustrates the way NetWare manages the memory pool, with one global allocation pool plus system cache. Each process also is assigned its own allocation pool.

Drew Major (chief architect of NetWare) is always trying to wring a few extra CPU cycles out of his code. He can count by hand the number of instructions it takes for NetWare to do a given core-filing task. Drew has a storybook full of interesting nights spent making a file read or write, or making some other operation a cycle or two shorter. He always has a delightful look on his face when he recounts these stories.

In meetings with Intel, Drew almost always brings out an instruction that he frequently uses in his code paths, and pleads with Intel to cut the number of cycles it takes to execute that instruction.

Once, I was quietly sitting in my office looking out the window (it overlooks a nice golf course; Ray Noorda is a frequent golfer there). I heard cries of excitement outside. Alarmed, I ran outside to find Drew and a few engineers celebrating. Apparently, they had received a Pentium microprocessor instruction manual from Intel that day, and discovered that Intel had cut down a few cycles from a few instructions. Drew (nearly frothing at the mouth, I must add) told me jubilantly how many extra cycles were saved in a file read.

I have had a tiff or two with Drew over the need for engineers to spend hours trying to wring a few cycles out of their codes (instead of doing some other productive task like, say, coding new features). For Drew, NetWare is like a sports car—it should be made to go as fast as the laws of physics allow.

Aside from its simplicity and elegance, Drew hastens to remind me, NetWare's chief strength has been its performance. No matter how fast the CPU can go, Drew adds, users will always make it run out of bandwidth by making it do more and more. NetWare should be lean and mean, and it should get the user the most "bang for the buck" from any hardware.

NetWare can be termed a *cache* machine. The memory sitting in the cache is used by NetWare to optimize reads and writes into the NetWare file system. The more memory available in the cache, the better it is for performance.

As revealed in figure 4.5, the operating system gives each process (and/or NLM) its own allocation pool. With each process managing its own memory, allocation is faster and much less complex. In previous versions of NetWare, each process was subject to the current condition of the global allocation pool, over which it had no control.

When the NLM—or processes executing within an NLM—requests memory, the NLM memory pool is checked first. If no memory is there, memory—in 4K-page chunks—is fetched from the cache. When memory is returned to the pool, it goes back to the cache. This enables NetWare to recycle all memory returned after use. Also, a new *garbage collection algorithm* is in place in NetWare 4.0 to avoid memory-fragmentation problems.

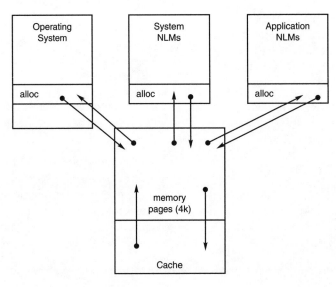

Figure 4.5:

NetWare 4.0 memory allocation.

Storage Management of On-Line and Off-Line Devices

NetWare's strong suit always has been its wide variety of supported on-line and off-line storage media, such as hard disks and tapes. NetWare 4.0 carries many new features that expand support for newer storage devices in the market and provide more efficient uses of the hard disks on the server.

One new feature is *block suballocation*, which provides a new mechanism to subdivide disk blocks among files that make up the file system. The block usage is more tuned to the size of a file, and it does not waste disk space.

Block suballocation divides any partially used disk block into 512-byte suballocation blocks. Thus, a 512-byte file uses 512 bytes only—as opposed to the full block size, which can stretch from 4K to 64K. If the default block size is 4K, for example, and a file takes 5K, one 4K block is used, plus a 1K-chunk of the second 4K block to make up the file. The rest of the second 4K block (3K) is then shared with some other file or files. Block suballocation is turned on by default when NetWare 4.0 is installed. Figure 4.6 illustrates the way block suballocation works within NetWare.

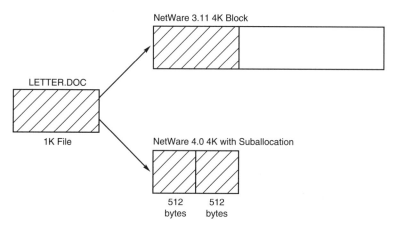

Figure 4.6:

Block suballocation.

Another feature is *data migration*, which enables administrators to move files from active on-line media (such as hard disks) to slower off-line media (such as tapes or jukeboxes) by using a set of migration rules. Although NetWare considers the files to reside on the primary medium, this scheme enables the administrator to make more efficient use of the hard disks by making the system automatically migrate rarely-used or huge files off to attached slower jukeboxes that can support large quantities of information storage. *Jukeboxes* in NetWare work like music jukeboxes, except that you have storage platters rather than music records. Users can request the mounting of any platter on demand.

Background file compression is another function that the NetWare server can undertake, during "idle" time, to compress files on the hard disks (see fig. 4.7).

Files are decompressed when they are accessed by the user or the application. Disk space of up to 70 percent can be freed if this feature is enabled at the NetWare server. This means that a 700M-volume that is full can regain up to 490M when the file-compression feature is enabled on the server.

Users can, however, flag files or directories that should never be compressed. After compression is enabled, files flagged for compression that are not accessed for a specific amount of time are compressed automatically. Files are decompressed on the server when accessed by a user.

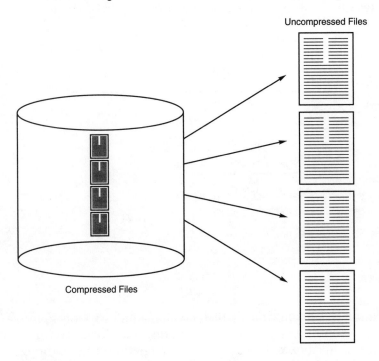

Figure 4.7:

File compression.

TIP

A volume is enabled for file compression by default when NetWare 4.0 is installed.

NetWare 4.0 also provides additional media-management functions through a new device interface called the *NetWare Peripheral Architecture (NPA)*. This device should enable many more storage devices that support CD-ROMs, flopticals (optical recording mediums that look like floppy disks), WORMs (Write Once, Read Many type media), and so on, to be supported under NetWare 4.0 servers. The NPA enables device-driver developers to develop drivers for newer storage devices in a much shorter time than before, and will reduce or eliminate the need to rewrite those drivers for future versions of NetWare.

Auditing of Server and Network Information

NetWare 4.0 enables an auditing function that is independent of the administrative function on a given NetWare server. By using this feature, an auditor account can be created that gives the auditor person the capability to monitor a variety of events relating to the file system, queue management, and even the global directory usage.

Some of the actions that can be audited are as follows:

❖ Logins and logouts

❖ Trustee modifications

❖ File and directory creations, deletions, reads, and writes

❖ Queue-management activities

❖ Events relating to the global directory services, such as the creation of global objects

❖ A variety of user actions on the network

Auditing can be enabled at the volume level for a given file server and at a container level for auditing global directory services objects. Audit data and history files are maintained to record all the auditing information. Auditors then can examine records to make sure that transactions are accurate, and that confidential information is secure.

The auditing function is distinctly different from the function of an administrator. An auditor can track only activities and events relating to a volume or a network—there is no authorization to perform any supervisory activities. An auditor's job is to observe and make sure that system integrity is not compromised by any of the users, including the supervisor.

As figure 4.8 illustrates, an auditor's relationship with a server/network administrator is similar to that of an independent auditor and a bank president.

Security of the Server and the Network

NetWare 4.0 enables users to log in to a network, as opposed to the NetWare tradition of logging in to one server at a time to find and use resources. The client workstation uses a background-authentication scheme by using highly secure public and private key cryptosystem algorithms that are licensed from RSA Data Systems.

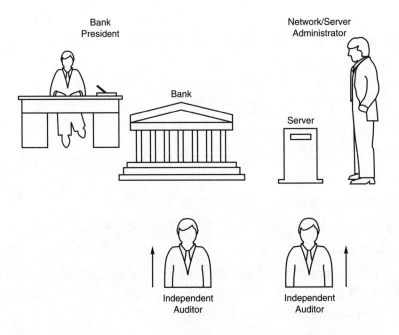

Figure 4.8:
The auditor and the administrator.

Under this scheme, the actual user password is not exchanged between the client workstation and the server, thus undermining any attempts to steal password-related information by eavesdropping on the LAN wire through network analyzers and other devices.

TIP
For more information on this public and private key technology, see Chapter 6.

Logging in to the network (instead of a server) is made possible by the newer NetWare client software on the workstation. This software can store password-related information in a highly secure form, called a *digital signature*, on the client workstation. This signature is used to "mint" new proofs of authentication every time a user attaches to a server in the network.

This authentication process is performed automatically by the client workstation, without any intervention from the user, whenever a user attaches to a new server in the network. As a result, the user never has to type in a password except the first time he logs in to the network.

NetWare 4.0 also uses a global access control system, which can be totally centralized or decentralized in varying degrees to control access to and better manage the network.

Optional Memory Protection

NetWare 4.0 provides the capability to "quarantine" NLMs (server-based applications) to run in protected mode. This prevents ill-behaved NLMs from running astray and crashing the server (see fig. 4.9). This memory protection is optional; the administrator can decide to forgo protection, run the application in the same memory as the server operating system, and gain added performance.

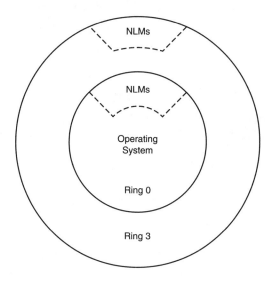

Figure 4.9:

Optional memory protection.

The NLMs that run protected actually are loaded into a memory domain that is separate from the server memory domain in which the NetWare operating system runs. This domain is called the OS_PROTECTED domain. The OS_PROTECTED domain can be located at any of the rings of the Intel architecture, such as ring 1, 2, or 3. The protection capability offered by NetWare does not differ across these rings, even though users expect to run protected applications at ring 3.

TIP

Under the Intel CPU architecture, the program with the highest privilege runs at the lowest ring (ring 0), and the program with the lowest privilege runs at ring 3. Normally, operating systems run at ring 0, from which they can exercise full control of the machine (memory, interrupts, and so on). Applications run at ring 3, from which they are allowed to use only the services provided by the operating systems.

Not all NLMs can be loaded into the OS_PROTECTED domain. Although all NLMs are capable of running at ring 0 with the NetWare operating system, not all NLMs can run in the OS_PROTECTED domain—only those NLMs that use the proper cross-domain function calls can run in this domain.

WARNING

Refer to the documentation that comes with the NLM to ensure that it can run in the OS_PROTECTED domain before actually loading the NLM in that domain.

If you load an application in the OS_PROTECTED domain, you can experience some performance degradation. The extent of performance degradation depends on the application. Applications that need to "talk" to the operating system frequently (that is, call many operating system-provided APIs) to do their jobs are the most hurt by the memory-protection scheme. To get high performance, as well as protection from server failures, the following guidelines are recommended:

❖ If the application is Novell-certified, and the user's prior experience with the application has been good, run the application at ring 0 at the same area as the operating system. No performance degradation occurs.

❖ If you have doubts about an application, run it at ring 3. Do this at load time. Note that not all applications can run at ring 3, and some may fail to load at ring 3. In that event, the user either can run it at ring 0 or wait until the application developer provides a new version that can run at ring 3. Running the application at ring 3 can result in some loss of performance.

❖ If the application has run at ring 3, and has demonstrated that it is
well-behaved (or the application is Novell-certified), the user can
unload the application from ring 3 and load it at ring 0. This is likely
to result in higher performance.

WAN Enhancements

In previous versions of NetWare, every packet that was transmitted had to
be acknowledged before the next packet was sent. The result was more
time taken overall for any data transmission, as well as more control
packets flowing between the source and the destination to accomplish any
data transfer. As a result, more time was taken to transfer data on slower
WAN links.

The new *packet burst* protocol improves performance for client workstations by efficiently transmitting multipacket messages between the client
and the server. Packets of data are transmitted in *bursts* between the server
and the client.

TIP
Packet burst must be enabled at the client through a statement in the NET.CFG
file on the workstation.

A *large internet packet (LIP)* capability was added to NetWare 4.0. It enables
larger packets to be sent across the network, and enhances throughput
across and between bridges and routers by increasing packet sizes being
transmitted.

The SPX protocol also has been enhanced under NetWare 4.0. A newer SPX
II protocol offers higher throughput and speed through a *windowing*
interface that allows multiple data packets to be sent between source and
destination with a single acknowledgement. SPX II offers a TLI interface. It
is backward-compatible with applications written to SPX, but it offers
higher performance and throughput only if written to its TLI interface.

In addition to these basic capabilities, Novell provides for several other
WAN products that offer links to SAA, IP tunneling, TCP/IP connectivity,
and so on. A forthcoming Novell offering is the software-based
Multiprotocol Router (MPR), which routes multiple protocol packets, varying
from IPX to IP through the use of an NLM on a NetWare server. These
offerings from Novell make NetWare 4.0 very suitable for an enterprise
network, in which the need for different types of WAN connectivity
options exists.

Competitors say that NetWare is a LAN-only solution, and perceive it as weak when it comes to WANs. To correct this impression, as well as to give NetWare all the WAN capabilities that it needed, Novell acquired Excelan in 1989.

The Excelan division (now named the Interoperability Systems Group, headed by Kanwal Rekhi) provides a variety of WAN products: NetWare for SAA, LAN Workplace for DOS, CommServer, Multiprotocol Router (MPR), and many others.

Without this "weakness," competitors then said that IPX (NetWare's native protocol) was a LAN-centric protocol, and it was not really suited for a WAN. Weaknesses in IPX, some detractors point out, include its ping-pong style protocol that requires an acknowledgment for every packet sent, its inability to send packets larger than 512 bytes across the network, and the ever-growing SAP (Server Advertising Protocol) packets that eat up a large bandwidth of the network traffic. Novell has addressed the first two weaknesses of IPX through the packet burst feature and the LIP feature. How about SAP? Before I answer this, let me give you some background on SAP.

SAP is the way that services (Novell-written NLMs, third-party NLMs, and basic NetWare servers) make themselves known in the network. SAP packets are broadcast every few seconds, and are collected and kept in the bindery by every NetWare server that gets them. When a service is gone and stops "SAPing," the NetWare server removes the entry from the bindery. The UNIX Internet expects all services to advertise themselves in the Internet Domain Naming Service and remove themselves when they stop giving out that service. A service that has gone away may never remove its entry, and users find this out only when they try to locate that service after looking up the DNS (Domain Naming Service) entry for that service. SAP is more dynamic, and gives a more accurate representation of the state of the service.

To enable customers to better manage the SAP traffic, Novell provides a service called the *SAP filter* (an NLM that runs on the NetWare server), which administrators can use to monitor SAPs from other LANs and filter out those that they don't want proliferated into their local LANs. This requires more administrative effort, though, and is a short-term solution, not a long-term one.

With the NDS global database, I believe that Novell has provided the long-term answer for SAPs (such as what is prevalent in the DNS—UNIX Internet—community). All services should advertise themselves in the NDS database instead of putting out their own SAPs. I expect that in the next couple of years all services will follow this procedure. To make the service state more dynamic, Novell may opt to release a feature that will let NDS "ping" the service periodically and remove its entry from the NDS database if it is no longer active.

Internationalization

By separating all messages from the server and the applications; and by isolating all locale-related information, such as date, time, and currency into separate modules, NetWare 4.0 becomes an *internationalized* operating system. A toolkit also is provided to developers that enables application development to be adapted to any country and/or language.

English is the default language bound into the server and the applications, and also is enabled by default in the event that designated language message files and/or information is absent on the server (see fig. 4.10).

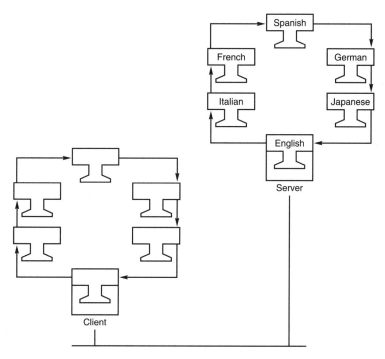

Figure 4.10:

Multiple language support.

The initial release of NetWare 4.0 supports the English, French, Spanish, Italian, German, and Japanese languages. The minimal work involved in translating NetWare 4.0 to other languages almost certainly means that NetWare will be released in many other languages in the future.

SOAPBOX

While we were making NetWare localizable for different countries and languages, one of the engineers in my group found a way to make multiple NLMs run on the same server, but in different languages. When he demonstrated this feature to me, I thought it was neat, but I didn't really think it was a feature to be touted because who in the world would want to run multiple NLMs in multiple languages on the same server? Because it made for an interesting demo, however, I kept it in the script of an internal milestone demonstration to the Novell executive staff.

As it happened, Uncle Ray (Noorda) came to this demo, saw this feature, and liked it a lot. Some marketing people (I guess) took their cue from this and started touting this feature to customers. I laughed it off at first, but (embarrassingly) found myself "demo-ing" this feature in my briefings with customers as well.

Print Services

NetWare uses a print queue and print server to enable several network workstations to print to a network printer. The print jobs then are routed to a queue, in which a print server picks them up and prints on a printer.

To accomplish this, NetWare uses three NDS objects: the print queue, the print server, and the printer objects. Under previous versions of NetWare, these objects were server-centric, and they were defined in a given server's database (the *bindery*), which was accessible only to that server and to the users who are attached to that server. Under NetWare 4.0, these are global NDS objects, accessible to all in the network from anywhere in the network.

When a network workstation sends a print job to be printed on a network printer, NetWare temporarily stores the print job in a network directory called a *print queue* until the print server can relay it to a printer. The *print server* monitors print queues and printers. It takes the print jobs and sends them to the assigned printer. The print server consists of software that can be loaded either on a NetWare server, or on a DOS or OS/2 workstation.

Printers can attach directly to the network, to print servers, or to DOS or OS/2 network workstations. In previous versions of NetWare, users could print only to print queues. They had to figure out, with some effort, which printers the print queues actually serviced. Under NetWare 4.0, the destination for a print job can either be the printer name or the print queue. This makes printing easier and more user-friendly.

To illustrate the way that printing has changed from previous versions of NetWare to NetWare 4.0, examine figures 4.11 and 4.12.

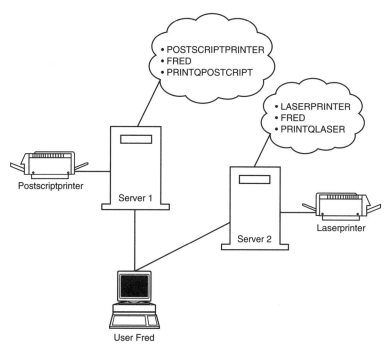

Figure 4.11:

Printing under previous versions of NetWare.

In figure 4.11, user Fred sends his print job to either queue PRINTQPOSTSCRIPT or to PRINTQLASER. Both of these queues are configured on different NetWare servers, and Fred has to configure his workstation's print-queue setting appropriately.

Fred also must be told by the department's system administrator about the way print queues map to printers, and where the printers are located in the department. Fred also must have duplicate user accounts created for him in both of these servers by the administrators of those servers, and have appropriate privileges granted to him.

In figure 4.12, user Fred can send his print jobs directly to the printers. In this case, Fred sends his print jobs to either queue POSTSCRIPTPRINTER or LASERPRINTER. Both of these printers (and their associated print queues) are defined under the department PAYROLL (where Fred works), and Fred can query the NDS database for more information about these printers (fonts supported, location, and so on). System administrators need to define Fred's user account only once (in the global NDS tree under department PAYROLL), and grant Fred access rights to both of these printers. The NDS logical tree and its user-friendly way of grouping objects makes it easy to set up and use from both the system administrator's and user's point of view.

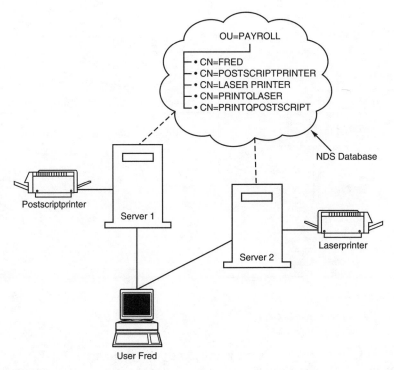

Figure 4.12:

Printing under NetWare 4.0.

Backup Services

Backup under NetWare is based on an architecture called *Storage Management Services (SMS)*. SMS has two major components: one for users and one for developers.

The user component, SBACKUP, provides basic backup, restore, and upgrade-migration capabilities for all supported versions of NetWare. The developer component, a set of NetWare NLMs, provides a standard, extensible architecture upon which developers can build their own backup and restore applications. *Target Service Agents (TSAs)* pass requests from SBACKUP to the NetWare server in which the data resides, and return the requested data to SBACKUP. TSAs are also provided for networked workstations to back up and restore data that reside on these workstations. A separate TSA is provided to back up the global NDS database.

SMS is designed to enable third-party developers to build sophisticated front-end applications without spending time studying the details of network file systems. SMS architecture is standardized across all versions of NetWare, and it is a reliable, open architecture that both ensures backward-compatibility and allows for future development. Figure 4.13 illustrates that SMS provides a storage-management solution for all Novell-supported client workstations and NetWare server versions, as well as backup/restore functions for the NDS database.

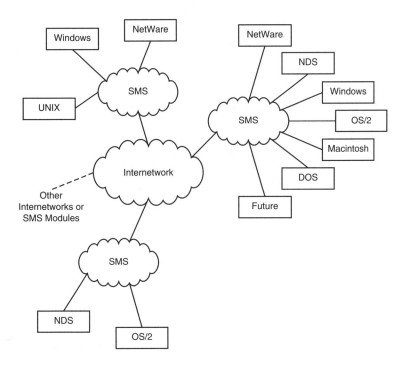

Figure 4.13:
SMS architecture.

Image-Enabled Server

Novell and Eastman Kodak (Imagery Division) teamed up in a project to *image enable* NetWare 4.0. The goal was to provide a set of back-end services for NetWare that allow the current image application vendors to build to a standard platform and provide a platform that allow non-imaging applications to become image-enabled (see fig. 4.14). Specifically, by using the services provided by *Image Management Services (IMS)*, applications can access and manipulate images in a variety of ways.

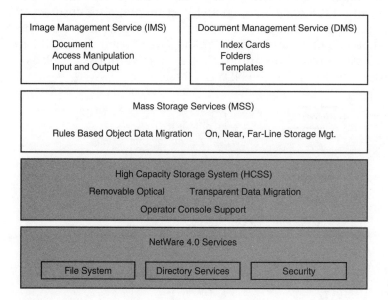

Figure 4.14:

Support for new breeds of image- or document-management applications.

Groupware, office automation, document management, electronic mail, and database applications are the types of applications that are primary targets to be image-enabled. These are the applications, prevalent on PC desktops, that provide information-sharing and communications. These applications need to be enabled to make image just another data type.

Many of these applications can store and manipulate bit maps in a rudimentary fashion, but they are not designed to deal efficiently with the large amounts of data that dealing with images regularly requires. Descriptions of products being co-developed by Novell and Kodak are presented in the following list.

❖ **High Capacity Storage Subsystem (HCSS).** The HCSS is based on the data migration and media-management capabilities of the NetWare 4.0 file system. This entry-level data migration application gives NetWare 4.0 administrators the capability to migrate data from primary storage to (slower) secondary storage, based on a high- and low-water mark.

The administrator sets a high and low percentage mark that indicates when HCSS will migrate files, based on the last accessed date. Each day HCSS migrates files to the low-water mark specification. If primary storage reaches the high-water mark, HCSS dynamically begins to migrate files to secondary storage. The migrated files appear to the user to be located on primary storage (the directory structure is kept intact), but when the migrated file is accessed, it will be de-migrated in real-time to primary storage for use. Secondary storage can be optical jukeboxes, DAT jukeboxes, and so on. Initially, HCSS provides the capability to utilize the HP 5 1/4-inch optical jukeboxes as secondary storage devices. Figure 4.15 illustrates the functionality of HCSS.

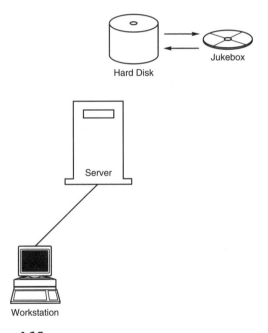

Figure 4.15:
Data migration, using HCSS.

❖ **Imaging Management Service (IMS):** The IMS provides the imaging-specific component of the product options. This is the service that provides access to various image-file formats and bit-map manipulations (compression, decompression, scaling, rotating, image enhancements, and so on) for bitonal, gray scale, and color images. The service also provides for image input/output. The scanner API is based on the TWAIN scanner device interface.

❖ **Mass Storage Service (MSS):** The MSS is a hierarchical storage subsystem that uses available NetWare file stores, including HCSS, to move files and data transparently across various types of media on the network. Most likely, the moves are from fast, high-cost hard disks to slower, lower-cost optical disks. The product enables relationships to be built between a set of files or objects (*object sets*), and for the set to move inherently as a unit through the various media types.

This functionality, although required for an effective image system, is not imaging-specific and, therefore, is useful for other data-intensive applications. Backup companies have expressed a strong interest in understanding the technology being built so that they can provide effective backup mechanisms. An administrator-user interface will be provided.

❖ **Document Management, Indexing, and Search Service (DMS):** When storing a large quantity of images, it is necessary to have a method for the application to index and subsequently search for the images. This service, built on NetWare SQL, provides for a configurable indexing paradigm of index cards, folders, and nested folders. The services utilize NDS to enable the application to find DMS databases on various servers to provide a distributed document-management environment. The service also provides versioning and security of index cards. As with MSS, this service is not imaging-specific. It also can be used as a foundation for a traditional (for example, word processing) document-management company to build a document-management system.

Note that HCSS is shipped with NetWare 4.0 basic release, and all the other components of imaging (MSS, IMS, and DMS) will be available later on, and must be purchased separately.

An Enhanced and Expanded Set of NetWare Utilities

In addition to streamlining the text utilities supported previously by NetWare, a new set of graphical utilities that support Windows and OS/2 operating systems has been developed. The highlight of these utilities is the *browser*, which enables the administration of the entire network from a workstation.

It can be difficult to remember an object's location in the directory because the directory can be large, hierarchical, and have many levels. Instead of trying to remember an object's location, you can use the browser to browse up and down the directory to find the object.

The initial release of NetWare 4.0 utilities supports DOS, Windows, and OS/2 workstations. Support for Apple Macintosh workstations will also be available. Meanwhile, Mac workstations can access and administer the NetWare 4.0 servers as if they are NetWare 3.11 servers because NetWare 4.0 is fully backward-compatible.

A highlight of the menu utilities is that they now feature help key lines on every screen, and the command-line utilities also feature improved on-line help.

Some utilities that were considered redundant have been eliminated, and some utilities have been combined. A few new utilities also have been introduced.

Both the NetWare 4.0 server and the NetWare 4.0 for OS/2 server support a variety of utilities that run as NLMs on the server. The server utilities are primarily used to manage memory allocations, monitor the way the server is used, and manage the workstations' use of resources on the server.

On-Line Documentation

An electronic version of the printed documentation is available through a Windows or OS/2 interface. This documentation can be accessed on client Windows and OS/2 workstation screens through the use of the NetWare Communication Services browser. All NetWare 4.0 manuals are available on-line, except for the quick access guide.

The browser enables the reader to do the following:

❖ Scroll gradually or sequentially through a book

❖ Move between parts of the book to follow cross-references

❖ Return to sections of the book that were previously viewed

❖ Search for specific words or phrases

❖ Print sections of the book or the whole book

❖ Display several views of a book at any time

❖ Open several books and view them at the same time

❖ Set a predefined viewing path so that only desired sections of the book are covered during a reading session

An Easier Platform to Develop NLMs

Novell introduced NLMs as a way to unleash powerful new services on NetWare 3.x operating systems. Many third-party developers now offer applications on NetWare through NLMs. Novell itself releases many services on the NetWare platform in the form of NLMs. Some NLMs are shipped with the basic NetWare product; some can be purchased separately.

NLMs were designed to run as extensions of the operating system at ring 0 of the Intel architecture. Tools are available today from third-party companies for developers to write NLMs on the NetWare server. Novell provides a compiler toolkit for writing NLMs in association with a company called Watcom. The NLMs are written and developed on the MS-DOS or Novell DOS platform, and then made to run on the NetWare server.

The major strength of NLMs is the nonpreemptive nature of the operating system that enables a task to run to completion. Well-written NLMs can take advantage of this by providing high performances that could not possibly be obtained under a preemptive operating system.

WARNING

Badly written NLMs have the potential to eat away too much CPU time without properly yielding the CPU, and can cause an overall server-performance degradation.

The other strength of NLMs is that they run as extensions of the operating system itself. This provides higher performance than comparable operating systems do because it is easier for the NLM to use operating-system services. No "protection" layer examines the interaction between the application and the operating system, causing decreased performance. The disadvantage of this feature is that it allows a badly written application to violate the operating system integrity by overwriting key memory areas and bringing the server down.

With the introduction of NetWare 4.0, Novell addressed the weaknesses to a great extent, while retaining all the key strengths, as the following list outlines:

❖ The memory-protection feature (as described earlier in the chapter) is optional, and enables the user to determine whether an application is safe at a protected area in ring 3. After an application is proven safe, the user has the option to unload it from ring 3, and then reload it at ring 0 to gain additional performance.

❖ Novell has a certification process in place for NLMs that enables Novell to certify NLMs as "good" and "free" from trouble. This certification process, however, costs time and money for developers. Novell is now looking to provide self-certification procedures for developers so that they can self-certify their NLMs at less cost, and have faster access to the market.

❖ With NetWare 4.0, Novell provides a server-based NLM that enables the system administrator to find those applications that consume more than their fair share of CPU, and "handicap" them—thus giving the user the option to enforce good behavior.

❖ Novell actively works with its industry partners to provide more tools for writing and debugging NLMs on the NetWare platform. Novell also has invested a considerable amount of money and time to developing quality documentation for Application Program Interfaces (APIs) and other information needed by third-party developers. With NetWare 4.0, Novell has put in place an SDK (Software Development Kit) process, ensuring that developers get the operating system, documentation of functional interfaces, and tools for writing NLMs long before the operating system actually is released to the market.

TIP

Novell has expanded its industry presence by signing agreements with Sun and HP to provide NetWare on their RISC workstations. Although this is expected to result in a significantly enhanced performance for NetWare, the other less-known feature is the superior development platform that these RISC workstations bring to the marketplace.

On HP workstations, you can compile, code, and debug more than one server-based NLM at the same time! In essence, you can tap into and debug multiple NLMs that run on multiple NetWare servers (which can either be Intel-based or RISC-based) from multiple windows on your workstation screen. HP RISC workstations, for instance, also provide for source-code level debugging, as well as a very sophisticated full-featured debugger. The tools provided on these workstations seem clearly superior to anything I have seen on PC-based operating systems.

SOAPBOX

History has shown that every new operating system has been too big, too unreliable, and too slow. OS/2 and the first release of LAN Server are some examples. Will NetWare 4.0 follow in their footsteps? No!

A lot of reports in the press have said that NetWare 4.0 was written from scratch to provide the global directory and other features. This is incorrect—this statement applies to the NetWare client software and the utilities that were totally rewritten to make them network-centric. Novell followed a different strategy for the operating system.

At the onset of v4.0 development, I commissioned my chief engineer to find out if he could take the v3.11 operating system, break the bindery-name service away from it, and define a "naming" interface between the core operating system and an external naming service.

At the same time, another engineering team was given the charter to find out if memory protection could be provided for NetWare applications through a separate NLM. Later on in the process, another group was given the charter to find out if licensing could be broken out of the operating system into a separate NLM module.

The licensing project was initiated because NetWare 4.0 will provide for network licensing in the future. Wouldn't it be nice if you could just drop in a new licensing NLM on an existing NetWare 4.0 server so that you could take advantage of network-licensing capabilities? What resulted in the end was a 4.0 operating system, as illustrated in figure 4.16.

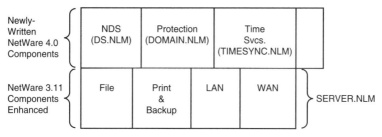

Figure 4.16:

NetWare 4.0 architecture.

The traditional SERVER.EXE now contains the core OS (SERVER.NLM), the NDS name services (DS.NLM), and the licensing extension (POLICY.NLM). The other pieces needed for operation are NLMs that are loaded automatically, such as the one that provides for memory protection (DOMAIN.NLM), and the global time services (TIMESYNC.NLM).

Thus, the heart of NetWare 4.0 is the proven v3.11 core-operating system, aided by other "enterprise-type" extensions. In benchmarks, NetWare 4.0 may actually turn out to be faster than v3.11! None of the v3.11 code paths for filing and printing (the traditional target for benchmarks) have been touched much, and NetWare 4.0 also features a server-based read-ahead cache that significantly enhances the performance for many filing activities.

Summary

NetWare 4.0 is well-suited for the enterprise network, and it promises to make network administration much easier. It also promises to improve user productivity by making networks more friendly, and making network resources easily accessible and usable.

NetWare 4.0 has high performance, good scalability, wide-ranging hardware support, and wide-reaching client support. What made NetWare 3.11 the platform of choice for workgroup computing also is present in NetWare 4.0. With NDS, NetWare now has become the platform of choice for enterprise computing as well.

Understanding NetWare 4.0 Services in Detail

This chapter explains some key features and services of NetWare 4.0 in detail. The information you read in this chapter is usually overlooked in the NetWare 4.0 marketing information provided by Novell, but is important to evaluators of NetWare 4.0's architecture.

In this chapter, you learn about the following:

- ❖ Memory management and protection
- ❖ The NDS schema
- ❖ The Media Manager
- ❖ Data migration

Understanding Memory Management and Protection

For years, Novell did not include memory protection in its NetWare operating systems because of two factors. First, memory protection requires CPU overhead, thus decreasing performance. Second, as a specialized server operating system, NetWare is not used in the same way as other general-purpose operating systems. This non-traditional role reduces the importance of memory protection in NetWare's capability to function robustly.

Memory protection in traditional general-purpose operating systems serves two purposes. First, on a multiuser operating system, each user runs his program concurrently with other users. Memory protection "quarantines" each user's session so that one user's session cannot bring down the entire system. In traditional operating systems, each user has the power to establish a session and run programs on the host computer's CPU.

NetWare is different because users run their programs on workstations attached to the server. Workstation-based programs request services from NetWare, but these services are obtained by using operating system code paths. Even on traditional operating systems, operating system code paths are not subject to memory protection because they are considered *trusted*, or free from programming errors. Only the network adminstrator can run server-based programs on the server's CPU. Because the administrator has complete control over programs loaded on the server, memory protection is less critical for the operation of the server.

The second use of memory protection under traditional operating systems is to detect and isolate programming bugs during the software-development process. Programming errors that cause memory-protection violations are trapped by the memory-protection system and isolated immediately, which enables the developer to correct the error.

Novell, therefore, recognizes memory protection first as an aid to software developers, and second as an aid to network administrators. The inclusion of memory protection in NetWare enables NLM developers to produce bug-free NLMs more quickly. It also enables network administrators to test commercial NLMs themselves, ensuring that such NLMs do not have memory-related programming errors.

TIP

Regardless of the way memory protection is implemented on an operating system, it decreases performance because of the CPU overhead required to check and enforce memory protection. This is true even for CPUs that have hardware-based memory-protection mechanisms, including Intel CPUs.

Intel CPUs base their memory protection on privilege levels and exception handling. When a program running in a less-privileged level attempts to reference memory of a more privileged level, the CPU generates an *exception*. An operating system exception handler must then take over and decide whether to deny the memory reference. Even though this is handled mostly by the Intel hardware, it introduces significant overhead into operating-system execution.

Intel hardware also features page-based memory mapping. *Pages* are 4K-chunks of memory. Each process running on an Intel CPU has its own *page map* that defines which 4K blocks of memory that process can address. When a process tries to address a page of memory that is not contained in its page map, the Intel CPU generates a special exception called a *page fault*. The operating system must then handle the page fault by altering the process's page map so that the memory reference can succeed, or by denying the memory reference.

Most UNIX systems use page maps to implement memory protection. Page maps also are used by operating systems to implement virtual memory. OS/2 uses *privilege levels* (sometimes called *rings*) to implement memory protection, and it uses pages to implement virtual memory.

NetWare 4.0's memory protection is unique because it uses both paging and privilege levels. Novell also decided to make memory protection optional, thus giving developers and administrators the choice of whether to run an NLM in protected or unprotected memory. NLM developers should always use memory protection as a debugging and testing tool.

TIP

Chapter 4 gives network adminstrators some guidelines for deciding when to use memory protection.

When implementing NetWare 4.0's optional memory-protection system, Novell reworked the operating system's basic memory allocation and management routines. The result is a page-based memory allocation and management system that is much faster and more flexible than in previous versions of NetWare. The most important aspect of the new memory management and allocation scheme is that memory can be returned to the NetWare 4.0 file-cache system when it is freed by an NLM.

The capability to run mission-critical applications is a much-needed feature in LAN-based systems, especially for corporate users. I remember asking an airline company once what their cost of downtime was. I expected an answer that quantified server downtime in terms of hundreds or thousands of dollars. In this case, however, the airline answered that they could not possibly quantify the cost of downtime. The goodwill lost—the airline representative explained to me—when a customer is left waiting at the ticket counter because a server is down is difficult to quantify.

An essential requirement then is protecting the server from misbehaving applications. Protecting the operating system from misbehaving applications is a key element; protecting applications from each other is the other key element. Providing this level of reliability without compromising server performance was a big challenge, however. The main text of this chapter illustrates some of the reasons why performance is affected by memory-protection schemes.

"Why not make it optional?" was a comment made one day by a fine engineer. The customer could turn it on or off. Better yet, the customer could load the application in "protected" mode and develop a trust for the application's good behavior. When the customer was assured of the application's good behavior, he then could unload the application, reload it "unprotected" as an extension of the operating system, and get all the performance back. Thus a scheme was devised that works in an optional manner.

Expect Novell to have higher levels of protection in the future so that the applications themselves also are protected from other applications. We could have done this in v4.0, but we ran short of time.

Page-Based Memory Allocation

Memory allocation in NetWare 4.0 is based on the Intel paging hardware. Memory pages are 4K-chunks of memory. Each process addresses memory by using a special data structure called a *page table* and a special register in the Intel CPU. The memory that can be addressed by a process is defined by the entries in that process's page table. Memory allocation then becomes a simple matter of adding or removing page entries from a process's page table.

TIP

Paging is available on most CPUs, including Motorola and RISC. The upcoming RISC-based versions of NetWare might use the same memory management scheme as native NetWare 4.0.

Page-based memory allocation enables the NetWare operating system to return freed memory to the NetWare file-cache system. This is a great improvement over previous versions of NetWare, which generally did not return freed memory to the file-cache system. Freed memory remained available for allocation by NLMs, but was permanently removed from the NetWare file-cache system. The file-cache system, therefore, becomes depleted over time, which reduces overall server performance.

Aside from page-based memory allocation, other changes were made to NetWare 4.0's memory-management scheme. These changes include a more optimized linked-list method of managing free memory and a more efficient garbage-collection algorithm.

TIP

Garbage collection is the procedure of collecting small and fragmented chunks of memory and consolidating them into larger chunks of memory, which can speed the memory-allocation routines.

RPC-Based Memory Protection

NetWare 4.0's memory-protection system is based on Intel paging, privilege levels, and Remote Procedure Call (RPC) technology. By using the console command line, developers and administrators can establish memory domains. (A *memory domain* is a page map associated with a privilege level.) The page map defines the memory that can be addressed by NLMs loaded within the domain. The privilege level determines how and under what circumstances NLMs loaded in the domain can call operating-system APIs.

When an NLM is loaded in a protected domain, that NLM's page map allows memory references only within the domain. Memory pages outside the domain are flagged as *not present*, meaning that any attempt to reference pages outside the domain causes a page fault. When such a page fault occurs, the NetWare 4.0 page fault handler quarantines the offending NLM by not allowing that NLM's code to execute, and the operating system immediately unloads the offending NLM.

TIP

Marking memory pages as not present is a commonly used technique for implementing virtual-memory systems.

When an NLM is loaded in a protected domain, the NetWare 4.0 loader substitutes special RPC labels for standard OS API entry points. The RPC labels are special entry points for operating-system routines. These special entry points check parameters passed to them by the NLM, copy the parameters into the operating system's domain, execute the OS API, and copy the results back to the calling NLM's domain. Thus, an NLM running in a protected domain can call operating-system routines without causing a page fault or privilege violation.

TIP

A protected domain can be assigned a less privileged ring.

When an NLM is loaded into the operating system (unprotected) domain, the NetWare 4.0 loader links the NLM to normal OS API entry points, which enables the NLM to call operating-system routines without going through the special RPC entry points. In addition, the NLM's page map shows all pages as being *present*, which provides the NLM access to all system memory.

Avoidance of Page Faults

Under NetWare 4.0's memory-protection system, page faults occur only when an NLM refers to memory outside of its protected domain—not when the NLM calls operating-system routines. This is different from other memory-protection schemes, which use page faults to handle calls to operating-system routines. Novell discovered that RPC-based entry points into OS routines provide greater performance than the generation and handling of page faults on Intel hardware.

Page faults still occur when the NLM refers to memory outside of its protected domain; however, page faults are appropriate in these cases because they arise only as the result of programming errors. In these cases, page faults protect the system from programming errors, and alert the developer to these errors.

Understanding the NDS Schema

Frequently, you may hear people speak of the NDS schema. They are referring to the structure of information stored in the NDS Directory Information Base (DIB). NDS ships with a base schema in place. This base schema is extendible by software developers, who can control the structure of information stored in the DIB, and expand the base schema to store and process new types of data.

Defining the Schema

The *Netware Directory Services (NDS) schema* is the collection of object definitions stored by the global, distributed NDS Directory Information Base (DIB). For example, people, FAX machines, printers, servers, workstations, tape-backup units, and others are all types of objects defined in the NDS schema. The schema determines not only which objects are created and added to the NDS DIB, but also how these objects are created and maintained by NDS.

The NDS schema has the scope of an entire Directory tree. That is, if you expand the base schema by defining a new type of object, that object definition becomes available automatically to all NDS partitions that are part of the NDS tree with which you are working.

Object Classes

The NDS base schema is a collection of *object classes*, which are definitions of objects that can be stored in the NDS DIB. The existence of an object class does not entail the existence of an actual object in the DIB. Rather, the existence of an object class means that an object of that class potentially can be added to the DIB. When an object is added to the DIB, it is *instantiated*—an instance of that object has been created.

Object classes consist of *attributes*. For a particular object class, attributes can be either required or optional. A *required attribute* of an object class must be included in the creation (instantiation) of any new object of that class. *Optional attributes* can be included in the instantiation of a new object, added at a later date, or not added at all.

For example, a required attribute of all object classes is a *common name*, which identifies both that specific object and, when combined with the full name of that object, defines the location of that object within the NDS tree.

An object of type Person requires a common name attribute. An optional attribute for an object of type Person is a FAX number—some people have FAX numbers; others do not. Each object class in the base schema has both required and optional attributes.

Attributes

Attributes are complex data types that, when combined, form an object class definition. When an object is instantiated, that object's attributes contain data about that object. Examples of attributes include common name, phone number, serial number, address, full name, network address, and so on.

Syntaxes

Syntaxes are the DIB's scalar (or basic) data types. Attributes consist of one or more syntaxes. Examples of syntaxes include character strings, unsigned long integers, linked lists of strings or byte streams, and so on. In some cases, part of a syntax also is a function used for comparison and a function used for collation. For example, although a Case Ignore String and String both consist of a string of characters, the case of each character in a Case Ignore String is not important to the comparison or collation of that string.

TIP

An address attribute consists of a linked list of Case Ignore Strings. A network address consists of an address type code, an address length, and a byte stream.

Object Instances

When you use NDS, you read, update, and search for instantiated objects. For example, your network may have 100 user objects, and each of these user objects is of the class Person. Although each user object is of the same class, 100 *instances* of that object class are in the NDS DIB—one instance for each user.

Each instance has unique information stored in it. For example, the full NDS (distinguished) name of each user object is different, and each user object has a different phone number.

Instantiated objects represent the "real stuff" of your organization: people, computers, organizations, printers, phones, and so on.

Inheritance

Now that you know the difference between object classes and object instances, you are ready to learn about *inheritance*. You can define new object classes by *inheriting* the definitions of object classes in the base schema.

For example, the base schema contains an object class for people, but not for animals. (Most organizations do not have animals.) What if your organization happens to be a circus or a zoo? You need to create a new object class of type Animal!

When creating the new Animal class, you can cause the new class to inherit the attributes of the Person class. Automatically, your new class has attribute definitions for name, organization, and so on. Now add a new attribute called Species, and you are set.

New object classes can inherit attributes from more than one existing object class. This is called *multiple inheritance*. NDS allows multiple inheritance so that it is easier for you to create sophisticated object definitions.

Object Orientation

The NDS DIB is a true object-oriented database. It allows multiple inheritance, extension of the schema to define new complex data types, and the inclusion of routines within the object definition for processing that object's data. These are the three common denominators for object-oriented systems.

Understanding the Media Manager

Versions of NetWare prior to version 4.0 were optimized for use with magnetic hard disk media. This allowed for many performance optimizations surrounding reading from and writing to magnetic media, and also allowed for fault tolerance such as hot fix and drive mirroring.

You may note that NDS has a *global schema*, which means that all user type objects are the same in the whole network. If a department is participating in a global NDS enterprise network, it cannot choose to have an implementation of schema different from the one employed by the rest of the network. Thus, all departments that participate in an enterprise network are forced to have one common schema dictionary. There is a good reason not to have this flexibility.

We went through a battle on this design feature. As you read this book, you will notice that NDS has oriented itself towards a decentralized management structure, as opposed to a centralized

one. This is obvious when you look at partitioning or access-control management. Yet the schema is centralized.

The reason for making the schema centralized was our worry that applications that provide services to every user in the network could not update multiple schema dictionaries with the same object information. In the words of one NDS engineer, an application could go "bonkers" if it had to find and update multiple schema dictionaries in different parts of the network before providing services to everybody in the network. With one global schema, the process is easy—you make the schema update once, and NDS applies it to the whole network.

When designing NetWare 4.0, Novell decided to redo the architecture of the NetWare drive subsystem to make it easier to support nonmagnetic media such as tape, CD-ROM, magneto-optical, jukeboxes, and more. The result of this redesign effort is the Media Manager, which provides a support architecture for all types of media without sacrificing the media optimization and fault tolerance of previous NetWare operating systems.

Internally, the Media Manager is an object-oriented database. Each object stored by the database is some type of media device. Examples of media devices include controller cards, hard drives, CD-ROM drives, jukeboxes, and tape drives. Developers can define custom devices and add them to the Media Manager. The Media Manager database resides completely in server RAM, and is initialized when you start a NetWare 4.0 server. Objects stored by the Media Manager are persistent for as long as the server remains running. You can, however, explicitly remove Media Manager objects from the database by unloading device drivers.

TIP
Each object stored in the Media Manager has a series of relationships with other objects. For example, a controller object is the *parent* of one or more physical devices attached to that controller. Two physical devices attached to the same controller are *siblings*. Tape cartridges installed in a tape jukebox are *children* of the jukebox object; the jukebox object is a child of the controller card to which it is attached.

Each object contains data and routines used by the operating system to manipulate that object. For example, a controller object contains entry points to its device driver. Objects also contain data describing their characteristics. The operating system can use the Media Manager to retrieve information about all device objects stored by the Media Manager.

NetWare 4.0 maintains special objects that define NetWare-specific data structures. For example, a mirror object establishes a set of mirrored partitions; a hot fix object establishes a hot fix area on a device object and contains routines for remapping bad media sectors on that device. Through the use of special objects, such as the mirror and hot fix objects, NetWare 4.0 continues special magnetic media-oriented features that have proved successful in the past. These features are redesigned to fit well into the Media Manager architecture.

Media Manager Support Layers

The Media Manager features two support layers: a device driver support layer and an application support layer. The *device driver support layer* presents a uniform application-programming interface to all device drivers, regardless of device type. Driver-code portability makes it easier for device vendors to develop NetWare 4.0 drivers. Idiosyncratic features of specific devices or device types can be supported more uniformly by using the Media Manager device driver support layer than in previous versions of NetWare. Device-driver code is more portable, and can be reused more easily. This enables NetWare to support alternative or new types of media more quickly after a new operating system release than it did previously.

The *application support layer* enables software modules to gain access to Media Manager objects by using a single uniform application-programming interface. Idiosyncratic characteristics of specific media or controllers are hidden from applications by the Media Manager. The NetWare 4.0 file system uses the Media Manager application support layer. This layer makes it possible for third-party developers to write alternative file systems for use with NetWare.

TIP
One of the first examples of an alternative file system that is based on the Media Manager is the Novell/Kodak HCCS image retrieval system.

Streamlined Code Paths

One beneficial side effect of the Media Manager in NetWare 4.0 is that most of the code paths to and from physical media devices are shorter and more optimized than in NetWare 3.11. This optimization occurs because Media Manager objects contain device driver entry points. A Media Manager application, such as the NetWare file system, therefore, can call a device driver directly instead of through a multilevel dispatch table, as in NetWare 3.11. The result is better overall performance for all types of media, while still retaining the magnetic media-specific optimizations and features of NetWare 3.11.

Understanding Data Migration

The typical NetWare server stores thousands (perhaps millions) of files. Typically, only a small percentage of the files stored on a NetWare server have been updated or read within the past 30 days. The possibility exists, however, that a user will attempt to read or update an older file at any time.

Data migration enables you to store files not accessed recently on slower or near-line media. These files remain available to users at all times because their directory entries are still resident on the NetWare volume. When a user attempts to gain access to a migrated file, the NetWare 4.0 file system detects that the file's data has been migrated to an alternative media; the file system retrieves the migrated file's data from the alternative media, and restores it to the NetWare volume. The user then gains access to the file in the usual way.

By using data migration, you can set up a multitiered data storage system. Frequently accessed files are stored directly on NetWare volumes by using fast magnetic media. Less frequently used files are migrated from the fast media to slower on-line media such as magneto-optical. Migrated files remain accessible to users because they still have directory entries on a NetWare volume; their data resides on the second-tier migration media, however. Finally, least frequently used files are archived to off-line media by using Novell's Storage Management System (SMS).

TIP
Data migration in NetWare 4.0 is not an actual product; it is a set of developer's tools. It remains for developers to create products that perform data migration. Such products consist of at least two components: a data migration support module, which controls the storage, retrieval, and format of migrated data on the alternative media; and a migrating NLM, which scans files on a NetWare volume and determines which files to migrate.

Migrating NLM

In the data migration system, the migrating NLM determines which files are suitable for migration to an alternative media. Developers should allow network administrators to configure the migrating NLM so that they have complete control over which files are migrated and which are not. Configurable parameters for the migrating NLM should include the file's last access date, the size of the file, the file's last archival date, and others. NetWare enables an administrator to flag files as not eligible for migration.

Data Migration Support Module

The *data migration support module*, the most complex component of the data migration system, is responsible for formatting, storing, and retrieving all migrated file data. When the migrating NLM calls the NetWare operating system to migrate a file, the operating system calls the support module. The support module must store the file on the alternative media by calling the Media Manager.

To store and retrieve files, the data migration support module must implement its own file system. This file system must store directory information for each file, store files using all name spaces supported by NetWare, and support extension and truncation of the files it stores. The file system implemented by the support module does not have to be fast or complex, just simple and reliable. Because of the way data migration works, the support module file system can be a single-user file system, and therefore does not need to worry about concurrency controls (record and file locks). The support module file system should have routines for migrating and restoring entire subdirectory trees, as well as for returning statistics about the migrated files stored on the alternative media.

In essence, the data migration support module is an alternative file system for NetWare. The support module, however, is a special file system because of the specific conditions under which it is called. The support module typically is called only by the migrating NLM (via the operating system) and by the NetWare file system when a user requests access to a migrated file.

Migration and Retrieval

All migrated files are migrated by the migrating NLM. The migrating NLM should be a perpetual background process that scans file attributes and, according to criteria set by the administrator, selects files for migration. After the migrating NLM selects a file for migration, it calls an operating-system routine to actually migrate the file. The operating-system routine calls the data migration support module, which places the file's information in the support module's file system, and calls the Media Manager to write the file's data to a physical storage device.

Migrated files remain migrated until a user requests access to the migrated file. The user knows about the migrated file because the NetWare volume maintains a directory entry for that file, even though the file's data is stored on another media device. When a user requests access to a migrated file, the NetWare file system calls the migration support module to retrieve the file's data. The migration support module restores the file's data to the NetWare volume, and the user gains access to the file in the normal way, except that it takes slightly longer to do so than if the file were not migrated.

TIP
The migration support module can contain routines for manually migrating and retrieving files or subdirectory trees, which enables an administrator or user to selectively migrate or retrieve batches of files all at once.

Image-Enabled NetWare

Image-Enabled NetWare, with its High-Capacity Storage System (HCSS), is a product based on data migration. Many others certainly will appear in the future as developers become familiar with the benefits of data migration. Potential applications include perpetual backup systems, anti-viral software, disaster-recovery systems, and more.

Understanding Auditing

Chapter 3 discussed auditing as an auxiliary security feature. Actually, NetWare 4.0 auditing is much more than an auxiliary feature: it is an entire subsystem built into the NetWare 4.0 operating system that enhances security and provides you with information about how users are making use of your NetWare 4.0 installation.

Information Provided by Auditing

The NetWare 4.0 auditing system enables you to track all types of file access on a NetWare volume by user and type of access (open, close, scan, delete, create, and so on). In addition, the auditing system tracks NDS activity, including the creation of new objects and object classes, modification of objects, object searches, and more.

File-system auditing occurs on a per-volume basis; NDS auditing occurs on a per-partition basis. The auditing system creates audit logs, which report all audited events, including the time and description of the event, and the user who performed the event.

The Auditor

The auditing system provides for a user to be designated as the system *auditor*, who should not also be the supervisor. The auditor has a special password that she must use to configure the auditing system and to view audit logs.

The auditor has complete control over which file system and NDS events are audited. The auditor can choose to limit the scope of audited events to a specific subdirectory tree in the file system or a specific container in the NDS DIB. The auditor also can expand the scope of audited events to an entire NetWare volume or NDS partition, but only for certain events, such as the modification of a file or NDS object.

The Audit Log

The *audit log* is a special file that only the auditor can view. Not even the Admin object can view the audit log without the auditor's password. The auditor can make the audit log be a circular file. That is, when the audit log becomes a certain size, the auditing system begins to overwrite audit records at the beginning of the file with current audit records. This prevents the audit log from becoming so large that it fills the volume on which it resides.

Generating Audit Records

Audit records are generated by internal routines of the file system and NDS. All routines that open, close, delete, modify, or create files or NDS objects check the audit attributes of the file or object being processed. The *audit attribute* is part of the file or object's attribute list, and determines whether the file or object is subject to auditing for the event being processed.

If the file system or NDS determines that the impending event is subject to auditing, it calls a special routine in the operating system that generates an audit record. The code for checking audit attributes and generating audit records is embedded into the lowest-level routines of the operating system. No alternative entry points to these routines exist and, as a result, no way exists to bypass the generation of audit records.

Audit records themselves are *binary-encoded* structures, which means that they store information about audited events in a compact format. This makes the audit log as small as possible and also causes the auditing system to have a minimal impact on operating-system performance. In addition, only software that recognizes the format of audit records (such as AUDITCON.EXE) can interpret audit records.

Security Provided by Auditing

Auditing does not prevent unauthorized access to files or NDS objects. It does, however, report such access, including the user and network station that makes the unauthorized access. If a user gains unauthorized access to a file or NDS object, he certainly will be discovered, albeit after the fact.

TIP

Although auditing does not prevent unauthorized access (that is the job of NetWare 4.0's other security systems), it serves as a powerful deterrent to snooping on the network. Even if a user successfully bypasses NetWare's other security measures, she generates an audit record when gaining access to audited files or NDS objects.

Users (including Admin) have no way of knowing when auditing is active for a volume or NDS partition or which files, NDS objects, users, and operations are subject to auditing. Only the auditor knows this information.

Data Provided by Auditing

Remember that the NetWare 4.0 auditing system generates audit records for authorized or unauthorized access to files and NDS objects. This means that the auditing system is a powerful source of data regarding the use of the NetWare installation. Auditing can tell you how frequently files or NDS objects are accessed, which files or NDS objects are accessed the most, and who is accessing the files or NDS objects.

Audit records can help you to design your NetWare installation more effectively. For example, you might determine from auditing records that the creation of a read-only NDS partition replica cuts down significantly on internetwork traffic. Or you might determine that certain frequently accessed files should be moved to a different volume, in which users of those files can access them directly instead of via a network bridge.

Understanding the NDS Printer Object Class

In Chapter 3, you read about the new NetWare 4.0 printing architecture. Users of NetWare 4.0 will notice immediately that they send print jobs to printers, rather than to print queues. This change was made because printers are physical objects that have a visible location, and print queues are logical objects without physical substance. A user can send a print job to "the Apple Laser printer by Debbie's office" much more easily than to a print queue.

This section explains the definition of the NDS Printer object class, enabling you to see how much more printer-related information is available to users in NetWare 4.0. The Object Class Definition for Printers is as follows:

Super Classes:	Device
Containment:	None
Named By:	None
Mandatory Attributes:	None
Optional Attributes:	Cartridge
	Default Queue
	Description
	Host Device
	Host Server

Optional Attributes:	Memory
	Network Address Restriction
	Notify
	Operator
	Page Description Language
	Printer Configuration
	Queue
	Status
	Supported Typefaces

Note that the Super Classes attribute defines the inheritance of the Printer object class. The Printer object class inherits the following attributes from the Device object class:

Containment:	Organization
	Organizational Unit
Named By:	Common Name
Mandatory Attributes:	Common Name
Optional Attributes:	Description
	Locality
	Network Address
	Organization Name
	Organizational Unit Name
	Owner
	Also
	Serial Number

Each of the optional and mandatory attributes in the preceding lists can contain information about actual printers located on the NetWare 4.0 internetwork. This information is available to users and administrators. You can, for example, search NDS to find a printer with the following attributes:

Apple LaserWriter II

4M of RAM or greater

Supports Palatino typeface

After the user finds a printer or printers matching the search criteria, she can call up that printer's location, owner, description, serial number, queue, host server, and more. Moreover, that user can read the printer's network address restrictions to see if she can send a print job to that printer from the user's workstation. Or the user can read the phone number of the printer's operator to ask permission to send a print job to that printer.

The containment attribute (inherited from the Device class) requires that all Printer objects be contained by an organization or organizational unit. This means that Printer objects must be located directly under organizations or organizational units in the NDS tree.

Understanding Storage Management Services (SMS)

Storage Management Services, or *SMS*, is a collection of services and specifications designed to make cross-platform network backup easier and more effective, both now and in the future.

Novell has three goals for SMS: to make it easier to back up NetWare data, to make it easier for third-party developers to support new versions of NetWare, and to make the archival and retrieval of data completely media- and platform-independent.

The components of SMS include the *System Independent Data Format (SIDF)*—a high-level device interface, and a group of services designed to enable different types of archiving and restoring of data. SIDF is a general-purpose data format that is suitable for the archival of data from any operating system, including future operating systems.

The *Storage Device Interface (SDI)* is a high-level API that enables SMS to store and retrieve data from archive hardware without knowing the hardware's configuration. SDI makes it easier to develop SMS archiving software and device drivers by separating hardware drivers and archive logic, thus making them independent of each other.

SDI enables users to restore old data by using new hardware. For example, a user must be able to archive her data today, and then restore that same data ten years from now by using hardware that did not exist when the data originally was archived.

SMS provides to applications a core group of services for archiving and restoring data. These services include different types and scopes of archival and restoration operations.

SMS Implementations

An implementation of SMS consists of a service provider and one or more service responders, called *Target Service Agents*, or *TSAs*. The *service provider* is the actual archive unit that consists of hardware and software. You can think of the service provider as an "archive server." The TSA is any network resource that has data to be archived. Think of the TSA as a an "archive client."

When archiving data, the TSA provides a stream of SIDF data to the service provider. The service provider archives the SIDF data. When restoring data, the process works in reverse.

SMS does not require service providers to be NLMs—they can be DOS EXEs, Macintosh programs, UNIX processes, or any other executable program running on any operating system. The only requirement is that a service provider must be capable of communicating with TSAs.

By the same token, TSAs may be implemented in any executable format, provided that they can communicate with the service provider. Hence, SMS enables archiving of client workstation local data, provided that the client workstation is running a TSA. The NetWare 4.0 implementation of SMS supports archiving and restoration of v4.0 and v3.11 servers, in addition to DOS and OS/2 workstation data.

TIP

The capability to archive and restore Macintosh and UNIX workstation data is built into the SMS specification, and Novell has plans to introduce those capabilities in the future.

Novell expects third-party vendors to introduce SMS-compliant products that add value to Novell's implementation. Specifically, some vendors are developing TSAs that support specialized network servers, such as database servers, e-mail servers, and so on.

Novell has also been working with third-party vendors to assist their SMS development by providing engineering support and even source code when appropriate. This support is especially critical because of recent changes to the SMS specification that might cause problems for existing SMS-compliant products.

The NetWare 4.0 implementation of SMS enables archiving of NetWare 2.x, 3.x, and 4.x file systems. In addition, users can archive DOS and OS/2 local data. Coming later is the capability to archive UNIX and Macintosh local data, in addition to future file systems such as Microsoft's Windows NT.

Archiving NDS

NDS is based on a distributed database of network resources. Novell provides a special TSA that enables the archiving and restoration of a distributed and replicated NDS DIB, which would be extremely difficult without the NetWare 4.0 implementation of SMS.

Summary

This chapter dealt with the features of NetWare 4.0 in detail. You learned about memory management and protection, the NDS schema, the Media Manager, and data migration.

The next chapter discusses NetWare directory services in detail.

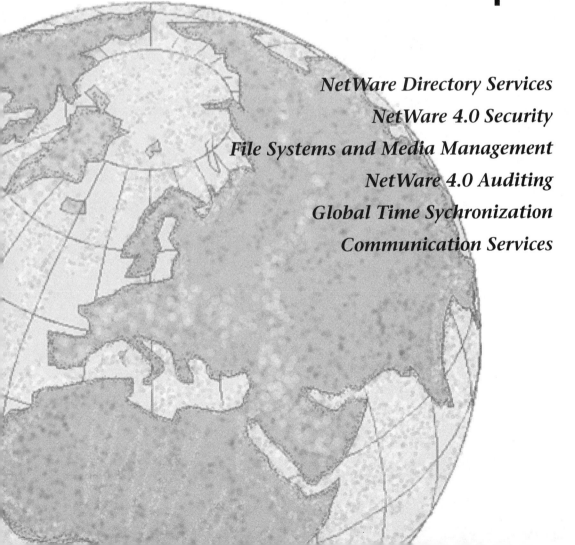

PART 3

NetWare 4.0 in Depth

NetWare Directory Services

NetWare 4.0 Security

File Systems and Media Management

NetWare 4.0 Auditing

Global Time Sychronization

Communication Services

NetWare Directory Services

NetWare Directory Services (NDS) introduces a new component to the NetWare environment: the *directory,* which is a distributed database of network objects. It replaces the bindery, which served as the system database for previous releases of NetWare. Although the bindery was designed to support the operation of a single server, the directory supports an entire network. The directory is accessible by all users, administrators, servers, workstations, and applications in the network. NDS promises to shift the paradigm for users from the server to the network and its resources.

For system administrators, NDS offers the capability to manage the whole network from a single workstation. For large organizations, NDS provides the capability to organize and distribute management authority to each department while retaining a centrally defined logical framework for the network.

This chapter examines the many features of the NDS, including the following:

❖ The directory versus the bindery

❖ The hierarchical nature of NDS

❖ The organization of information stored in NDS

❖ The naming of objects stored in NDS

❖ The authentication services provided by NDS

❖ The distributed operation of NDS

❖ The different services provided to applications by NDS

❖ The backwards-compatible bindery-emulation feature of NDS

❖ The interoperability features of NDS with other databases

❖ The migration and upgrade strategies provided by NDS

Comparing the Directory to the Bindery

Previous versions of NetWare are based on the bindery, which is a server-centric flat database without a data dictionary or schema (no set of rules enforces guidelines for the definition and storage of objects in the bindery). A single user can have multiple accounts on multiple binderies (rather than one account held in common between multiple servers) carried by multiple servers because no synchronization happens between binderies to share common information. Novell released a product called NetWare Name Services (NNS), which extends the bindery to serve an entire local area network. This enhancement uses application software to combine numerous binderies, creating a "superbindery," which is then copied to each participating server. The family of servers that shares this super-bindery is called a *domain*.

TIP

A *domain* is a group of servers that shares a superbindery created by NetWare Name Services (NNS). The number of servers contained in a given domain is limited.

NNS extended the scope of the bindery's operation, but it is a partial solution at best. Because NNS was not scalable to the entire network, multiple domains had to be constructed to manage the whole network. These multiple domains could not interact or share information. In addition, the excessive overhead generated to maintain the flat, non-hierarchical bindery databases in synchronization was too expensive in terms of both disk space and CPU time. NNS became too slow as the information within the binderies grew and the number of servers contained in a domain increased.

Furthermore, the application was responsible for keeping the binderies synchronized in a given NNS domain by updating all binderies within that domain. Inconsistencies resulted if the application did not perform this domain-update task, or if only a partial set of binderies was updated before the responsible application failed because of a network failure or other failure. No automatic retries or consistency checks were built into NNS to avoid the problems resulting from such failures.

NDS solves the shortcomings of NNS in the following ways:

❖ It is hierarchical (not flat)

❖ It provides for a robust distribution scheme through logical partitioning (thus avoiding redundant storage)

❖ It enforces a data dictionary or schema across the whole network (unlike NNS or bindery)

❖ It makes synchronization happen in the background by the server (rather than the application)

❖ It has automatic retries and consistency checks

Exploring the Hierarchical Nature of NDS

A big advantage of NDS is that it is a *hierarchical database*—that is, relationships between objects can be shown hierarchically. With the flat files used by the bindery, it is difficult to understand bindery data because it contains objects whose nature and purpose are unclear. The hierarchical structure of NDS, however, makes the relationships between objects clear.

Figure 6.1 illustrates the hierarchical relationship between objects in the NDS database. The tree structure in the figure makes it intuitive for users to locate an object according to its position within a particular organization. Note that the tree provides a dynamic logical mapping or context for an object, apart from its physical location. Therefore, no matter how often an object's physical address changes, the user can logically find the object by navigating through the tree.

SOAPBOX

If most Novell engineers and marketers privately admit that NetWare Name Service (NNS) was, indeed, "broken," then why build it in the first place, and why not fix it and ship a better NNS? After all, many people think that NDS is too much technology, and that Novell could have just "fixed" NNS and solved many customer problems.

Why did Novell build NNS the way it did, and then make NDS a completely different story? Well, it goes back to what Ray Noorda calls "market pressure," which is the obligation to respond to customer needs quickly and to ensure a smooth migration and upgrade strategy. Novell marketing decided too late that customers needed a bindery synchronizer, and demanded that engineering build a synchronizer product fast. After all, many big customers were screaming bloody murder.

The second big caveat that Novell marketing imposed on the product design was not to require the customer to upgrade the server software to a new release. This was perceived as being a weak selling point. In other words, NNS had to be a client-based tool—servers could not track bindery updates and synchronize among themselves—meaning that the clients who updated one bindery had to update the other binderies in the domain. This caused

Novell's super architect, Kevin Kingdon, to nearly come unhinged because he felt that he was being forced to build a "broken" product.

So, knowing the many weaknesses of the product, Kevin designed the product to ship early and not require a server upgrade. Then he busily set to work on what he perceived as the "real" product: NetWare Directory Services (NDS). Three years and a few months later, it happened as part of NetWare 4.0.

In defense of Novell marketing people: they perceived the difficulty of building a "true" synchronizer, and concluded that it could not be done in any current timeframe. To keep the customers satisfied while the "real" product was being built, they did not want to invest too much in what they perceived to be a stopgap product.

Could a better NNS be built? Certainly! Look at Banyan's ENS For NetWare product. That's what a true NNS should have been. But is NDS a better solution for the customer than either NNS or ENS For NetWare? Certainly! NDS has hierarchical, distributed, replicated database scales for any kind of large and complicated network; NNS and ENS For NetWare have scaling problems because they must synchronize flat databases without a data dictionary.

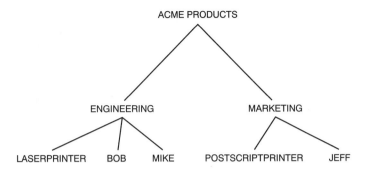

Figure 6.1:

NDS hierarchical tree.

Understanding the Organization of Information Stored in NDS

The foundation for constructing, organizing, and storing objects in the Directory Information Base (DIB) is the NDS schema, which uses the standard set of attribute types to construct object classes. The different attribute types, from which a particular class is constructed, determine which attributes can or must be associated with the objects of that class. Therefore, although a user references and accesses objects of various classes, the schema provides for constructing, organizing, and storing those objects.

The schema also controls the relationship among objects in the NDS hierarchical tree by defining subordination among classes of objects. For example, for an object of any given class, a limited group of classes exists to which the object can be subordinate. The schema limits the pairs of superior and subordinate objects, and guides the development of the NDS hierarchy.

NDS is *extensible*, which means that new information types can be added to existing ones. Although NetWare 4.0 utilities do not have the capability to display or add user-defined attributes to standard NDS objects, this capability will exist in a future release of the utilities.

For now, any user-defined extensions must be added and then viewed through custom-written software programs. All NDS objects, and information about them, can be accessed through the standard Novell APIs provided on the NetWare 4.0 server and all supported client platforms.

The object class and the attributes that make up the class provide information about objects of that class. Object-class definitions carry attributes that provide information about the object. These attributes can range from a login script for a user to the network address for a server. The objects in NDS correspond to objects in the real world such as users, printers, organizations, organizational units, file volumes, applications, and so on.

The primary purpose of NDS is to store information about all network resources and users. NDS also provides for the use of organizations and organizational units as objects to organize network resources logically. This is similar to the relationship between files and directories on a hard disk. For example, you can organize all payroll files under a directory called Payroll.

TIP

In figure 6.1, the organizational units named Marketing and Engineering provide an intuitive way to organize information about network resources for Acme Products.

Naming Objects in NDS

For every object class, one attribute (or more) is selected as a naming attribute, and makes up the object's name. A *name* is an object's most significant attribute because it uniquely identifies an object within the NDS database. Names are keys to the information stored in NDS. A user who wants information about a given object can navigate the NDS tree to find the object, and then query for information or give the name of the object to NDS and ask for information.

The user also can search the directory through the "yellow-paging" mechanism, in which he supplies the description of an object, and NDS retrieves it. NDS becomes more appealing than many other databases today because it supports simple and intuitive definitions of names that users can read and remember.

SOAPBOX

Although many appreciate Novell for building NDS with an X.500 framework in mind, Novell paid a couple of big costs to adhere to standards. The first big cost was with the so-called "contexts," and the second was with the way the NDS names objects by type in the NDS tree.

In figure 6.2, you can see that user Bob's name is `CN.Bob.OU=Engineering.O=Acme Products`. Imagine logging in with this name! To solve this problem, Novell provides a partial solution: you can designate a context in the NET.CFG file that can be appended to the names that you type in if they are incomplete (if they do not define all the way to the root of the tree).

Novell also provides *default typing*, in which the name that you supply is affixed with the proper types (OU, O, and so on) automatically before being used by the NetWare client and server software.

These are partial solutions at best, however. For example, suppose that user Jeff in Marketing (see fig. 6.2) walks over to a workstation in the Engineering department and logs in as follows:

```
F> Login Jeff
```

The name first is default typed as `CN=Jeff`. Then the context in the NET.CFG file is appended to the name, and used by the NetWare client and server software. It is likely that the

context set on the engineering workstations is OU.Engineering.O=Acme Products, so Jeff's name is formed as:

```
CN=Jeff.OU=Engineering.O=Acme
Products
```

This is not Jeff's correct NDS name. His correct name is:

```
CN=Jeff.OU=Marketing.O=Acme Products
```

This becomes a bigger problem for Jeff if he were to travel around and use workstations in different divisions of Acme Products. To ensure that he is logged in with the proper name, Jeff is better off typing the following:

```
F> Login CN=Jeff.OU=Marketing.O=Acme
Products
```

What's with all these naming types, such as O, OU, and CN? Why are these needed? As was explained in the main text, these are needed because under X.500 each object has a naming attribute and a type. X.500 has types because conceivably an organizational unit called Jeff and a user called Jeff can exist in the same level of the tree.

Under X.500, duplicate names are permitted at the same level in the tree only if they have different naming types. Although two CN=Jeff objects cannot exist in the same part of the tree, a CN=Jeff and an OU=Jeff can exist in the same part of the tree! Big deal! Not worth having naming types just to get this extra flexibility, huh?

continues

Full Name or Distinguished Name (DN)

Users see NDS as a tree of names; each name in the tree represents an object in the directory. As shown in figure 6.2, the full name of an object is formed by taking a path to the object all the way from the root.

The full name also is referred to as the *distinguished name (DN)* of the object. Figure 6.2 illustrates the naming conventions used in a typical NDS tree. Each object name in the figure has a type. For example, names such as Bob, Mike, and LaserPrinter are of type CN. NDS has defined the following standard abbreviations for most commonly used name types:

- ❖ Organization Name = O
- ❖ Organizational Unit Name = OU
- ❖ Common Name = CN

The distinguished name forms a unique name by which the object can be referenced, and a unique path that enables users to locate the object in the NDS tree. For example, the complete distinguished name for Bob is as follows:

    CN=Bob.OU=Engineering.O=Acme Products

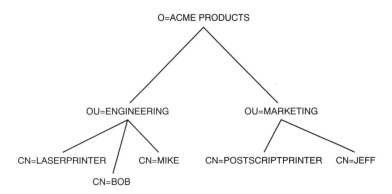

O=ACME PRODUCTS

OU=ENGINEERING   OU=MARKETING

CN=LASERPRINTER   CN=MIKE   CN=POSTSCRIPTPRINTER   CN=JEFF

CN=BOB

Figure 6.2:

Naming conventions used in NDS.

Relative Distinguished Names (RDNs)

The short name for each individual object is its *relative distinguished name (RDN)*. An object's RDN is unique, relative to its superior object. In other words, no two objects sharing the same immediate superior can have the same RDN. In figure 6.2, for example, CN=Bob is a unique name, relative to its superior OU=Engineering. No other object immediately subordinate to OU=Engineering can be named CN=Bob. Likewise, OU=Engineering is a unique name, relative to its superior O=Acme Products.

Partial Names

Partial names are used to identify and access objects, making it easier for users to deal with NDS objects. Partial names are based on a name context, and assume a portion of the naming path. For example, if the name context is OU=Engineering.O=Acme Products, the name CN=Bob.OU=Engineering.O=Acme Products can be expressed simply as CN=Bob. The NetWare-resident software on the client workstation appends the name context (OU=Engineering.O=Acme Products) to the name input (CN=Bob).

The name context simplifies your work with NDS. By analogy, suppose you are standing on a street corner in Provo, Utah, giving someone the address of Novell's offices. It is unnecessary to specify the city or state; they are obvious by your context.

If you direct someone to Novell's Developer Relations, however, you certainly include information about Austin, Texas, as part of your instructions. Thus, travel directions and NDS names both rely on context to simplify location descriptions.

Default Name Types

A user is not always required to enter a name type with a name. If the name input does not include a name type, the NetWare-resident software on the client workstation applies a default sequence to the name. The default type sequence assumes one common name, zero or more organizational units, and one organization name.

The default sequence is applied to the object's complete distinguished name under the following conditions:

❖ The context is null, that is, it is not specified.

❖ The context is not null, but the RDN does not correspond to the default naming context.

If the context is null, the name input must include the complete name path. The user also can use the type sequence found in the name context as the applied type sequence. To do so, the user precedes the name input with a single period. For example, suppose that the name context is as follows:

```
OU=Engineering.O=Acme Products
```

The user inputs the following name (note the period preceding the name):

```
.Bob
```

The entered name is assigned the following name type, and is completely formulated, as follows:

```
CN=Bob.OU=Engineering.O=Acme Products
```

Note that the regular default type sequence is applied to any RDNs that do not correspond to the name context. Therefore, the name Bob is given the type Common Name.

SOAPBOX

To X.500 zealots, one thing is obvious by looking at all the illustrations of NDS trees in this chapter. Whatever happened to the Country object? Where are the Locality objects?

X.500 specifications always assume that the tree starts with a Country object under the invisible root, followed by Organization(s), and then followed by Organizational Units and/or Localities. The bottom objects are almost always Common Names. The NDS installation does not assume a Country at the top; rather, it assumes an Organization object. Also, Locality objects are not supported.

Why?

Well, for a couple of reasons. Having the Country at the top scared too many loyal Novell customers in usability testing. Mr. Joe from Joe's Bike Shop did not see why he needed to have a Country=US instead of Organization=Joe's Bike Shop to start the tree.

Obviously, given Novell's current customer mix, more Joes buy NetWare than do Mr. Smart Guys of the international business conglomerate, who want to standardize on NetWare 4.0 and need a country object to start the tree. Too bad. NetWare 4.0 installation and the accompanying documentation start out with an organization at the top of the tree. Also,

the last that I knew about the status of Novell's utilities on the workstation, they worked only if an organization object was at the top of the tree. It is questionable whether they could handle one or many countries at the top of the tree—at least, I don't remember anyone testing such a configuration at Novell.

The other reason for not supporting a country or a locality in the name was because it made it too difficult to default type the name. Suppose Bob enters his login name as `Bob.Engineering.Acme Products`. The name easily can be default typed as `CN=Bob.OU=Engineering.O=Acme Products`, wherein you assume that the bottom most component is a CN; the top component is an O; and the middle ones are OUs.

How do you default type it if the topmost name is a C (country), and the middle components became a combination of OUs and Ls (localities), ending with an O? Novell engineers who thought that the NDS naming already was complicated simply could not tolerate any more headaches for the user. Also, NDS architect Kevin Kingdon found by reading the X.500 specifications closely that the tree really did not need to start out with a Country object. So both the Country and the Locality were quietly dropped, and the documentation went mum on both.

Alias Objects

Alias names are used to reference and represent existing NDS objects. For example, user Bob is an object under OU=Engineering in O=Acme Products. All information related to object Bob is kept under this name. If Bob is a frequent visitor to the Marketing organizational unit, and uses client workstations located there to log in and use the network, the system administrator for Marketing might want to create an alias for Bob under OU=Marketing in the NDS tree. Bob then has a local representation for his name in Marketing's local context. Any object in NDS can have an alias. If an object has subordinates, its alias appears to have the same subordinates. The alias itself must be a leaf object, however, and is not allowed to contain any more objects underneath.

Aliases are a convenience that system administrators can use to their advantage and for the benefit of the network users. For example, as in figure 6.3, a system administrator can assign aliases to all servers in the network, and group the aliases under a particular NDS object. In such a case, a user has to search only one area of the NDS tree to find out how many servers are available in the network.

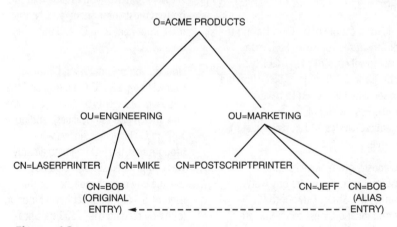

Figure 6.3:

Alias objects.

Understanding Authentication Services Provided by NDS

Authentication services under NDS use RSA public/private encryption technology, and provide the foundation for network security. NDS authentication provides a mechanism to prove objects' identities to each other before they begin exchanging further information. When logging in to the network, a user goes through an authentication process before the network acknowledges him as a valid user, and enables the user to use network resources. The authentication process includes two major steps: initialization and authentication.

Initialization

Initialization begins when a user logs in to the network at a client workstation by entering a user name and password.

TIP

Prior to the login attempt, the NetWare-resident software on the client workstation automatically finds and attaches to the nearest NetWare 4.0 server at the installation of the software to memory. (It attaches to a specified server when the NET.CFG file on the client workstation—the configuration file on the workstation that specifies many required parameters of the NetWare client-resident software—specifies a preferred server.)

After the name and password are entered, the client workstation sends only the user name (without the password) to the NDS software on the server. The NDS software on the attached server sends the user's private key to the client workstation, encrypted with that particular password. The client workstation then decodes this encrypted key with the user's password that was entered at login. After the private key is decoded, the password is erased from memory (see fig. 6.4). With the decoded key, the client workstation creates an *authenticator*, which contains information such as the user's full distinguished name, the workstation address, the validity period, and so on. The client signs the authenticator with the private key to create a signature.

TIP
The *validity period* is the period of time during which the authenticator is valid.

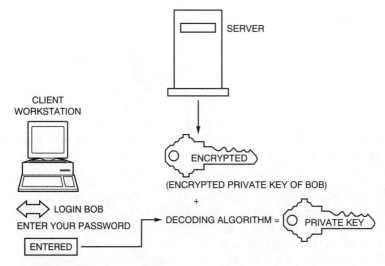

Figure 6.4:
Process of decoding encrypted private key obtained from server.

The resulting signature reflects values stored in the authenticator. Typically, a proof accompanies a message and enables the recipient to verify that a message originated from the purported sender. After the signature is created, the private key is erased from memory, but the signature and authenticator are retained. Figure 6.5 shows the principal items used to form the signature.

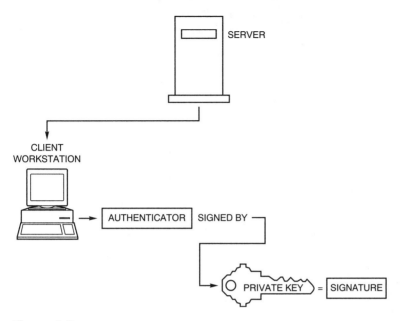

Figure 6.5:

Creation of the signature during the initialization process.

Authentication

The authenticator and the signature enable the client workstation to *authenticate*, or prove, the user to the network during the authentication process.

To authenticate the user to the network, the client workstation creates a *proof*, which is constructed from the values derived from both the signature and the request itself. Using the proof avoids having to send the signature across the network, thus risking exposure.

Figure 6.6 shows the principal items that are used to construct the proof. The *proof* is the essential mechanism in the NDS authentication scheme, and is used in all authentication dialogs. It ties the client's signature to both the current request and the current session, making each proof unique to the request it accompanies. Figure 6.7 illustrates the way the request for confirmation is sent to the server NDS software with the proof and the authenticator.

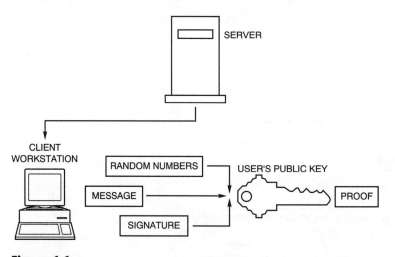

Figure 6.6:

Constructing a proof.

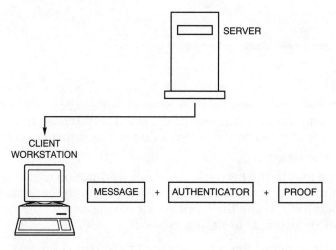

Figure 6.7:

Request for confirmation.

When NDS receives the packet, it verifies that the proof contains evidence of the signature and the message. The proof always assures the recipient that the message has not been modified since it was sent. Authentication can be accomplished in the same manner with other participating services on the network. A validated authentication request confirms the following:

❖ The proof was constructed by using a valid signature of the authenticator.

❖ The client knew the correct password to obtain the key because the client used the private key to build the signature.

❖ The request came from the station at which the authenticator was signed.

❖ The request pertains to the current session (the request does not contain information counterfeited from another session).

❖ The information in the request has not been changed or corrupted.

The highlights of NetWare 4.0 authentication are as follows:

❖ The process of initialization and authentication is completely transparent to the user and happens in the background. The user types in only his or her name and password. This information is taken up by the NetWare client-resident software to perform network authentication. The user does not need to enter the password except when logging in to the network.

❖ Authentication is a network service: applications on the NetWare server and supported client workstations can use authentication functions through a programmatic interface. Thus, applications can set up authenticated sessions between themselves and/or their clients.

❖ Authentication is session-oriented, and always is performed relative to a given session. For a user logged in to the network, the authentication is valid only for the duration of that session. If the user terminates the session and desires to log in again, the entire process of initialization and authentication is performed again.

❖ Authentication can be mutual and ongoing. Both sides of a session can be required to authenticate themselves, and authentication can proceed throughout the session. Both of these features are optional.

Understanding the Distributed Operations of NDS

NDS distributed operations divide the database into units, and store it across multiple servers in multiple locations. Important topics related to distributed operations include partitions, replication, and tree-walking (the method used by the NetWare-resident software on the client workstation to traverse the NDS tree and locate resources).

Partitions

A physical division of the directory database is called a *partition*. Partitions form the major subtrees of the directory. Although any region in the NDS tree can be considered a subtree, a partition subtree forms a distinct unit of data for storing and replicating directory information. Because partition boundaries cannot overlap, each object in the directory tree appears in only one partition (see fig. 6.8).

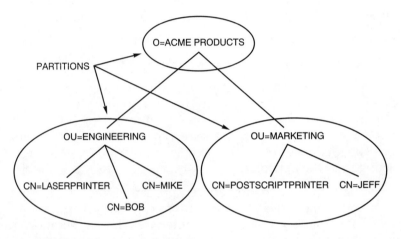

Figure 6.8:
Directory partitioning.

Multiple partitions can be stored on a given NetWare server. The partitions stored on a server can contain data from any part of the tree—that is, the partitions do not have to be contiguous. The group of partitions stored on a server can duplicate, supplement, or intersect the group of partitions on another server. A given NetWare server also is not required to have a partition stored on it unless bindery emulation is enabled on the server. A partition is named by the name of the object that forms the subtree.

TIP

For more information on bindery emulation, see the section on backwards compatibility, later in this chapter.

Replicas

A copy of a partition in a directory is called a *replica*. The three types of replicas are as follows:

❖ Master

❖ Secondary

❖ Read-only

Only one master replica exists. The secondary and read-only replicas are formed from the master, and a directory can have many of these. Tree-structure operations, such as creating a subordinate partition, can be performed only on the master copy of a given partition. Master and secondary replicas are used to read or update directory information. Read-only replicas are used only to read directory objects.

One example of a partition-location scheme is shown in figure 6.9. Note that multiple copies of a single partition are located on multiple servers.

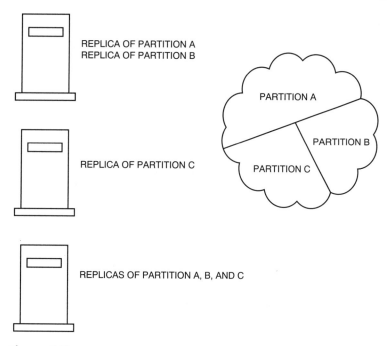

Figure 6.9:

Location of replicas of partitions.

SOAPBOX

Parts of the Novell documentation (and some articles on NetWare 4.0 in the trade journals) refer to the "skulk" process. Where does this name originate?

The first time that I came across a process that Novell's NDS architect, Kevin Kingdon, called the "skulker" was in the very early copy of the NDS design documents. I asked Kevin why he called the process the "skulker." The *skulk* process synchronizes different replicas of a given partition with update information.

Kevin said he found that term in a DEC document that referred to a "midnight skulker" that ran in the middle of the night to perform its tasks when the network was "dead." Apparently, Kevin's original intent was to synchronize NDS replicas with update information every 24 hours, possibly during the night. So he called the process the "skulker."

Note, however, that NetWare 4.0 NDS does not support "skulking" at timed intervals. When a replica of a partition is updated, the "skulker" tries to synchronize other replicas of the partition immediately, and if it fails, it tries every five minutes or so thereafter. A future release of NDS is likely to enable the "midnight skulker" to be true to its name by offering "timed" skulks.

Tree Walking

Tree walking is the process of the NetWare client-resident software "walking" through the NDS tree of partitions to obtain information about a particular object at the request of the workstation user. The client software may have to follow a number of points through the directory before it obtains the information it needs. The amount of walking depends on where the client software begins in the tree, relative to its destination.

In its process of "walking" the tree to find an object, the client software may encounter helpful hints that are cached by a server. These hints can contain the name of the partition at which the desired object is located and the name of the server that holds that partition. Otherwise, the client software walks from one partition to the next until it reaches the "root" partition, and then walks all the way down to the desired object.

If the process of locating a object involves walking up the tree to the root partition, the client software then needs to locate the server that holds a copy of the root partition. This process can be accomplished by querying the nearest NetWare server that is holding any copy of a partition in the NDS tree, and following the up pointer until a server that holds a copy of the root partition is encountered.

The client software is likely to "hit" the cache and locate the name of the server carrying the desired partition. It does not have to "walk the tree" all the way up to the root, and then down to the desired object. The process of walking down to the desired partition is accomplished by following a down pointer from each server to the next server.

TIP

A *down pointer* is information kept by a given server that points to another subordinate partition on another server.

NDS processes that run on the NetWare server are continually checking the up pointer, down pointer, and other link information to make sure that the tree is always connected and "walkable" by the client software. When partitions or replicas are deleted or added, all relevant information is updated accurately to reflect the changed structure of the tree.

The client contacts a NetWare server only once to locate a desired object. The NetWare server then "walks the tree" on behalf of the client until one of the following events occurs:

❖ The object is found. A handle to that object (called the *object ID*) and the address of the server holding the object are then returned to the client software. The client software then does further operation(s) on the object with the information that was returned.

❖ The object is not found. A fatal error is returned to the client software.

Understanding the Services Provided to Applications by NDS

Application Program Interfaces (APIs) are provided to applications on the NetWare 4.0 server and all supported client workstations. They access and use the NDS services through programmatic interfaces. The different sets of services that NDS provides to applications are the following:

❖ **DIB Services.** DIB services APIs actually access the Directory Information Base (DIB) and return information. These conform closely to the CCITT X.500 set of directory-abstract services. These services include Add Object, Compare, List Subordinates, Modify Object, Modify

Name, Read Object, Remove Object, and Search. These services also include APIs used to manage security information that controls access to objects.

❖ **Authentication Services.** Authentication services APIs actually have two layers. The first layer provides for network login, generating RSA key pairs, and changing object password, among other things. The second layer is a lower level that enables third-party application developers to adapt RSA authentication services to non-NCP, non-IPX type protocols, and provides the flexibility to build simpler authentication services than the one used by NetWare. At the time of writing this book, Novell has not yet put together a release format for providing these APIs to third-party developers.

❖ **Schema Services.** Schema services APIs access and maintain the directory schema, which defines the rules for adding objects (and object attributes) to the directory. The rules are specified through a data dictionary that provides a standard set of data types from which objects can be created. The different APIs provided for schema manipulation include creating classes, defining attributes, adding new attributes, and so on.

❖ **Partition Management.** Partition management APIs include functions that partition and replicate the directory. These APIs include adding partition, deleting partition, splitting a given partition, and joining two partitions.

Providing Backwards Compatibility with Bindery Emulation

Bindery emulation is provided by NetWare 4.0 servers so that they can interoperate with previous versions of NetWare servers and bindery-based clients. The bindery-emulation feature enables bindery-based NetWare clients and servers to access and use the NDS database as if it were a bindery. The bindery-emulation feature also provides access to dynamic objects, the local server's objects, and the supervisor objects, which are present for backwards-compatibility reasons only, and cannot be accessed through NDS APIs.

The bindery-emulation path can be set at a NetWare 4.0 server that specifies a context within the NDS tree to be shown as a bindery to previous versions of NetWare servers and clients. (The actual process of translating the directory objects to look like bindery objects is done by an emulation code layer in the NetWare 4.0 server.) The whole NDS tree is not flattened and made to look like a bindery, but only a selected context within a tree is made to look like a bindery for a given server.

SOAPBOX

Even knowing that nonstandard APIs almost certainly mean that big industry gurus will come down hard on Novell, I still permitted Kevin Kingdon (architect of NDS) to implement nonstandard NDS APIs, for some good reasons.

At the time that Kevin was designing NDS, the 1988 X.500 specifications (on which Kevin was basing his work) had no API definitions. X.500 defined just the abstract application service layer, but not the application program interfaces, or APIs. AT&T and X/Open, however, did have API definitions.

On closer review of both AT&T and X/Open APIs, Kevin found that they were practically unusable by the typical PC hacker or programmer. They were designed by UNIX gurus, who took

great pleasure in making things so complicated that only their kind understood each other. Kevin argued that these APIs would never fly, and that we had to have simpler APIs.

Finally, I worked out a compromise with Kevin, who wanted simpler APIs, and Novell marketing, which wanted standards-based APIs. Kevin would design a protocol layer beneath these APIs that would enable development of other APIs such as X/Open on top of it in the future. For now, Kevin could design his simpler APIs.

In the final run, I admit that I don't really know if Kevin's APIs are any simpler than the standards-based APIs, but Kevin certainly had a good argument to do it his way.

A bindery-emulation SET command specifies the context of a partition that supports bindery emulation. This partition must exist for bindery emulation to function. Figure 6.10 illustrates the way bindery emulation works on a given server.

All servers are not required to specify the same bindery-emulation context; the administrator is free to specify different bindery-emulation contexts on different servers, as long as actual physical copies of those partitions referenced by the context reside on those servers.

Bindery emulation is optional. Administrators can choose not to apply emulation by not specifying a context on NetWare 4.0 servers for bindery emulation.

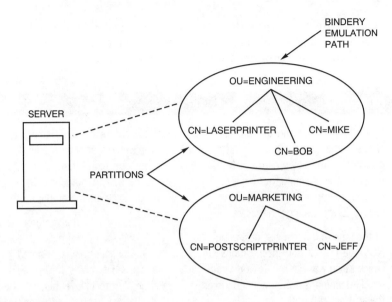

Figure 6.10:
Setting bindery emulation.

Using the Interoperability Features of NDS

Given that multiple standards exist for building a global name service, the database, and the very process for distribution of such a database, it is imperative that NDS interoperate with other standards-based and propri-etary databases. To accomplish this, Novell has taken the following steps in building the NDS:

❖ NDS database schema is a superset of the X.500 definition. Thus, an alien X.500 service always can query an object in the NDS database and expect to receive a satisfactory reply.

❖ NDS operates on NCP, which is Novell's service protocol that is based on the IPX protocol. Novell has not provided for an OSI protocol interface, or any other protocol interface for an alien directory ser-vice, to come in and query information about NDS database objects. This means that gateways must be built to provide the bridge for alien X.500 services to interact with the NDS database. This is certainly a feasible task that can be undertaken by Novell or interested third-party developers.

❖ Novell's security services for NDS are homegrown and do not follow the 1992 CCITT X.500 recommendations. The problem is that Novell's implementation of NDS is based on the 1988 CCITT X.500 specifications, which do not define an access-control scheme. The standard allowed third parties to adopt their own schemes. This gap may be tough to bridge because a suitable match may not be found for access-control implementations adopted by alien X.500 systems and that of Novell. Novell's engineers feel that objects that do not have security restrictions (objects in the public domain) can be shared easily between NDS and alien X.500 services, but it would be difficult to share information about objects that have security access control lists defined around them.

❖ Novell's distribution scheme for deploying replicas of partitions and the control messages that servers send to each other to accomplish NDS functions are proprietary; they do not follow either 1988 or 1992 CCITT X.500 specifications. This may not be relevant in bridging NDS with alien X.500 services, in which the primary need is to share information—not pass other command packets between the two dissimilar systems.

❖ Novell uses the RSA authentication scheme, which the X.500 standard also recommends. Multiple flavors of RSA-authentication implementations, however, may exist between two X.500 systems. It happens that the X.509 standard defines *certificates* that enable cross-authentication between two systems. Novell's implementation of these certificates is close to X.509, but not fully compliant with X.509. However, the certificates are close enough to X.509 so that a third-party developer can work with Novell to exchange certificates between an alien X.500 system and NDS.

❖ Many name services in the industry have adopted the Kerberos authentication scheme instead of RSA, which presents major problems if integration is desired between a Kerberos-based name service and the RSA-based NDS. This process might require extensive work by both Novell and the third-party developer trying to bridge NDS with a Kerberos-based name service.

❖ Novell has defined an API set that enables NDS to exchange information dynamically with other name services. A third party can write an NLM to run on a NetWare 4.0 server that uses the APIs to filter information in and out of NDS to and from other name services. By using this set and some form of X.509-based certificate exchange, you might bridge NDS with another standards-based or proprietary name service.

TIP
Novell provides tools for NetWare 2.x and 3.x installations to upgrade easily to NetWare 4.0. Chapters 12 and 13 shed more light on this process.

Summary

NetWare Directory Services (NDS) provides a comprehensive view of the enterprise network, and makes it both manageable and usable. NetWare 4.0 makes NDS the entity that administrators manage—not a server as a collection of servers. The same is true for users who log into the network and deal with NDS to locate and use resources.

This chapter explained the differences between the directory and the bindery. You learned about the hierarchy, organization, and object naming in NDS, as well as its various features.

Applications now also can use NDS to advertise their services. In essence, NDS offers a good infrastructure for an enterprise network, and has bandwidth enough to grow with an organization and meet all its growing computing needs.

NetWare 4.0 Security

NetWare 4.0 features greater security than any previous version of NetWare. This enhanced security comes from three new features: NDS authentication, based on RSA public-key cryptosystem; the auditing system; and NCP session authentication. These new security features work together with the excellent file-system security that has been part of NetWare since the release of v3.0 to make the most secure networking system on the market. For this reason, Novell is seeking Class F2 security certification for NetWare 4.0.

Understanding the Details of Class F2 Security Certification

Class F2 is a security criterion specified by the Information Technology (IT) security standards. The IT security standards and criteria are established and maintained by the German Information Security Agency (GISA). Class F2 is a concise, yet complete, security criterion, a summary of which is presented in the following sections.

Identification and Authentication

A system complying to Class F2 identifies and authenticates users uniquely. This identification and authentication occurs prior to all other interactions between the system and the user. Further interactions between the system and the user are possible only after the user has been identified and authenticated. Information that is used to authenticate the user is stored by the system so that only authorized users can gain access to the information. For each additional interaction between the system and the user, the system establishes the identity of the user.

Administration of Rights

A system complying to Class F2 can distinguish and administer access rights between users or user groups, and objects subject to administration of rights. The system can deny users or user groups access to an object completely, and also can restrict access to nonmodifying access. The system can grant access rights to an object down to the granularity of a single user.

The activity of granting and revoking access rights is allowed by the system only when such activity is performed by authorized users. The system provides controls to limit the propagation (inheritance) of access rights. Similarly, the creation of new users and the deletion of users is possible only when performed by authorized users.

Verification of Rights

Each attempt by users or user groups to gain access to objects is subject to verification by the system of the user's or group's rights to gain such access. Attempts to gain unauthorized access to objects are rejected by the system.

Auditing

A system complying to Class F2 must have an auditing system that logs the following events and data:

❖ Use of the identification and authentication mechanism (login): date, time, user identity supplied, identification of the equipment on which the identification and authentication mechanism was used (node address), and success or failure of the attempt.

❖ Attempted access to an object subject to the administration of rights: date, time, user identity, name of the object, type of access attempted, and success or failure of the attempt.

❖ Creation or deletion of an object subject to the administration of rights: date, time, user identity, name of object, and type of action.

❖ Actions by authorized users affecting the security of the system: date, time, user identity, type of action, name of object to which the action relates.

Examples of actions affecting the security of the system include the creation or deletion of users, the introduction or removal of storage media, and the startup or shutdown of the system.

Only authorized users can have access to data generated by the auditing system. The system makes it possible to restrict access to audit data to one or more users. The system provides tools to examine and maintain data generated by the auditing system, and such tools are documented. The format of data generated by the auditing system also is documented.

Object Reuse

All storage objects returned to the system must be treated before reuse by other subjects so that no information regarding the preceding content of the object is available. (Identification and authentication information must be erased from the object before it is recycled by the system.)

NetWare 4.0 Implementation of Class F2

With the exception of auditing, most of the requirements for Class F2 certification are present in NetWare 3.11. Auditing is a major component of Class F2 certification, however, and is very important to the security of the NetWare 4.0 environment. Many mechanisms of NetWare's security system are important to F2 compliance and are carried forward from NetWare 3.x, including the following:

❖ Trustee assignments (file system)

❖ Inherited rights mask (file system)

❖ Space restrictions (file system)

❖ User-account restrictions (login)

❖ Security equivalence/group membership (bindery)

Because of the introduction of NetWare Directory Services (NDS), all bindery-related security features of NetWare have been redesigned to become consistent with NDS. Most of the bindery-based security concepts, however, still apply to NetWare 4.0 and NDS. You will read more about NDS security mechanisms shortly.

As you read about specific security features that are present in NetWare 4.0, keep in mind the information you just read concerning Class F2 security. Novell is in the process of gaining F2 certification for NetWare 4.0, and an understanding of the Class F2 certification criteria may shed light on why NetWare 4.0's security mechanisms work the way they do.

Components of NetWare 4.0 Security

The major components of NetWare 4.0 security include the following:

- ❖ Authentication, using RSA public-key cryptosystem
- ❖ Access control for all NDS objects
- ❖ File system trustee-based access control
- ❖ Limits on the propagation of access control for both NDS and the file system (inherited rights mask)
- ❖ Auditing of NDS and file-system events
- ❖ NCP session authentication

Some of these components of security exceed Class F2 criteria, such as NCP session authentication and certain parts of NDS authentication. Each of these components provides a critical element of the overall NetWare 4.0 security architecture. Each of these elements works together with the others to make a NetWare 4.0 internetwork a highly secure system.

Understanding NetWare 4.0 Authentication

Authentication is the procedure used by NetWare 4.0 to verify the identity of a client submitting a request for some network resource. Verification of client identity entails the following:

- ❖ The sender of a message or request is a valid client.
- ❖ The sender actually built the message or request.
- ❖ The message or request originated at the workstation where the authentication data was created.
- ❖ The message or request pertains to the current session.
- ❖ The message or request has not been tampered with or corrupted.

It is important not to confuse authentication with rights enforcement. (The Level F2 criteria treat these two security components separately.) Authentication ensures that a client making a request is precisely who she claims to be. Rights enforcement ensures that the client cannot make a request for which he does not have rights. The network administrator's job is to establish security rights for users and groups so that users and groups are granted appropriate rights, but not granted inappropriate rights.

The NetWare 4.0 authentication procedure is highly secure, and is based in part on the RSA public-key cryptosystem. (*RSA* is a privately held firm that holds patents on a number of security algorithms. The firm is named after its founders: Rivest, Shamir, and Adleman.)

RSA Public-Key Cryptosystem

A *cryptosystem* provides methods for encrypting and decrypting messages. Messages are encrypted by *hashing* them (performing some mathematical algorithm) by using the message itself and the key to derive the encrypted messages. In most cryptosystems, messages must be encrypted and decrypted by using the same key. In such cryptosystems, the decryption process is exactly the inverse of the encryption process. Same-key cryptosystems, however, suffer from the weakness that keys must be distributed (both the encrypting and decrytping objects must know the key). Changing keys therefore becomes a complex problem.

Public-key cryptosystems use two keys: the *public key* is analogous to a user's phone number—it is published in a directory; the *private key* is known only to the decrypting object. To send a secure message, the system encrypts the message by using the destination object's public key. The destination object can then decrypt the message by using its private key.

The mathematics that enables the public-key cryptosystem to work is complex. To generate public and private keys, the computer system must derive three very large numbers (100 to 200 digits) from a random seed.

The first (and usually largest) number is used in both the encryption and decryption; the second number is a prime number and the public key; and the third number also is a prime number and the private key (n = first number, p = public key, s = private key).

Encryption of a message occurs by raising the message to the power of p, and taking the resulting number modulo n. Decryption of the same message occurs by raising the encrypted message to the power of s, and taking the resulting number modulo n. Decryption always results in the same message.

To break a public-key cryptosystem, a spy must be able to derive the secret key s, given the public key p. Deriving the secret key requires the spy to successfully factor the public key. If the public key is very large (and it always is), it should take years to factor it by using the best algorithms and the most powerful computers.

Login Authentication

When a user requests a login by issuing a user name and a password, the client software requests authentication from NDS. NDS generates a public and private key, encrypts the private key with the user's password, and sends the encrypted private key back to the user. The client software decrypts the private key; the user's password never crosses the network.

Information that is unique to the user, network station, and login session is then combined to form a unique signature. The *signature* not only identifies the user and network station uniquely, but also identifies the current NCP session. The signature is then combined with the private key to create a *credential*. After the credential is created, the private key is removed from the workstation's memory.

Full login authentication occurs when the client returns the request to complete the login process. This request contains the credential and a *proof*, which is derived from both the signature and the contents of the login-request packet, and is encrypted by using the NDS server's public key.

If the credential and proof derived by the client match those derived by NDS, authentication occurs, and the client is logged in to NDS. Figure 7.1 shows this process.

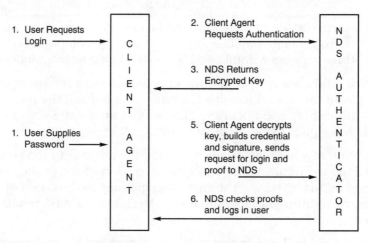

Figure 7.1:
NDS authentication is a complex procedure.

Background Authentication

Background authentication occurs whenever a logged-in client requests access to NDS objects that reside on a partition other than the partition to which the client originally logged in. When NDS requires background authentication, it sends a message to the client, asking the client to authenticate itself. The client then constructs a proof, combines it with the credential, and returns this information to NDS. If the proof and credential derived by the client match those derived by NDS, background authentication occurs, and the client gains further access to NDS.

All communications related to authentication make use of the RSA public-key cryptosystem. The inclusion of the signature, credential, and proof in the authentication procedure are designed to fulfill the requirements of the Class F2 security criteria. Specifically, this ensures that all authentication information for an ongoing session originates at the same network station, that the sending station is indeed the originating station, and that the message has not been tampered with en route to NDS.

During the life of an NCP session, the user's password and signature never cross the network. Both of these unique identifiers are derived independently by the client software and NDS.

Examining NDS Security Architecture

NDS security is based on a special object attribute called the *access control list (ACL)*. Each NDS object contains an ACL. The ACL itself contains a list of NDS object IDs that are allowed access to the object in question.

For example, an NDS tree has the following user objects:

User Name	User ID
ADMIN	00000001
MDAY	0e137ab1
MKOONTZ	001436ac
DMARSHAL	f00013c7

ADMIN is a special user created by NDS, and is always contained by the root partition of any NDS tree. By default, ADMIN has all rights to objects throughout the NDS tree. (You can modify the rights assigned to ADMIN to allow for delegation of NDS administration.)

The default ACL for user object MDAY is as follows:

```
00000001      (ADMIN)
0e137ab1      (MDAY)
```

SOAPBOX

Kerberos is an authentication scheme that is widely used in the academic community (and lately in the business world). I believe that Kerberos got its big start when OSF (Open Software Foundation) gave its blessing to this security scheme by making it part of the DCE (Distributed Computing Environment) standard.

Novell's architecture for the directory service relies on the X.500 specification, which recommends an authentication scheme based on the RSA cryptosystem. That's one strong reason for Novell's adoption of this standard into NetWare 4.0. Strong consideration was given to the Kerberos authentication scheme, however, and Novell's super architect, Kevin Kingdon, decided to forgo Kerberos in favor of RSA.

At the time that Kevin pulled the plug on Kerberos (1990), the Kerberos scheme still had some scalability problems. Kerberos provides for an authentication scheme that relies on tickets issued by an agent that the bearer can use to obtain a service from another entity (for example, an entity that offers a service that the ticket-bearer wants to use). For the Kerberos authentication scheme to work, the ticket-granting agent has to communicate with both the bearer and the service-provider through a three-way dialog in a somewhat complicated fashion.

At that time, Kerberos also designated ticket-granting domains, which limited the validity of a ticket to a domain assigned to a ticket-granting agent. The real problem (as Kevin perceived it) was the scalability of these ticket-granting domains to a large network. The RSA scheme that he devised, he felt, was more peer-to-peer—the authentication process was mostly performed by the requester of a service and the service-providing entity without a mediating third party, such as the Kerberos ticket-granting agent.

A later revision of the Kerberos scheme solved the scalability problems associated with ticket-granting domains. Unfortunately, by this time it was too late for Novell to consider adopting Kerberos as an authentication standard.

I do not particularly regret having chosen an RSA-based authentication scheme for NetWare 4.0. It works well, and more importantly, it scales quite well for large networks. The only disadvantage that I perceive is the fact that RSA is a technology owned by a for-profit private company (see text). Unless Novell works out an appropriate licensing arrangement with RSA, third parties that want to attach intelligent devices to NetWare servers may have to pay a licensing fee to RSA to use RSA code so that such devices can authenticate themselves to NetWare 4.0 servers.

In the default ACL for user object MDAY, only the ADMIN object and the MDAY object itself are inserted into object MDAY's ACL. That is, only ADMIN and MDAY have sufficient rights to gain access to object MDAY. If ADMIN decides to grant user object MKOONTZ access to object MDAY, the ACL for user object MDAY is modified to contain the ID number of object MKOONTZ, as follows:

```
00000001    (ADMIN)
0e137ab1    (MDAY)
001436ac    (MKOONTZ)
```

ACL Rights Mask

The ACL of each NDS object is a list of object IDs that can gain access to the ACL's object. For example, ADMIN, by default, has access to all NDS objects because the ID of ADMIN is (by default) inserted into the ACL of every NDS object. The ACL also contains a rights mask, however, that determines which types of access are allowable for each object ID contained in the ACL.

The various access rights that can be granted for each NDS object are as follows:

❖ **Browse.** Grants the right to see the object in the directory tree. This does not allow the objects to view the ACL itself.

❖ **Create.** Grants the right to create a new object below this object in the directory tree. Granting the Create right automatically causes the Browse right also to be granted.

❖ **Delete.** Grants the right to delete the object from the directory tree.

❖ **Rename.** Grants the right to change the name of the object.

❖ **Supervisor.** Grants all access privileges to the object.

Because of the ACL rights mask, each object that is granted access to a specific object can have different actual rights to that object. Consider the following example:

```
00000001    (ADMIN)      Supervisor rights
0e137ab1    (MDAY)       Browse, Delete, Rename rights
001436ac    (MKOONTZ)    Browse right
```

In this example, only ADMIN has full access to user object MDAY. User MDAY can browse, delete, or rename his own object. User MKOONTZ only can browse the user object MDAY.

Object Property ACL

NDS objects contain properties. The properties of a user object include such things as full name, login script, phone number, and so on. All NDS objects contain multiple properties. Just as each NDS object has an ACL, each property of each object also has an ACL. The property ACL works just like the object ACL: it contains ID numbers of NDS objects that can be granted access to the object property in question.

Although the property ACL works just like the object ACL, the property ACL rights mask is different from the object ACL rights mask. Property rights are as follows:

- ❖ **Compare.** Grants the right to compare any value to a value of the property. With the Compare right, any comparison can return true or false, but the comparing object cannot see the value of the property.

- ❖ **Read.** Grants the right to read the values of the property. Granting the Read right automatically entails granting the Compare right.

- ❖ **Write.** Grants the right to add, change, or remove any values of the property. Granting the Write right automatically entails granting the Add or Delete Self right.

- ❖ **Add or Delete Self.** Grants an object the right to add or remove itself as a value of the property. This right is only meaningful for properties that contain object names as values, such as group membership lists and mailing lists.

- ❖ **Supervisor.** Grants all rights to the property.

The ACL in Action

The Object and Property ACLs work together to define access rights for each NDS object. *Access rights* determine who can create, read, write, and delete NDS information. The NetWare 4.0 operating system always checks access rights before any NDS operation can proceed. This is a primary element of the Class F2 security criteria.

Most NetWare 4.0 users require only the Browse right for NDS objects other than their own. In terms of the object ACL, this means that all NDS user object IDs should be present in the ACL of most NDS objects, including other user objects. The ACL rights mask associated with user objects should limit their access to Browse, however. In the preceding example, user MKOONTZ has Browse rights to the user Object MDAY.

Network administrators require at least Browse, Create, Delete, and Rename rights to the objects for which they are responsible.

In terms of property ACL rights, network adminstrators require Write or Supervisor access to object properties. For a user to be able to modify her login script, she must have Write rights to her object's Login Script property. If a user is to view a specific property belonging to her object, she must have Read rights to that property. The same idea holds true for all objects and object properties.

The Admin Object

Admin is a special object that is always contained by the root of every NDS tree. The Admin object is granted Supervisor rights to the root of the tree, which enables the Admin Supervisor to access every object and property in the entire NDS tree. A user can modify or delete the Admin object, however, just as she can any other object. A user also can remove the Admin Object ID from object or property ACLs throughout the NDS tree. This means that NDS has no "Super User."

TIP
Novell defined the Admin object to be modifiable and even deletable so that a user can establish different network adminstrators for different partitions of NDS. This reflects the role for which NDS was defined. Because an NDS tree spans all divisions of an organization, it is reasonable to expect that only persons within a division have full rights to that division's area of the NDS tree.

The Public Object

Public is a special object definition that enables a user to grant global access to NDS objects or properties. For example, if you want to establish an object for which all users have Browse access, you can assign Browse access for that object to the Public object, and all users automatically have Browse access. This is significantly easier than manually adding each user's object ID to the new object's ACL.

Groups

You can establish user groups by creating a *Group* object. To include a specific user in a new group, include her user's ID in the new group's ACL. When that person grants object or property rights to the group, NDS automatically transfers those rights to each user who is a member of the group.

Rights Inheritance

By default, object and property rights are inherited downward through the NDS tree. For example, if a person creates an Organizational Unit called Engineering, and the Engineering object is contained by the root object, the user Admin automatically inherits Supervisor access to the new Engineering object.

```
[Root] (Admin has Supervisor Access)
    [Organization Unit Engineering]
    (Admin inherits Supervisor Access to the new object)
```

What if the Admin user object was not to have Supervisor access to the new Engineering object? To prevent Admin from inheriting Supervisor access to the new Engineering object, you can block inheritance by using a special property called the *Inherited Rights Filter (IRF)*, which is a mask that blocks the inheritance of access rights downward through the NDS tree. By placing the Admin access right in the IRF of the root object, a person automatically can block user Admin from inheriting Supervisor access to any new objects contained by the root.

TIP

The IRF can be used throughout the entire NDS tree. The IRF can block the inheritance of any object or property access right. By induction, the IRF also can grant unintentionally inherited rights to new objects if the network administrator ignores the IRF. Therefore, it is important for the network administrator to understand and make use of the IRF when working with NDS objects.

Login Restrictions

Login restrictions have been a feature of NetWare for several years. NetWare 4.0 continues to feature login restrictions as an important component of its overall security system. Login restrictions supported by NetWare 4.0 include the following:

❖ Account restrictions

❖ Password restrictions

❖ Station restrictions

❖ Time restrictions

❖ Intruder limits

Account restrictions enable the network administrator to disable specific accounts. This completely prevents the user from logging in to the NetWare 4.0 system. The network administrator also can set expiration dates for accounts. Expiration dates are appropriate in environments in which users are transient, such as educational institutions or commercial on-line database systems. When the expiration date arrives, NDS automatically removes the account.

Password restrictions enable the network administrator to enforce the correct use of passwords. The network administrator can require passwords, set a minimum length for passwords, force periodic changes of passwords, or require unique passwords.

The network administrator also can limit *grace logins,* which occur when a user mistypes her password, and the system allows her to attempt to log in to the system again. Limiting grace logins can prevent hackers from systematically discovering passwords by trying repeatedly to log in to the system by using different passwords.

Workstation restrictions enable the network administrator to control the stations from which a specific user can log in to the system. For example, the administrator can choose to prevent user MDAY from logging in to the system from any station other than MDAY's own computer.

Login time restrictions enable the network administrator to set specific times of day when specific users are not allowed to log in to the network. For example, user MDAY can be prevented from logging in to the network between 12 a.m. and 5 a.m.

Intruder limits control the temporary disabling of accounts when a specific number of unsuccessful logins occur. For example, a hacker attempts to log in to the network by using MDAY's account. If the intruder limit for MDAY's account is set at three, NDS temporarily disables MDAY's account when the hacker has made three unsuccessful attempts to log in as user MDAY. The network administrator can set the time during which user MDAY's account is disabled. At the end of that time period, user MDAY's account is enabled once more.

Exploring File-System Security Architecture

The NetWare 4.0 file-system security architecture is essentially unchanged from NetWare 3.11. Like the NDS security architecture, file-system security is based on a list of objects that have rights to specific files or directories. In NDS, these lists are called *access control lists (ACLs),* and are attributes of each object and object property. In the file system, these lists are called *trustee lists*, and are components of directory entries for both files and directories.

For example, the file SYS:\USERS\MDAY\TEST.ONE resides in user MDAY's home directory. The trustee list of file TEST.ONE contains the IDs of users ADMIN, MDAY, and MKOONTZ, as follows:

```
00000001    (ADMIN)
0e137ab1    (MDAY)
001436ac    (MKOONTZ)
```

Users ADMIN, MDAY, and MKOONTZ are said to be trustees of the file TEST.ONE because their object IDs are present in the file's trustee list.

Each trustee can have a different level of rights to a specific file. The trustee list contains a rights mask for each trustee that is present in the list. The rights mask enumerates the different types of operations for which a specific trustee is granted access to the file in question. Specific rights enumerated by the trustee list rights mask include the following:

❖ **Supervisor.** User has all rights to files and directories.

❖ **Read.** User can read the file's contents.

❖ **Write.** User can alter the file's contents.

❖ **Create.** User can create further files and subdirectories.

❖ **Erase.** User can delete file(s) or directories.

❖ **Modify.** User can modify the directory.

❖ **File Scan.** User can scan for files.

❖ **Access.** User can change access control for trustees of the file or directory.

The Read and Write rights apply only to files, but the remaining rights apply to directories and files. To continue the example of file TEST.ONE, the rights masks for that file's trustees can be similar to the following:

```
00000001    (ADMIN) Supervisor (all rights)
0e137ab1    (MDAY) Read, Write, Create, Erase, Modify, Scan
001436ac    (MKOONTZ) Read, Scan
```

According to the trustee rights shown in the preceding example for TEST.ONE, user ADMIN has all rights to the file. User MDAY has all rights except the ability to change access control for the file.

User MKOONTZ can see the file's directory entry (by using the Scan right), and can read the contents of the file, but cannot alter or delete the file TEST.ONE.

File Ownership

Each file and directory has an *owner*, which is indicated by a user ID contained in the file or directory's directory entry. File ownership implies that the owner had sufficient rights to create the file or directory. Those rights can subsequently be revoked from the owner, however.

File Attributes

Each file or directory has attributes that control permissible operations for that file or directory. File attributes always take precedence over trustee rights. For example, if a file has the Delete Inhibit attribute, no user can delete that file, even if a user has Delete rights to the file. Similarly, if a file has the Read Only attribute, no user can alter the file, even if a user has Write rights to the file. File attributes defined in NetWare 4.0 include the following:

- ❖ Read Only
- ❖ Hidden
- ❖ System
- ❖ Execute Only
- ❖ Archive
- ❖ Sharable
- ❖ Transactional
- ❖ Purge Immediately
- ❖ Rename Inhibit
- ❖ Delete Inhibit
- ❖ Copy Inhibit

Although most of the file attributes are self-explanatory, some need further discussion. The Hidden attribute prevents files from showing up in directory listings. Users with sufficient rights can still open the file to alter its contents, but they must know the file's name, and they cannot discover the file's name by using a directory listing.

The Execute Only attribute means that a file can be executed, but it cannot be read, written, copied, or otherwise altered. Files with the Execute Only attribute can be deleted. Execute Only is designed for executable software programs that are stored on a NetWare server, and it prevents unauthorized copying of software. Execute Only also prevents infection of the file by virus programs because NetWare prevents any attempt to alter the contents of the file.

The Transactional attribute is used with the NetWare Transaction Tracking System (TTS), which is a highly robust implementation of transaction control for use by database management software.

The Purge Immediately attribute causes a file to be purged when that file is deleted. Most deleted files continue to reside in the NetWare file system for a period of time after their deletion, which enables you to recover mistakenly deleted files. Files with the Purge Immediately attribute, however, are not only deleted from the file system—their contents are also written over with null bytes upon deletion.

The Delete Inhibit and Copy Inhibit attributes prevent files from being deleted and copied, respectively.

New NetWare 4.0 File Attributes

NetWare 4.0 has several new file attributes, only one of which has implications for security. These new file attributes enable you to control the compression and data migration of specific files and directories. A new file attribute also controls the auditing status of a file or directory. The Auditing attribute is part of the NetWare 4.0 auditing system. Users can never view the auditing status of a file or directory—only the system auditor can set or view the Auditing attribute of a file or directory.

Learning About NetWare 4.0 Auditing

System auditing is a major element of the Class F2 security criteria. The NetWare 4.0 auditing system was designed specifically to meet Class F2 requirements, but also to maintain the performance and efficiency standards that have been part of the overall NetWare design philosophy for years. The design goals of the NetWare 4.0 auditing system are as follows:

❖ High level of security

❖ Auditor separate from Supervisor or Admin

❖ Low impact on system performance

❖ Selective auditing

❖ File and directory Auditing attribute

❖ Auditing of NDS objects

❖ Auditing of data storage resources

NetWare 4.0 system auditing achieves a high level of security by allowing any operation involving the file system, storage resources, or NDS to be audited. Users have no way of knowing which operations or resources are being audited. Therefore, even if a user successfully bypasses NetWare's other security measures, unauthorized operations performed by a user may leave an audit trail.

TIP

The auditing system is designed so that the system auditor should be a different person from the system administrator. This follows the time-proven business tradition of performing independent audits of business-accounting data. In business, persons with a vested interest in the financial status of a company are prevented from performing audits; business audits are performed by an independent auditor who has no vested interest in the outcome of the audit.

The NetWare 4.0 auditing system achieves efficiency and has a low impact on system performance because of the methods used to generate audit records. Code for generating audit records is resident in the low-level routines of the operating system. The audit records themselves are compact, and they are stored in binary format. The generation of an audit record is quick, and it has a slight impact on overall system performance.

Efficiency is further increased by the capability of the system auditor to select specific operations and objects that are subject to auditing. For example, it makes little sense to audit a public area of the file system. Areas of the file system that contain private or critical data should be audited, however. The system auditor can choose to forgo auditing of public or nonsensitive data, but can choose to audit sensitive data.

By using a combination of audited events, NDS object properties, and file-system attributes, the system auditor can implement auditing by user, operation, NDS object, file or directory, or any other combination.

The auditing of storage resources also is necessary for Class F2 certification. When auditing is activated for a NetWare volume, the operating system does not mount that volume until the system auditor enters the auditing password for that volume. If a user dismounts a volume, that operation generates an audit record of the dismount. Likewise, bringing the operating system down and restarting the operating system both generate audit records.

The NetWare 4.0 auditing system features a utility called AUDITCON.EXE that the system auditor can use to establish and configure auditing for a file system or NDS partition. AUDITCON also enables the system auditor to read and maintain audit logs.

The auditing system also features an Application Programming Interface (API) that developers can use to build system auditing into their applications. This API fully documents the format of audit records (a requirement of Class F2 certification), and enables developers to create their own audit-record formats.

Understanding NCP Session Authentication

NCP session authentication is a new security feature recently added to NetWare 3.11, and is integrated fully into NetWare 4.0. NCP session authentication renders obsolete a sophisticated method of breaching security on networked systems that was demonstrated during 1992 in an academic setting.

The so-called *forged packet* method of breaching the security of networked systems involves taking over a network session after authentication has occurred. In other words, the forged-packet method does not try to compromise the authentication procedures of a network system—it waits until authentication occurs and then effectively blocks the authenticated user from further use of the authenticated session by taking the session over from the authenticated user.

Although the forged-packet method of hacking a network session is not unique to NetWare, NetWare is the only network system to date that provides immunity to this method.

RSA MD4 Message Digest

NCP session authentication involves maintenance by both the client and the server of a session state. The state of a session reflects the prior and current activity of that session. Hackers using the forged-packet method to breach security must capture a network packet and alter that packet so that it causes the server to perform an otherwise legitimate modification of server security settings.

To successfully forge a packet when NCP session authentication is active, however, the hacker must have tracked the complete history of the session. Moreover, a portion of each NCP packet is intentionally altered by the sending station by using a special algorithm similar to encryption. The hacker must therefore know the algorithm for altering packets and also a 64-bit session key, which is derived independently by both the client and the server. Finally, the algorithm for intentionally altering NCP packets changes dynamically with each additional packet sent or received by the client or the server.

TIP
NCP session authentication is based on the RSA MD-4 message digest algorithm. This algorithm is similar to encryption, but it does not change the actual contents of the packet, except for a special packet signature that the sending station inserts into the body of the packet. The receiving station uses the prior activity of the NCP session as a factor for calculating the expected signature of a received packet. If the expected signature of a received packet does not match the actual signature that is inserted into the packet by the sending station, the packet is not accepted by the receiving station.

Session activity is factored into the calculation of the packet signature, along with a secret session key known only to the sending and receiving stations. Because this session key never crosses the network, it is impossible for a hacker to discover the session key by snooping on the network.

As stated earlier, NCP session authentication renders obsolete the forged-packet method of breaching system security. The system administrator can determine, on a user-by-user basis, which NCP sessions are subject to authentication. Typically, only sessions in which users have supervisory rights present an opportunity for a hacker to use the forged-packet method. The administrator can, therefore, subject supervisory users to NCP session authentication while allowing other users to have unauthenticated sessions. Novell is currently implementing further security for NCP sessions, including the total encryption of all NCP packets.

Summary

NetWare 4.0 is the most secure operating system that Novell has ever produced. Features such as authentication, auditing, and NCP session authentication improve on the security of NetWare 3.11, which is an impressively secure environment.

The additional security provided by NetWare 4.0 is necessary if this operating system is to be the primary computing platform for large organizations. NetWare 4.0 provides a security environment similar to that found on very secure mainframe systems, as evidenced by Novell's application for Class F2 security certification.

File Systems and Media Management

The heart of a good enterprise platform is its file system. The file system must have a prodigious capacity, be robust and tolerant of faults, and be very, very fast. In addition, a file system that runs legacy applications must be a multiuser system (files must have owners and be secure from access by users who should not view or manipulate the file). The NetWare file system is all of these.

The NetWare 4.0 File System

The NetWare file system offers certain services that are usually associated with database management systems, such as transaction control. The existence of these services at the kernel level is evidence that NetWare's designers were thinking of downsizing before they wrote a line of code.

A single NetWare 4.0 server can have up to 32T (terabytes) of storage space.

TIP

A *terabyte (TB)* is 1024 gigabytes, or one million megabytes. However, because of file-entry caching, the real limit on NetWare storage space is installed RAM.

Many NetWare servers are in the field right now, sporting multigigabyte storage systems. The important thing to note is that the NetWare file system was designed to support multigigabyte storage systems without slowing performance. All low-level file system routines in NetWare are optimized to perform well with super-large file systems. This is evident throughout the array of system maximum limits, including concurrent file handles, file and record locks, and concurrent transactions. Each and every one of them is prodigious, just as the file system as a whole is.

The Volume

The basic structure of a NetWare 4.0 storage system is the *volume*, which is a logical structure, analogous to a *file system* under UNIX. NetWare servers can have up to 64 volumes, and a single volume can consist of up to 32 segments. A *segment* is an area of physical storage stamped for use by NetWare.

TIP

Stamping consists of writing information directly to the physical media. This information consists of the size of the segment and other control items.

Segments that make up a NetWare 4.0 volume reside on different physical-storage devices. That is, you can create segments using up to 32 different storage devices and combine those segments into a single NetWare volume. When you do this, NetWare will *stripe*, or spread, data among all the different physical devices, which gives NetWare a built-in split-seeking capability. For example, on a volume consisting of four segments, each of which resides on a separate hard drive, the reading and writing of data is close to four times faster on the multisegment volume than on a single-segment volume.

Volumes consist of *blocks*, which are logical storage-allocation units. Blocks are analogous to DOS clusters—they provide a mechanism whereby the low-level file system routines within NetWare can translate a logical file offset given in a read or write command into a physical disk sector. Within the NetWare file-system logic, blocks are mapped to a volume segment, which is in turn mapped to a physical drive; the block number and physical drive are then resolved to an actual sector or sectors on that physical drive (see fig. 8.1).

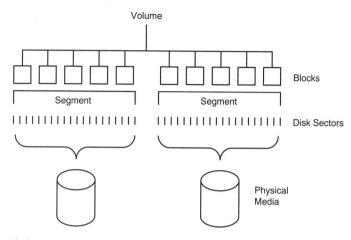

Figure 8.1:

Basic structure of the NetWare file system.

Extending a Volume

One advantage of NetWare 4.0 volumes is that you can extend them at any time. To extend a volume, add a prepared segment to it. NetWare extends its logical volume data structure so that all physical disk sectors on the new segment are addressable through the (now extended) volume. NetWare can do this at any time, even when the server is up and running or when the server is being used for heavy disk I/O.

Data Striping

When a volume consists of more than one physical segment, NetWare 4.0 automatically arranges files so that they are spread evenly across all segments allocated to that volume. This enables read and write operations to occur simultaneously because they are being accomplished by multiple physical storage devices. This phenomenon is called *data striping*, and it allows for *split seeking*, or splitting a seek among multiple physical devices.

The File Allocation Table

The second primary data structure of the NetWare 4.0 file system is the *File Allocation Table (FAT)*. The FAT is a collection of information about every single block within the volume. Each block within the volume exists as an element within the FAT. Moreover, the entire volume FAT is cached in server RAM for as long as that volume is mounted. Figure 8.2 shows the way the FAT tracks each block on the volume.

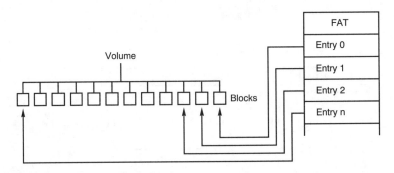

Figure 8.2:

The FAT tracks the way each block on the volume is used.

Files in NetWare are chains of FAT entries. That is, a large file consists of a series of FAT entries that are linked together, in sequential order, to form a chain. Although the actual data of the file is located on volume blocks that resolve to physical disk sectors, the FAT chain provides information to the NetWare file system that enables the file system to read or write the file into or out of memory from the correct physical disk sectors, and in the correct order.

Free space on a NetWare 4.0 volume shows up in the volume FAT as *unallocated entries*, which represent physical disk sectors that do not contain any file data. Because the entire volume FAT is cached for as long as that volume is mounted, unallocated FAT entries are cached with allocated ones. This enables the NetWare file system to find and allocate empty FAT entries (and their corresponding volume blocks and physical disk blocks) very quickly.

Mirrored FATs

Each NetWare 4.0 volume contains a redundant volume FAT. Only one copy of the volume FAT is cached while a volume is mounted, but the uncached (mirrored) copy of the volume FAT is kept up-to-date by the file system. This protects the integrity of the volume in the face of I/O errors or physical device malfunctions. If one copy of the volume FAT becomes corrupt, NetWare can restore the FAT by using the redundant copy. NetWare usually can restore the integrity of the FAT, even if both copies are damaged, provided that they are not damaged in the same location.

The Directory Table

The third primary data structure of the NetWare 4.0 volume is the *directory table*, which contains an entry for each file located on the NetWare volume. An entry in the directory table consists of file information, such as the file name, creation date and time, last access date, file owner, users who have access to the file, their access levels, and more.

A key element of each directory entry is a *pointer* to an entry in the volume FAT, which enables the operating system to locate the first block of a given file. After the first block is located, the operating system can read the entire file because each entry in the FAT contains a pointer to the next block (see fig. 8.3).

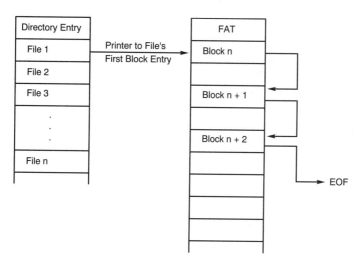

```
Block n:       First block of file
Block n + 1:   Second block of file
Block n + 2:   Last block of file
EOF:           End-of-file marker
```

Figure 8.3:

The directory table keeps track of files on a volume.

The last FAT entry in a file chain contains an *end-of-file (EOF)* marker, which informs the operating system that it has just located the last block of the file.

Directory-Caching

Every time NetWare 4.0 is instructed to open a file, it must search the directory table to find the directory entry for that file. After NetWare locates the directory entry, it can then read the file by traversing the file's FAT chain. This is all pretty simple, but it can take time for the operating system to search the directory table because a volume typically contains thousands of files (which results in a directory table with thousands of entries).

Because of this time delay, NetWare 4.0 caches the directory table on an as-needed basis. The entire directory table is rarely cached. The first time NetWare opens a file, however, it copies that file's entry in the directory table to cache memory in server RAM. The next time that NetWare must gain access to that file, it does not need to search the directory table because the entry for that file is located in RAM.

NetWare 4.0 manages cached directory-table entries according to an intelligent Least-Recently Used (LRU) algorithm. First, you can set an upper limit to the amount of memory that NetWare uses to cache directory-table entries by using a special server console command (SET maximum directory entries = n). When NetWare has reached its upper limit of cached directory-table entries, it caches further entries by flushing the least-recently used entries from cache memory, and replaces them in cache with the new entries.

NetWare 4.0 limits the number of cached directory-table entries specifically so that more server RAM is available for caching the files themselves. NetWare's file-caching algorithms are discussed in more detail shortly.

Directory Hashing

Despite the performance gains offered by cached directory table entries, it still takes some time to locate a file's directory-table entry the first time that the operating system must gain access to the file. This is where directory hashing comes in to play. To hash a directory entry, the file system constructs a numeric key by processing the file's name.

TIP

Hashing is computer science jargon for the method used to generate a numeric key from a string of bytes, such as a file name.

When searching for a file entry in the directory table, NetWare 4.0 performs an indexed search on a numeric key, which is an order of magnitude quicker than searching on the file's name. After the file's entry in the directory table is located, it is immediately cached, making subsequent searches even quicker than the first one.

It is not uncommon for NetWare 4.0 volumes to have hundreds of thousands of directory-table entries. Because of directory hashing, first-search times through the directory table increase on a logarithmic scale instead of on an exponential scale. This is the same type of performance metric that is achieved by tree-based (rather than table-based) file systems, such as those implemented by mainframes and minicomputers.

That is just the beginning, however. The real fireworks occur after the NetWare 4.0 operating system locates the file's first block and begins read/write operations on that file.

File-Caching

After the NetWare 4.0 operating system loads, initializes itself, and mounts volumes, it allocates all remaining server RAM as file-cache buffers. *File-cache buffers* hold volume blocks that are in use (or that have been in use) as the result of file access by a network client (or by a program running on the server operating system). When the operating system needs to read or write a volume block (as part of some file I/O operation), the read or write occurs hundreds of times faster if it can read from or write to a cache buffer instead of physical storage media.

TIP

A *cache hit* occurs when the data can be read from or written to a cache buffer instead of a physical disk sector.

The NetWare 4.0 file system is so highly optimized that a read or write operation that generates a cache hit executes by using only one hundred or so machine instructions, and it occurs in microseconds. Although this is impressive, it is made more so by the sheer size of the file-cache memory on the typical NetWare server.

For example, a server machine with 16M of memory typically has at least 10M of that memory dedicated to file-cache buffers. This means that the server can hold 4,000 volume blocks in cache. Thousands of files can reside in cache concurrently. On a server with 32M of RAM, it is likely that at least 28M of server RAM is devoted to caching data files.

The NetWare 4.0 file-system cache algorithms use an intelligent LRU algorithm to manage the flushing and filling of file-cache buffers, just as the directory-table caching algorithms do. This means that only the most recently used volume blocks remain in cache when the server is using all its cache buffers.

NetWare 4.0's allocation and use of file-cache buffers is dynamic—running processes or programs allocates memory from the file-cache system. When another process or program needs memory, the NetWare operating system removes that memory from the file-cache system, and allocates it for the process or program. Thus, NetWare uses all available memory for file-caching, but it does not prevent other processes or programs from "borrowing" file-cache memory for their own uses.

The size of NetWare 4.0's file-cache memory is the single greatest variable in determining how fast a NetWare server performs. When the file-cache is large, the NetWare server performs very well. When the file-cache is too small relative to the level of file I/O on the server, performance slows significantly. By definition, the greatest thing you can do to improve the performance of a NetWare server is to give it plenty of RAM, which translates into plenty of file-cache buffers.

When file-cache memory is equal to 80 percent of server memory (or greater), it is common to achieve a 90 percent cache-hit ratio. That is, 90 percent of all server read or write requests are fulfilled from file-cache buffers rather than from disk accesses. For an average server, 16M of RAM is usually sufficient to guarantee that 80 percent of all RAM is in use as file-cache. On a heavily used server, the more RAM the better, although 32M usually is sufficient.

NetWare 4.0's memory-management and file-cache management algorithms do not slow down significantly when server RAM reaches huge amounts (such as 128M). For most resource-management algorithms in the NetWare operating system, no significant penalty exists for configuring a massive server in regard to the amount of disk storage and the amount of RAM. Indeed, any slowdowns in internal operating-system algorithms resulting from huge volume sizes or numbers of cache buffers is more than compensated for by the ways NetWare uses massive hardware configurations.

File-Cache Integrity

When it comes to legacy applications, you may be concerned that so much file data is cached at any one time by the NetWare 4.0 operating system. What if the server fails? What happens to cached data?

Application designers can force cache buffers to be flushed immediately upon write operations, depending on the way the application opens the file. This is equivalent to a write-through cache. For critical database files, a write-through cache is the best way to go—read operations still occur in microseconds, but write operations are guaranteed to go directly to disk.

NetWare 4.0's file-cache system, however, is different from analogous systems in other operating systems. The file-cache system is an integral part of the NetWare file system; it is built into the file system at the lowest levels, and literally dominates most file system code.

In addition, three fault-tolerant features of the NetWare 4.0 file system work together with the file-cache system, making it rare that an application needs to open a file in write-through mode. These three fault-tolerant features include disk duplexing and mirroring, hot fix, and read-after-write verification. These features are described in the following sections.

Disk Duplexing and Mirroring

Disk duplexing and mirroring enables you to install redundant hard drives in a NetWare server. During normal operation, NetWare writes all data to both drives, and reads data from the first available drive. (This makes read operations faster, but it slows down write operations somewhat.) If one drive or drive controller suffers a failure, NetWare automatically switches to using the nonfailed driver or controller exclusively until the failed drive or controller is replaced. Upon replacement of the failed driver or controller, NetWare re-establishes the mirror by duplicating all the data on the non-failed drive to the new or restored drive.

TIP

You can mirror a single partition to many other partitions, up to 15. This enables you to implement a multiple redundant storage system.

Hot Fix

Hot fix refers to the NetWare 4.0 file system's capability to detect bad physical drive sectors and replace them with good sectors from a collection of reserved volume blocks. This process is similar to that of formatting a drive, except that it occurs transparently during the course of server operation. NetWare detects bad physical disk sectors when it suffers a read or write error, or when read-after-write verification fails.

TIP

Volume blocks correspond to physical drive sectors, although not necessarily in a one-to-one relationship.

Read-after-Write Verification

Read-after-write verification refers to the NetWare 4.0 file system's capability to verify that data it has just written to disk has, in fact, been recorded correctly on the disk's physical media. NetWare calls the disk's device driver, causing the device driver to write a buffer of data to disk. Immediately after the device driver returns to NetWare, Netware calls the device driver to read the just-written data back into a "check" buffer. NetWare then compares the data in the check buffer to the original data buffer. If the two buffers match, everything continues normally. If the two buffers do not match, NetWare uses hot fix to replace the block or blocks that correspond to the bad physical media.

Read-after-write verification slows write operations somewhat, just as disk mirroring and opening a file in write-through mode do. Most hard-drive manufacturers today produce drives that perform read-after-write verification by using software encoded on the drive's controller, however. When this is the case, NetWare recognizes that it does not need to perform read-after-write verification because the drive hardware is doing so. Hardware-based read-after-write verification does not slow write operations at all, so it is obviously the best option.

TIP

Even with hardware-based read-after-write verification, NetWare recognizes when it must use hot fix to replace a bad block or blocks, although such times are far less frequent.

Read-after-write verification complements hot fix nicely. In fact, both forms of file-system fault tolerance are less effective alone than when used together.

The combination of drive mirroring and duplexing, hot fix, and read-after-write verification ensures that cached data retains its integrity throughout its journey from server RAM to physical media. Hence, many of the traditional concerns you might have regarding file-caching are not as relevant to NetWare as they are to other operating systems. You can always ensure that your legacy applications open all their critical files in write-through mode. Another way to ensure write-through mode is to use the NetWare Transaction Tracking System (TTS), which is discussed shortly.

Elevator Seeking

Elevator seeking is an attack on the relatively long time it takes for a magnetic hard drive to move, or *seek*, its read/write head from one track to another. Although most hard drives on the market today can read or write around 1K of data in a single millisecond, it takes them (on average) around 16 milliseconds just to move their read/write heads into position for reading or writing data. As a result, most of the time consumed by a read or write operation is spent seeking the read/write head to the correct track.

Seek time is especially wasteful for multitasking operating systems, in which each different task contends for control of the hard drive. Moreover, each task has different files open, which markedly reduces the chances that a read or write operation can be fulfilled from contiguous locations on the hard drive's physical media.

Any mechanism whereby the operating system can reduce the amount of seeking required to perform read/write operations provides disproportionate gains in performance. Elevator seeking does this by reorganizing read/write requests to group them according to the track of the hard drive they target. Read/write operations targeted to the same track are grouped together, as are read/write operations targeted to contiguous tracks.

The *elevator* is a memory buffer in which NetWare 4.0 stores the reordered read/write requests. Under normal operation, NetWare flushes file-cache buffers by emptying them into the elevator. When the elevator is "full," the operating system flushes the elevator by executing the read/write requests in the optimal order (the order that results in the least amount of time spent seeking from track to track). In certain situations, however, such as a writes to a file opened in write-through mode, NetWare flushes the elevator before it is full, diluting the performance advantages of elevator seeking.

Even with a write-through file, NetWare 4.0's elevator seeking improves the performance of file I/O. Under favorable circumstances, elevator seeking produces dramatic gains in performance, sometimes reducing the time required to perform reads and writes by up to 90 percent.

More About Transaction Tracking

Because transaction control is such a vital component of a legacy application, NetWare's built-in transaction control should be discussed in some detail. This section is a technical discussion of NetWare's transaction-control system. Legacy applications can take advantage of NetWare's transaction-control system by using a very simple API.

Transaction Tracking Definitions

During this discussion, you come across the following terms:

❖ **Log file.** The transaction-control file that contains original data from database files. This original data must be restored to the database file in the event of an I/O error.

❖ **Target file.** The database file that contains transaction records. The target file is the target of write operations. If the write fails to occur completely, the target file must be restored to its prewrite state.

❖ **Back out transactions.** The process of restoring target files to their pre-error state.

Purpose of Transaction Tracking

The NetWare 4.0 *Transaction Tracking System (TTS)* is a component of NetWare's System Fault Tolerance (SFT). Specifically, TTS protects the integrity of data files by controlling whether and in what ways those files are modified. Also, TTS attempts to recover from system crashes and data errors, if they occur, by restoring affected data files to their pre-error state.

TTS works best for transaction-oriented data management applications in which modifications to data files must be an "all or nothing" proposition. That is, either an entire transaction gets added (or deleted or changed) to the data file, or none of the transaction gets added to the data file. When TTS is active, NetWare uses it to modify the the NDS DIB (Directory Information Base).

Transactions are clusters of data objects and read/write instructions that are grouped together for a specific purpose by the application. Every transaction consists of a beginning point and an ending point. Most transactions also have at least one data object and at least one read/write instruction.

For example, in a financial-accounting application, a transaction might consist of a series of debits and credits that are balanced (all the debits added together equal all the credits added together). In such an application, the database lacks integrity if a single transaction is out of balance. The possibility always exists that the system can start a transaction but not complete it because of an unforeseen event such as a power failure. This, in turn, leads to the possibility of the database being left in an out-of-balance state. TTS is a fail-safe device that prevents this from happening.

How TTS Works

TTS is simple in theory. It notes the beginning of every transaction and records the progress of that transaction. Before TTS enables a process to write data to the transactional target file, TTS reads the existing data from the target file at the offset of the impending write.

After reading the existing data, TTS rewrites that data to the TTS log file. Only after the original data from the target file is recorded in the TTS log file does TTS allow a process to write data to the target file. After successfully writing data to the target file, a process can end a transaction. If the transaction progresses through its end point successfully, TTS forgets about that transaction, and erases the original data from the TTS log file.

If, however, the transaction fails to progress through its end point for some reason, TTS restores the data file associated with that transaction to its pretransaction state. When possible, TTS does this immediately. In the case of a fatal error that shuts down NetWare, however, TTS can restore the data file to its pretransaction state as soon as the system comes back up.

TTS is implemented in several parts of NetWare 4.0. First, TTS exists as code segments in NetWare's low-level file routines. Second, TTS exists as code segments in NetWare's file and record locking routines. TTS code is embedded throughout the NetWare file system, and virtually all file-handling routines interface with TTS in one way or another.

Activating TTS

For TTS to become active, NetWare 4.0 must initialize the TTS data structures and a TTS log file, which has its system and hidden flags set. If TTS discovers an existing log file when initializing a new one, it tries to rename that file and back out the transactions recorded on it. If TTS cannot initialize a new log file, or if sufficient memory is not available to initialize TTS data structures, NetWare cannot make TTS active.

After TTS is active, it only engages a transaction for target files that are "transactional" (those that have their transactional bit set). TTS supports two methods of engaging a transaction: explicit transactions and implicit transactions.

Explicit transactions occur when an application calls the server API `TTSBeginTransaction()`, and the application tries to write to one or more transactional files before calling the server API `TTSEndTransaction()`.

During explicit transactions, TTS generates a physical record lock for each transactional file to which the application tries to write. As soon as the application ends the transaction by calling `TTSEndTransaction()`, and as soon as a record of the transaction exists in the TTS log file, TTS commits the transaction to the target file (or files) and releases any physical record locks generated by the transaction.

Implicit transactions occur whenever an application breaches a workstation's application threshold or causes a breach to the workstation's workstation threshold. The *workstation threshold* is the number of file or record locks that a workstation can have active before TTS begins a transaction for that connection.

The *application threshold* is the number of file or record locks that a specific application running at a workstation can have active before TTS begins a transaction for that connection. Applications can set these thresholds by calling `TTSSetWorkstationThresholds()` or `TTSSetApplicationThresholds()`. Applications can query the OS for current thresholds by calling `TTSGetApplicationThresholds()` or `TTSGetWorkstationThresholds()`.

As soon as either threshold (workstation or application) is breached for the active connection, TTS begins an implicit transaction. At that point, any time the active connection attempts to lock a transactional file, TTS generates a transaction. TTS does not, however, generate a physical record lock because such a lock begins the implicit transaction, and thus already exists. When the application tries to release the lock on the file or record, TTS generates a call to `TTSEndTransaction`. It retains the lock on the file until the log record for that transaction is complete, and the cache buffers holding the written data get flushed to the target file.

Because implicit transactions are triggered by file or record locks, TTS monitors all locking activity; because transactions are engaged only for transactional files, all file routines check a file's transaction bit for every write operation when TTS is active. NetWare automatically sets the transaction bit for the NDS DIB.

Whenever NetWare 4.0 initializes the TTS system, it creates a new TTS log file, which becomes the active log file. Only a single, active TTS log file can exist at a given time. The beginning of the log file contains a record of the Volume Name Table as the table existed when TTS initialized.

The *Volume Name Table* is a mapping of volume numbers to volume names. Because the state of a given volume is dynamic when NetWare 4.0 is running, TTS cannot assume that the Volume Name Table at transaction time is identical to the Volume Name Table at backout time.

TIP

The NetWare file system uses volume numbers when calling I/O procedures, but it uses volume names for command processing, alerts, and error messages.

Therefore, whenever TTS attempts to back out a transaction, it resolves the value contained in the volume table with the name associated with the TTS log file's copy of the old Volume Name Table. Next, it checks the current Volume Name Table and attempts to match the "old" volume name to a name in the current Volume Name Table. If it cannot match names, TTS assumes that the volume indicated in the TTS log file is not on-line. If the match is successful, TTS continues the backout.

TTS manages its log file much like NetWare 4.0 manages cache buffers. That is, TTS tracks which blocks within the log file are being used by a transaction. When a new transaction initializes a write to the log file by allocating blocks within the file, TTS first checks for blocks that were previously allocated but which are not currently in use.

If TTS finds such a block, it gets allocated to the new transaction. TTS only allocates new blocks if no previously used blocks are within the log file. Thus, the TTS log file remains as small as possible. In addition, managing access to the file by individual blocks (or chains of blocks) provides the most efficient record-locking possible. This is critical to NetWare's performance because transactional writes must wait for TTS to create a backout record within the log file before they can return to their calling procedure.

Recording Transactions

When NetWare 4.0 initializes TTS, it allocates a linked list of transaction nodes. Each transaction node represents a potential transaction, and it contains fields for associating the node with a specific station and task. To begin a transaction, the station makes a call to the API TTSBeginTransaction. TTSBeginTransaction scans the linked list of transaction nodes, and if it finds an available node, associates that node with the calling station and task. This makes the node at once unavailable and "active." An active transaction node is, in essence, an active transaction. If no transaction nodes are available, TTSBeginTransaction tries to allocate memory for a new node. If the allocation is successful, the new node becomes unavailable and active.

When beginning a transaction, TTSBeginTransaction always sets a bit within the transaction node, indicating that the transaction was started but not written to. The setting of this specific bit is important because it alters the behavior of the NetWare 4.0 logical file system, triggering some additional file-system events that are necessary to begin a transaction.

An active transaction node is the only thing that the NetWare file system needs to process and complete a transaction. Everything else that is required to do so is contained in the standard NetWare 4.0 logical file system.

Whenever the NetWare 4.0 file system writes data to a file, it first checks the file's attributes to see if it is a transactional file. If the file is transactional, NetWare finds the file's transaction node by looking at the address pointed to by an element of the file control block. If the transaction node indicates that the transaction has been started but not written to, NetWare correctly infers that it is about to perform the first write of a new transaction.

After setting up to perform the write, NetWare 4.0 checks the file's attribute field once again, this time to verify that it should generate backout information for the TTS log file.

If so, NetWare copies the original data from the target file and prepares to write that data to the TTS log file. Next, NetWare writes the original data to the TTS log file. Before writing the data to the log file, however, NetWare ensures that the write does not occur until the original data is logged to the backout file. As soon as the original data is logged to the backout file, NetWare allows the write operation to continue its normal course by writing the new data to the target file.

After NetWare 4.0 performs all writes for a transaction, it takes the transaction node and clears its TransactionActive bit. Next, TTSEndTransaction unlinks the transaction node from the active transaction list, and links the node to another list. This linked list contains transaction nodes that have logged, written all their data, but are waiting to be "completed."

At this point, the application that generated the transaction assumes that the transaction is complete. It has called TTSEndTransaction, which has returned successfully. Although the original data from the target file has been written successfully to the TTS log file, the transaction data currently reside in NetWare cache buffers, and have not been committed to disk. If the server were to go down at this point, the transaction would be incomplete, and TTS would attempt to back the transaction out when the server next booted.

As soon as TTSEndTransaction places a transaction node on the list of completed transactions, NetWare "wakes up" a special process to officially end each transaction. This process makes one final write to the TTS log file—in this case, a record containing an end-of-transaction code. The special process to end transactions then must wait until all transaction data that is currently in cache has been flushed to disk. Finally, this process unlinks the transaction node from the list containing logged and written transactions, and places the now-free transaction node on the appropriate list, thus recycling the transaction node.

Certain aspects of TTS are important to note. First, TTS guarantees that database files do not become corrupt through partial writes. Second, a transaction is not considered complete until all written data is flushed from file-cache memory and recorded successfully on physical media. This is important, especially for those who are wary of file-caching.

TTS provides an alternative to opening a database file in write-through mode. Although transactional writes do not occur as quickly as non-transactional writes, they do occur more quickly than write-through writes.

The TTS API is easy to use, especially because it automatically performs all file and record locks necessary for multiuser database access. This is an attractive feature for those using the NetWare API to construct legacy applications.

Finally, TTS is integrated completely into the NetWare 4.0 file system, and at the lowest levels. This ensures that TTS is robust, and that TTS cannot conflict with the NetWare logical file system in any way. They are one and the same.

TTS and NetWare 4.0 Directory Services

NDS uses NetWare 4.0 TTS to ensure the integrity of all updates to the NDS DIB. In fact, without TTS, the distribution and replication of the NDS DIB is impossible. The distributed nature of the DIB requires that a recovery method be built into the operating system for occasions when a remote update (an update to a remote NDS DIB partition) fails.

Although TTS has been part of all NetWare operating systems for years, NDS provides the perfect application for it. This demonstrates the usefulness of TTS for other distributed and replicated database management systems, including legacy applications.

Exploring NetWare 4.0 File-System Limits

As an enterprise platform, NetWare provides a file system with comfortable limits, even for large legacy applications. The limits of the file system are as follows:

❖ Up to 64 volumes

❖ Up to 32 segments on each volume

❖ Total volume capacity of 32T

❖ Up to 4G for a single file

❖ Up to 100,000 active file or record locks on a single NetWare server

❖ No hard limit on number of directories—500,000 is not uncommon

❖ No hard limit on number of files

These upper limits of NetWare 4.0's file-system capacity make NetWare a peer of the large host computers that organizations historically have used as platforms for their legacy applications. Although NetWare 4.0 has an architecture that is different from traditional host operating systems, the capacity of NetWare 4.0 is equivalent to those traditional workhorses. This supports Novell's positioning of NetWare 4.0 as the primary computing platform of the enterprise.

Ensuring Good File-System Performance

Despite the efficiency of NetWare 4.0's file system and its massive file-caching, NetWare remains a disk-bound operating system. Most hard drives on the market today have an upper data throughput limit of around 3M-per-second. NetWare itself can move data around at least 300 percent faster. To ensure good file-system performance with NetWare, you must take advantage of its performance-oriented features by doing the following:

❖ Always construct multisegment volumes.

❖ Make sure that at least 80 percent of server RAM is in use as file-cache; the more RAM in the server the better.

❖ Install caching drive controllers. When NetWare flushes its file-cache, it must flush the cache to some other media. Controller cache is the fastest media to which NetWare can flush its file-cache.

❖ Try to avoid opening files in write-through mode; use TTS instead.

Using NetWare 4.0 File-System Extensions

Earlier in this chapter, you read about volume blocks. Each NetWare volume is an array of blocks. Blocks are mapped directly to storage areas on physical media devices. In NetWare 3.11 and earlier versions, the block represented the smallest increment of storage that the NetWare file system could allocate for use by a file. For example, with the default block size of 4K, the amount of storage consumed by a file is a multiple of 4K. Even a one-byte file consumed 4K because the (4K) block was the smallest unit of allocation available for files. For example, a 10-byte file consumed three blocks (12K) of storage—all of the first two blocks allocated to that file, and half of the third block allocated to that file.

Block Suballocation

NetWare 4.0 uses a mechanism called *block suballocation* to make the storage of data by the NetWare file system more efficient. Volume blocks are subdivided by the NetWare file system into 512-byte sectors. With the default volume block size of 4K, a volume block consists of eight 512-byte sectors. In NetWare 4.0, you can enable block suballocation, which causes the block sector, rather than the block, to become the smallest unit of storage allocation.

For example, with block suballocation enabled, a one-byte file consumes one sector (512 bytes) rather than one block (4K). This leaves the remainder of the block (seven sectors) available for allocation to other files. Block suballocation, therefore, makes the NetWare 4.0 file system much more efficient than in previous versions of NetWare.

One interesting side-effect of block suballocation is that you can set the volume block size to a very large number, such as 64K, without compromising the efficiency of the file system's storage algorithms. Raising the block size above the default of 4K requires less server memory to have the volume mounted because the FAT for that volume is smaller. (A larger block size means that fewer blocks are on that volume and, hence, there is a smaller volume FAT.)

With block suballocation, the file system can store data efficiently, even with very large block sizes, because the smallest unit of allocation remains the sector (512 bytes). The network administrator can enable or disable block suballocation during the process of volume creation.

Background File Compression

NetWare 4.0 features *background file compression*, which means that a special thread in the file system executes in the background and compresses files that have not been read or updated for a fixed period of time. When a user requests access to a compressed file, the NetWare 4.0 file system decompresses that file automatically, and the user gains access to the decompressed file.

The network administrator can define the criteria for background file compression. For example, these criteria can cause the file-compression thread to compress only files that have not been read or updated for 30 days. In addition, the network administrator can flag select files as being ineligible for background compression.

Because the compression process runs in the background under a low priority, it does not affect server performance. This enables the compression process to make several passes through a file when compressing it, which yields very high compression ratios (frequently greater than 50 percent).

When a user requests access to a compressed file, the initial opening of that file takes longer than normal because the file system must decompress that file before granting the user access to the file data. All further requests for access to the decompressed file occur at their regular speed, however.

Background file compression provides the network administrator with the unusual experience of upgrading a 3.11 server to 4.0, leaving to do other work, and, after coming back to the 4.0 server several days later, seeing that the available storage space on that server has doubled.

File Monitoring

The NetWare 4.0 file system features a new programming interface called the *File Monitor*. By using the File Monitor interface, developers can create NLMs that receive callbacks from the file system when certain events occur. Events available for monitoring include file opens, closes, creations, deletions, renames, modifications, and more. Whenever one of these events occurs, the NetWare 4.0 file system calls the monitoring NLM and provides that NLM with information about the impending event.

Monitoring NLMs can register for one or more specific file-system events. Furthermore, NLMs can register to receive a callback from the file system either before or after the event occurs.

When a monitoring NLM receives a callback prior to the occurrence of the event, that NLM can disallow the event by returning to the file system with an error code. For example, a virus-protection NLM can use the File Monitor interface to disallow certain file operations.

Because the File Monitor is a programming interface rather than a feature or product, it remains for third-party developers to build products that use this new programming interface.

Installable File System

Another file system programming interface that is new with NetWare 4.0 is the *Installable File System*. By using the Installable File System, third-party developers can create new, specialized file systems and have those file systems be integrated with NetWare. Developers can construct their Installable File Systems so that those file systems show up as NetWare volumes that are capable of being mounted and accessed like the standard NetWare file system.

The Installable File System makes possible the construction of specialized file systems for use with NetWare 4.0, including synchronous multimedia file systems, file systems optimized for specific database management products, and more.

Like the File Monitor, the Installable File System is a programming interface, rather than a product or feature. Therefore, it will have little impact on the success of NetWare 4.0 until third-party developers make use of it to introduce new file systems for NetWare.

Media Manager and Data Migration

The *Data Migration* interface provides transparent movement and retrieval of file data to and from near-line or off-line storage media. The *Media Manager* is a new storage device interface that enables many different types of storage media to be installed for use with NetWare 4.0.

Although these two features are not part of the NetWare 4.0 file system in a strict sense, they are so closely integrated with the file system that they bear mentioning at this point.

Collectively, the File Monitor, Installable File System, Media Manager, and Data Migration interfaces represent an opening up of NetWare's file-system internals to an unprecedented degree. Third-party developers now have access to the low-level components of the NetWare file system as never before. This will lead to a new generation of network management and administration tools that will make the NetWare 4.0 file system much easier to groom and tune.

Read-Ahead Cache

The NetWare 4.0 file-cache system has been extended to perform *read-ahead caching*, which is the process of reading and caching additional file data beyond the specific data that the file system requests for the current operation.

Research performed by Novell revealed that most read operations for a specific portion of data are soon followed by a second read operation for file data, sequential to the data requested by the initial read operation. The read-ahead cache reads and caches data beyond the offset of the initial read request in anticipation of further read requests for the sequential data.

In practical terms, the read-ahead cache increases the cache-hit ratio, which improves file-system performance dramatically for read operations. The read-ahead cache has little or no effect on the performance of write operations.

SOAPBOX

We were getting pretty close to finishing up the work on the NetWare 4.0 operating system. If only work on NDS could be wrapped up, the operating system team that I managed would be home! Not quite so! Drew Major had this great idea that he wanted to run by me.

"What if we put background file compression into NetWare?" he asked. I thought it over for a few seconds. "Don't DOS-based products already provide that kind of compression?" I asked.

It turns out that compression software modules are available from third-party developers that can be run on the client workstations to compress files on the local hard disk. As the main text illustrates, a set of rules can be used to decide just how to go about compressing files. At the end of the compression, the user normally ends up with half the occupied space freed up on the disk. Compression is a great cost saver.

"Compression should really be done on a server!" Drew asserted. Thousands of

SOAPBOX

continued

our customers store almost all their data and applications on the server hard disk. It is very common to find gigabytes of hard disks on NetWare servers at a customer site. "If we offer compression, and it saves disk space by about 50 percent, that alone might act as a big incentive for many of our small customers to consider upgrading to NetWare 4.0!"

No argument there! But I was concerned that NetWare might suffer in file-system throughput because of compression. Drew assured me that it wouldn't suffer in throughput—decompression would be relatively fast, and the user wouldn't really feel the delay at all. In addition, you can disable compression selectively for those files that require absolutely the quickest access time.

Impulsively, I okayed the feature, and then ran over to get approval from my management, marketing, and other concerned parties. NDS was slipping behind, I reasoned. Maybe we can take some extra time and do things right in

the core operating and file system. Plus, Drew assured me that he would have the whole thing working in less than a month. (It actually took well over three months to get this feature coded, completely tested, and integrated into NetWare.)

NetWare's development history has many cases in which unplanned features were put in at the last moment. In many cases, these last-minute features have given NetWare a mighty edge over the competition.

For example, take the case of read-ahead caching under NetWare 4.0. Would you believe it if I told you that the feature was put in to the operating system (some would say sneaked in) at the very last possible moment? This feature alone gives NetWare 4.0 some of the whiz-bang speed that you will see in future benchmark tests.

For a multibillion dollar company, Novell is surprisingly agile and adroit in putting together state-of-the-art software products. Let's see IBM do that!

Summary

The NetWare 4.0 file system builds upon that of its predecessor, NetWare 3.11, to provide a fundamentally sound platform for legacy applications. Like its predecessor, the NetWare 4.0 file system has a prodigious capacity for storage of data, is very tolerant of hardware faults, and performs very well.

The NetWare 4.0 file system is much more efficient than its predecessor when it comes to storing data. Block suballocation and background file compression effectively increase the storage capacity of NetWare volumes by reducing the amount of physical media required to store files.

Finally, the NetWare 4.0 file system is much more extendable and flexible than its predecessor. Third-party developers have information, programming interfaces, and tools that allow them to extend the NetWare 4.0 file system in new directions; and to make the NetWare 4.0 file system easier to configure, tune, and manage.

NetWare 4.0 Auditing

In general, *auditing* means examining an organization's records to ensure that transactions are accurate and that confidential information is secure. Typically, auditors are independent of the organizations they examine. For example, an independent auditor examines a bank's records to see whether its transactions and records are accurate, that its confidential information is secure, and that the bank as a whole is sound. Auditing a NetWare 4.0 network is a similar process.

Understanding the Auditing Feature

NetWare's auditing feature enables designated individuals, acting independently of supervisors or users on the network, to monitor transactions that take place in specific server volumes or in specific containers in the network's Directory Services (NDS) tree. These auditors can monitor the following types of transactions:

- ❖ Transactions that are directly related to network accessibility, such as logins, logouts, or trustee modifications.

- ❖ Server transactions, such as changes in server date/time, or volume mounts and dismounts.

- ❖ Transactions involving files or directories, such as file creations and deletions, or reads and writes.

❖ Queue-management transactions, such as creating or destroying queues, editing or starting queue jobs, setting queue job priorities, and so on.

Auditing enhances security against unauthorized intrusion, and ensures that network records are accurate and secure.

SOAPBOX

Novell initially pursued the auditing feature for its NetWare 2.x operating system. This was to be based on the European F2 certification, and the goal was to gain acceptance in certain segments of the European marketplace. This certification process, however, was never pursued. Instead, Novell decided to provide these auditing capabilities in its forthcoming NetWare 4.0 operating system.

The goal was to provide auditing in a server-centric fashion so that users could audit whatever events happened within a server. Those events include all file-system activities (openings, closings, reads, writes, and so on), activities involving server-integrity violations, and more.

As the auditing feature was nearly completed in the NetWare 4.0 development process, it occurred to developers that something serious was lacking. Although you could monitor a user's actions (logins, attaches, and so on) on a server-by-server basis, you could not gauge these activities on a network-wide basis.

Even though NetWare 4.0 shifted the user's paradigm from *server-centric* to *network-centric* (with features such as network login, and accessing resources on a network basis by querying the NDS

database), the same perspective was seriously lacking on the auditing front from an administrator's point of view. To find out what the user did on a network, an administrator had to touch every server in the network and manually sort through the data. Besides, the scenario that a single auditor had such rights to servers in the entire network was not real. This was unacceptable.

Novell was also seriously pursuing C2 certification for NetWare, and decided that both network and server auditing were requirements to obtain C2 certification.

Thus, NDS auditing was introduced in NetWare 4.0, which turned out to be a monumental task because of the distributed nature of the NDS database. Before the auditor could obtain a report on a user's activities on the network, an audit process on the NetWare server had to collect auditing information from all servers in the network that held copies of the NDS database containing the user account, and then consolidate all the information into one report. In the end, however, a truly sophisticated auditing feature was implemented that provided network auditing capabilities to administrators.

Viewing the Auditcon Utility's Initial Menu

The user interface to NetWare auditing is a workstation utility called *Auditcon*. Typically, a supervisor on a network enables the auditing feature by going into Auditcon, setting the auditing password for either a specific server volume or an NDS container, and then giving the password to one or more designated auditors. The auditors then can go into Auditcon, change the password, and be independent auditors for that specific server volume or NDS container. Neither the supervisor nor any other user has auditing privileges unless the designated auditors provide the password to them.

The capabilities that NetWare auditing provides can be divided into two major areas: NDS-container auditing and server-volume auditing. As shown in figure 9.1, these options are the first items in the menu you see after you type **auditcon** at your workstation command line. (The menu lists them as Audit Directory Services and Auditor Volume Login.)

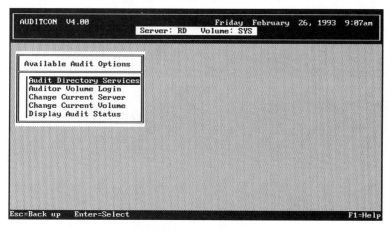

Figure 9.1:

The initial Auditcon utility menu.

Note also the three other options available in the Auditcon menu. If you select the option to change your current server, an additional menu showing available servers displays. If you select the option to change your current volume, a list of volumes on the current server displays, as shown in figure 9.2.

Figure 9.2:

The Volume List dialog box for server RD.

As already mentioned, an auditor is designated on a per-server volume or per-NDS container basis. If you are on server RD, for example, you might be limited to auditing only the TDOC volume on that server, so you know only the password for that one volume. Likewise, you might be limited to auditing only one container in the NDS tree, and know only the password for it.

The other option available in Auditcon's initial menu is Display Audit Status. As figure 9.3 illustrates, this option enables you to see auditing status information—such as whether auditing is enabled—and what the size, threshold size, and maximum size of the audit file is.

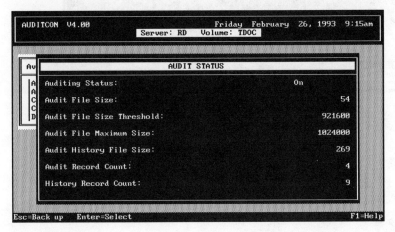

Figure 9.3:

The Audit Status screen.

As auditors use the Auditcon utility, and then go one or two levels beyond the intial menu, they often become interested in this status information. For this reason, the Display Audit Status option also is available in other menus.

Much of the audit-status information has to do with the audit file, which contains records of audited events. These are the events, or transactions, previously mentioned: user transactions directly related to network accessibility, such as logins and logouts; server transactions; file or directory transactions, such as file creations and deletions, and file reads and writes; and queue-management transactions, such as creating or destroying queues and editing queue jobs. You can view the audit file by going into the Auditing Reports option (explained later).

When you configure auditing, you determine the maximum size for the audit file, the threshold size for the audit file, and the type of action that occurs automatically when the audit file reaches the maximum size. The auditor can choose either of the following two actions:

❖ Discard auditing records

❖ Dismount the volume

When the audit file reaches its maximum size, one of these actions occurs, based on what the auditor selects during initial configuration or when making changes to the configuration.

The *threshold size* of the audit file is the size that the file must reach before the server console receives a warning that storage space for audited transactions is almost full. This warning message also is placed in a log file. In addition, auditing can be configured so that all logged-in users on an audited volume receive the warning. As with other configuration settings, auditors set the threshold size during initial configuration, but can change it later. The option to dismount the volume when the audit file is full is a drastic measure, and auditors who choose that option must keep watch on the status of that file.

All of this configuration information is stored in an *audit history file*. This file contains information about when the auditing is enabled; when the auditor logs in to auditing; when the auditor uses the ON/OFF switch to select a particular event, file, directory, or user for auditing; when the auditor changes the threshold size of the audit file; and so on. You can see the size of this audit history file when you select the Display Audit Status option (see fig. 9.3). You also can see the number of records in the audit history file and in the audit file. You can view the audit history file by using the Auditing Reports option, explained later in this chapter.

Auditing NDS

As mentioned earlier, one of the two major capabilities that NetWare Auditing provides is NDS container auditing. When you select the Audit Directory Services option from Auditcon's initial screen, and choose to audit the Directory Tree, a menu similar to that shown in figure 9.4 appears.

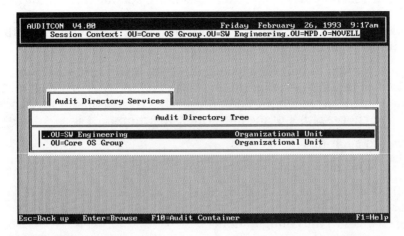

Figure 9.4:

Audit Directory Tree container list.

From this menu, you can select a particular container to audit. Remember that an auditor is designated on a per-server volume or per-container basis. By limiting an auditor to a certain area of the directory tree or to a certain volume on a server, you can create auditors within groups or departments. This is an advantage, especially for organizations in which the confidentiality of information varies from department to department.

For example, a security division in a large organization can be responsible for auditing the company as a whole. This division can maintain tight centralized control by handling all auditing itself. Or it can designate auditors in departments throughout the company, but work closely with those auditors. A security division also can delegate auditing completely, allowing each department to handle its own auditing. Whichever way the auditing is set up, however, a password is required for each server volume and each container.

After you select the container for which you have been designated auditor, and enter the password, a menu similar to that shown in figure 9.5 appears.

Notice that the Display Audit Status option also is available here. Two of the other three options, Audit Files Maintenance and Auditing Reports, are discussed later in the chapter. The Auditing Configuration option also is discussed later, but it is important to mention here because this option is different in a container.

Figure 9.5:

The Available Audit Options menu, when auditing a container.

When you are auditing a container, and you select the Auditing Configuration option, a menu similar to that shown in figure 9.6 appears.

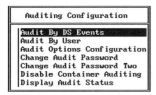

Figure 9.6:

The Auditing Configuration menu, when auditing a container.

The options in this menu enable you to do major auditing tasks in a container, and container auditors spend much of their time working in this menu. One task, for example, includes auditing NDS events, including Add Entry, Add Partition, and Add Replica (see fig. 9.7).

Without going into detail about the NDS tree and NDS events, note that many of the events in this menu are marked as AUDITED. This is because the execution of events—such as partition joins, splits, deletes, and moves— have an impact on network security and performance. An *audit trail* (a record of events that occur in the directory database) is critical because unauthorized tampering can do considerable damage.

Figure 9.8 shows another option in this Auditing Configuration menu— Audit By User.

This option provides an important capability that Audit By User on a server volume does not: seeing and being able to audit every user in the NDS tree.

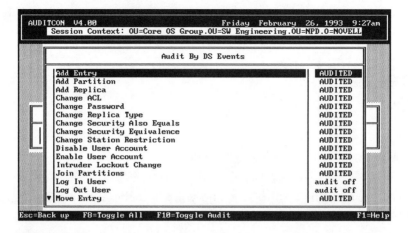

Figure 9.7:

The Auditing By DS Events menu.

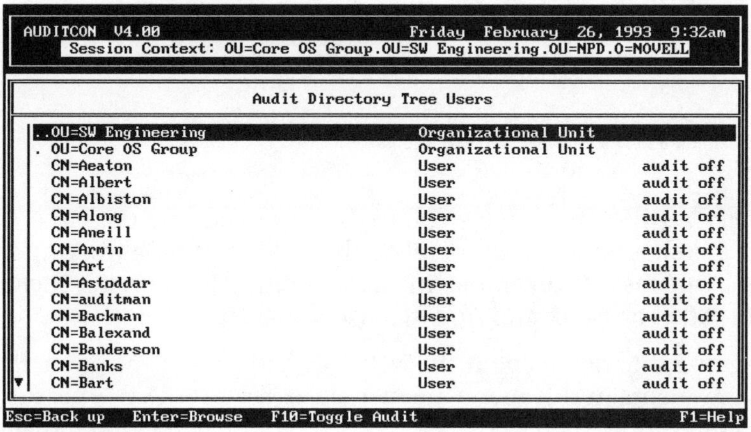

Figure 9.8:

The Audit Directory Tree Users menu.

All events automatically are audited globally, except for file events. Because file events are so pervasive, auditors can choose whether to audit them globally, by user and file, or by user or file. For example, if you choose to audit the event Open File by user or file, and you mark a file, that file will be audited globally. Auditing produces a record that displays every time that file is opened, and by whom—regardless of who opens it.

If you choose to audit the event Open File by user or file, and mark the user, every time that user opens a file, regardless of the file, the open will be audited.

When you audit a server volume, you cannot see every user in the NDS tree. Because of this, the NDS Audit By User option is critical; it enables you to see every user in the NDS tree, and to select any of them to audit when file events occur.

The Auditing Configuration menu also enables auditors to change the audit container password (One and Two) and disable auditing in the container. Auditors also can select options to display auditing information. The options to display information include the familiar Display Audit Status and a new information option called the Audit Options Configuration.

The Audit Options Configuration menu, shown in figure 9.9, displays the audit file maximum size and threshold size, and enables you to specify whether to allow concurrent auditor logins, to broadcast errors to all users, or to force dual-level audit passwords.

```
AUDITCON  V4.00                     Friday  February  26, 1993  9:21am
         Session Context: OU=Core OS Group.OU=SW Engineering.OU=NPD.O=NOVELL

                          Audit Configuration

   Audit file maximum size:                              1024000

   Audit file threshold size:                            921600

   Allow concurrent auditor logins:                      Yes

   Broadcast errors to all users:                        No

   Force dual-level audit passwords:                     Yes

                 Error recovery options for audit file full
                        or unrecoverable write error.

   Disable audited events:                               No
   Disable event recording:                              Yes
   Minutes between warning messages:                     3

Esc=Back up    Enter=Select                                    F1=Help
```

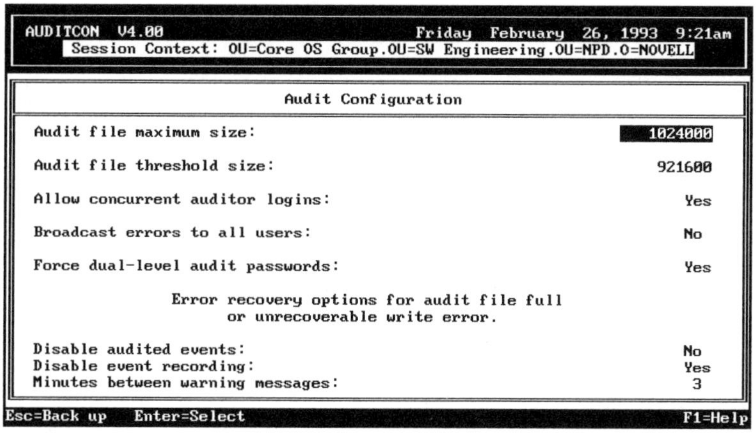

Figure 9.9:

The Audit Options Configuration menu.

The *dual-level password* is not only another way to ensure tight security; it also provides an additional level of control as you manage network auditors. As its name indicates, it enables you to set two passwords.

The first-level password enables an auditor to use Auditcon to see auditing information, but not make any changes to the auditing configuration. The second-level password (Password Two in the preceding screen) enables an auditor to use all of Auditcon's capabilities. When you enter the Auditcon utility, it prompts for only one password. You can enter either the level-one or level-two password, and then perform auditing tasks.

By using this menu, you can determine the action to take place when an audit file reaches its maximum size. As mentioned earlier, two actions are possible: dismount the volume or discard the auditing records. You also determine the number of minutes between warning messages that are broadcast to the server console or, if enabled, broadcast to all users.

Auditing a Server Volume

When you select the Auditor Volume Login option from Auditcon's initial screen and enter the appropriate password, a menu similar to that shown in figure 9.10 appears:

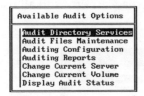

Figure 9.10:

The Available Audit Options menu, when auditing a server volume.

Notice that some options in this menu also are included in the intial Auditcon menu shown earlier. These options are Audit Directory Services, Change Current Server, Change Current Volume, and Display Audit Status. Several of the other options are described in the following sections.

Audit Files Maintenance

When you select the Audit Files Maintenance option, you see a menu like the one shown in figure 9.11.

Figure 9.11:

The Audit Files Maintenance menu.

This menu enables you to see the familiar Audit Status screen and do cleanup work on the audit file and the audit history file. You can copy, close, delete, or reset the old audit file (also called old audit data file), and you can reset the audit history file.

When you reset the audit file, the old audit file is deleted, the current audit file becomes the old audit file, and a new audit data file is created. If you are deciding whether to delete or reset the old audit file, determine the size of the file and how useful its information is. When you configure auditing, you specify how large this file can become and what action the system takes when this file reaches its maximum size.

The audit history file, which contains information about the way the auditing is configured, also can be reset (it is deleted and a new audit history file is begun). The Audit Files Maintenance option enables you to manage the auditing files as they grow—when they are deleted or reset, it is because you choose explicitly to delete or reset them.

Auditing Reports

Auditing Reports is an option you use to filter certain information from an audit file to create a smaller, more manageable report. Although the audit file already contains a limited amount of information (depending on the way you configure auditing), this option gives you another tool for organizing that information.

For example, you already know the general kind of information that the audit file contains because you have chosen certain users, files, directories, and events to audit. With Audit Reports, you can create a number of reports that contain limited audit-file information organized by date, time, or event; or by including or excluding certain paths, files, or users.

When you select Auditing Reports from the Available Audit Options menu, another menu displays (see fig. 9.12).

Figure 9.12:

The Auditing Reports menu.

As with other auditing menus, this menu gives you quick access to audit-status information without exiting to a previous menu. The primary purpose of the Auditing Reports menu is three-fold, as follows:

❖ To define and edit a report filter

❖ To send reports to a file on any network directory in which you have sufficient rights, or to a file on your floppy or hard drive

❖ To see reports, whether they are filtered or not

Figure 9.13 shows the kinds of filters you can use when you select the Edit Report Filters option.

Figure 9.13:

The Edit Report Filter menu.

To use a filter by date or time, for example, select the date or time you want to begin collecting information, and the date or time you want to stop collecting information. Figure 9.14 shows how to set up a report filtered by Date/Time.

```
                 Report By Date/Time

   Start date:          2-26-1993

   Start time:          6:48:07pm

   End date:            3-1-1993

   End time:            11:00:00am
```

Figure 9.14:

Defining a Report Filter by Date/Time.

With a Date/Time filter, the system builds a report containing auditing information within those start and stop dates.

The other options available in the Audit Reports menu enable you to send created reports to a file on a network directory in which you have sufficient rights, or to a file on your floppy or hard drive. You also can select from the Audit Reports menu to view reports you have created, or you can view the unfiltered audit file and audit history file.

Auditing Configuration on a Server Volume

When you are auditing a server volume, and you select the Auditing Configuration option, you see a menu like the one shown in figure 9.15.

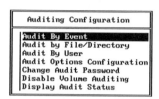

Figure 9.15:

The Auditing Configuration menu, when auditing a server volume.

The options in this menu enable you to do major auditing tasks on a server volume (auditors spend much of their time working in this menu). These tasks include auditing events, files or directories, and users.

By using this menu, auditors can change the audit password for the volume and disable auditing on the volume. Auditors also can select options to display auditing information. These options include the familiar Display Audit Status and Audit Options Configuration, which already have been explained.

As illustrated in figure 9.15, the first three Auditing Configuration options are Audit By Event, Audit by File/Directory, and Audit By User.

When you audit by event (transaction), you see a the Audit By Event menu (see fig. 9.16). This menu enables you to audit by file, QMS, server, or user events.

Note, however, that the option to audit by server and user events is limited to auditors on volume SYS because server and user events are system- or server-centric transactions. In other words, they are transactions that affect the server rather than a particular volume on the server. This is evident, in figure 9.17, which shows the server events or transactions for which an auditor can turn auditing on or off.

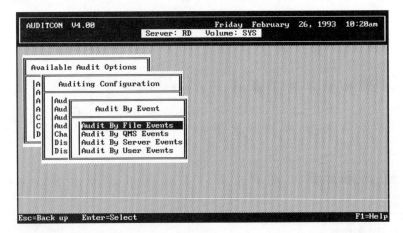

Figure 9.16:

The Audit By Event menu on volume SYS.

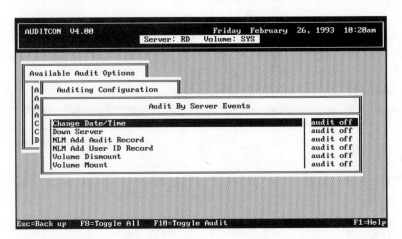

Figure 9.17:

The Audit By Server Events menu on volume SYS.

Figure 9.18 also shows the user events, or transactions, for which an auditor can turn auditing on or off. When you mark any of the server or user events to be audited, those events are audited for every instance. If you choose, for example, to audit the server event Change Date/Time, every change to the date or time in the system is audited. Likewise, if you choose to audit the user event Log In User, that event is audited every time a user logs in to the server.

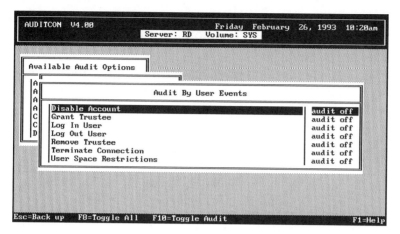

Figure 9.18:

The Audit By User Events menu on volume SYS.

File events, as shown in figure 9.19, are transactions involving files or directories. These transactions include creating, deleting, salvaging, opening, closing, reading from, writing to, and modifying files or directories.

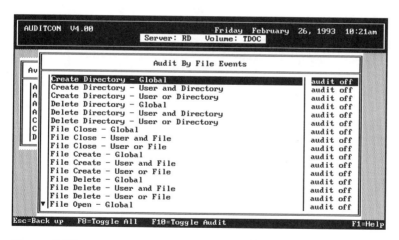

Figure 9.19:

The Audit By File Events menu.

When you select the Audit By Event option, a menu appears that enables you to select the kind of event or transaction to audit (creating, opening, reading from, and so on), rather than the particular file or directory to audit. In some cases, you also must select the file or directory (from another menu) on which the event is performed, and the user who performs the event.

Note that you can audit most of these file events in three different ways: globally, by user and file, and by user or file. Table 9.1 lists the events and the different ways they can be audited.

Table 9.1
File/Directory Access Events

Event	Auditing Options		
	Global	User and File	User or File
Directory Create	x	x	x
Directory Delete	x	x	x
File Close	x	x	x
File Create	x	x	x
File Delete	x	x	x
File Open	x	x	x
File Read		x	x
File Rename/Move	x	x	
File Salvage	x	x	x
File Write		x	x
Modify Directory Entry	x	x	x

The Global option in table 9.1 means that all files and directories are audited, regardless of the user who performs the event on the file or directory.

The User and File option specifies that the event is audited on the basis of a specific user and file or directory. You must select the event (File Open-User and File, for example) from the File Events menu, but you must also choose the specific user and file.

You select the specific user (the individual to be audited when this event occurs) by selecting the Audit By User option in the Auditing Configuration menu (see fig. 9.20). A list of users appears, from which you select one.

Select the specific file to be audited when the event occurs by choosing the Audit by File/Directory option in the Auditing Configuration menu (see fig. 9.20). A list of files and directories appears.

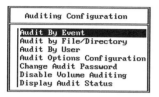

Figure 9.20:

The Auditing Configuration menu, when auditing a server volume.

Suppose, for example, that you choose to audit the File Open-User and File event. In the Audit By File Events menu, you mark that event, exit the menu, and then select Audit by File/Directory from the Auditing Configuration menu. As shown in figure 9.21, this option displays a list of files and directories from which you can select one to audit.

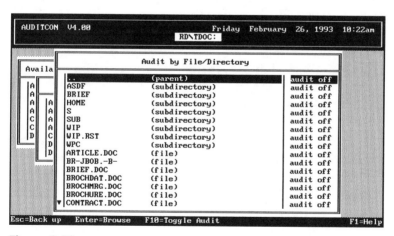

Figure 9.21:

The Audit by File/Directory menu.

Then, you also must select Audit By User from the Auditing Configuration menu. This option displays a list of users, from which you select one to audit (see fig. 9.22).

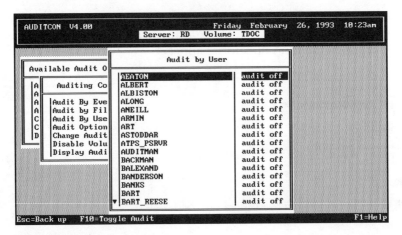

Figure 9.22:

The Audit by User menu.

The result in this scenario is that you have a specific, customized audit trail. The audit trail shows when a specific file is opened by a specific user. It does not show when the file you marked is opened by other unmarked users, and it does not show when the user you marked opens other unmarked files.

The User or File option in table 9.1 is slightly different. You must select the event, of course, such as File Open-User or File from the File Events menu. But you need only to select either a file, directory, or user. You could select both, but you do not have to.

For example, in the Audit By File Events menu, you mark the File Open-User or File event, exit, and then choose either the Audit by File/Directory option or the Audit By User option from the Auditing Configuration menu.

The result is again a specific, customized audit trail, showing only the information you want. Depending on whether you marked a file or a user, it shows one of the following:

❖ Every time a specific file is opened, and who opens it, regardless of the individual

❖ Every time a specific user opens a file, regardless of the file

From these two scenarios, remember that unless you audit events globally, you also must select a specific file or directory and/or a specific user. Remember also, that as table 9.1 shows, not all events can be audited globally. You cannot audit file reads and writes globally because of the frequency of these events; your audit file would become too large too quickly.

When you audit by QMS Events (Queue Management System Events), as figure 9.23 shows, you audit events that affect the queue.

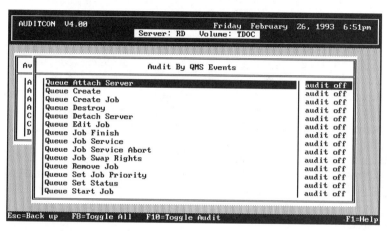

```
AUDITCON  V4.00                   Friday  February  26, 1993  6:51pm
                    Server: RD    Volume: TDOC

 Av                         Audit By QMS Events
   A     Queue Attach Server                              audit off
   A     Queue Create                                     audit off
   A     Queue Create Job                                 audit off
   A     Queue Destroy                                    audit off
   C     Queue Detach Server                              audit off
   C     Queue Edit Job                                   audit off
   D     Queue Job Finish                                 audit off
         Queue Job Service                                audit off
         Queue Job Service Abort                          audit off
         Queue Job Swap Rights                            audit off
         Queue Remove Job                                 audit off
         Queue Set Job Priority                           audit off
         Queue Set Status                                 audit off
         Queue Start Job                                  audit off

Esc=Back up   F8=Toggle All   F10=Toggle Audit               F1=Help
```

Figure 9.23:
The Audit By QMS Events menu.

Summary

NetWare 4.0 provides powerful security capabilities. The Auditcon workstation utility taps in to, and takes advantage of, these auditing capabilities. Auditcon is designed to give you more control and to make security management simple, yet complete. Designated auditors, acting independently of users or supervisors, can use the Auditcon tool to monitor transactions that take place, both in specific server volumes and NDS tree containers.

These auditors can monitor user events that are directly related to network accessibility, such as logins, logouts, and trustee modifications. They can monitor transactions that affect the server, such as changes of server date or time, mounts or dismounts of volumes, and server downs.

Auditors also have a great deal of control and flexibility in monitoring transactions that involve files or directories. They can track file and directory events globally, by user *and* file, and by user *or* file. These file/directory events include creations, deletions, opens, closes, reads, writes, renames, moves, modifications, and salvages.

SOAPBOX

What is frightening about the auditing feature in NetWare 4.0 is its wide encompassing scope: you can audit not only a given set of servers, but the whole network! In essence, you can audit user Joe's activities throughout the network. This is true, even if the network spans continents and is connected by a myriad of WAN links. If user Joe is a mobile user and travels from one country to another, an auditor still can generate a report that tells accurately what Joe has been doing to the network. In the future, maybe a Hollywood movie will be made in which an international criminal is tracked through his use of network computing resources.

You can also audit many things on a given NetWare server, such as opening and closing a file, or reading from and writing to a file. While enabling auditing on a NetWare source code server, I found an engineer assigned to a particular project opening and reading files quite frequently on an unrelated project. When I asked that engineer for an explanation, he told me that he had spare time on his hands and was looking for "things to do" on other projects. He also was shocked that I had this information. Of course, I gave that engineer more "things to do" related to his assigned project , but it occurred to me that the auditing feature, if used improperly, can result in misuse of authority by auditors.

Auditors also can monitor transactions that involve queue management, such as creating or destroying queues, editing and starting queue jobs, and setting queue-job priorities.

To simplify and enhance auditing reports and records, Auditcon also enables auditors to view and create customized reports of audited events, users, files, and directories.

All of these features and capabilities enhance NetWare 4.0 security and discourage unauthorized tampering with sensitive network information. They provide to designated security personnel the kind of tools necessary to track and keep records of various transactions as they occur on server volumes or in the the NDS tree.

Global Time Synchronization

NetWare 4.0 provides the *global time synchronization* service to keep correct time on all servers in the NetWare 4.0 network. The client workstations that query the NetWare servers for time are also given the correct time. This chapter explains the architecture of the global time synchronization service provided under NetWare 4.0.

Understanding Why NetWare Needs Global Time Synchronization

Time synchronization ensures that all NetWare servers report the same time, within a few seconds. If all servers in the network are connected through a LAN, the accuracy is better—within the range of few milliseconds. If the servers are connected through both LAN and WAN links, accuracy is likely to suffer.

Absolute accuracy was not the chief reason for designing and developing global time synchronization for NetWare 4.0. Instead, the goal was to provide fairly reliable timestamps to NetWare servers so that they could synchronize different replicas of the NetWare Directory Services (NDS) partitions. NDS defines a partition and its replicas to function in a "loosely consistent" fashion, and guarantees that conflicting updates to a given entry are resolved so that the most recent update almost always wins.

TIP

See Chapter 6 for more information on NetWare Directory Services.

As an example, suppose that an update is made to the entry LASERPRINTER—first on a partition replica on server S1, and a few seconds later on server S2 (see fig.10.1). The update on S2 happens before S1 has had a chance to share its update with the replica of server S2. If the clocks on both servers display the same time, the entry on server S2 wins because it happened a few seconds after the update on server S1. On the other hand, if the clock on server S1 is ahead by five minutes from the correct time, the update on server S1 wins, even though the update on server S2 happened a few seconds later.

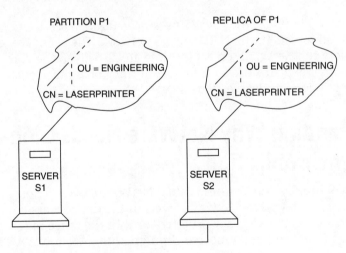

Figure 10.1:

Multiple updates at the same time.

In test cases at Novell, simulations of real-world networks showed that clocks on different servers were off by a maximum of 10 to 15 seconds (in the worst case). This interval can be defined as a *get caught interval* because updates that happen to multiple copies of the same NDS entry within this interval are resolved in an unpredictable fashion.

Although the get caught interval can result in unpredictable update behavior, it never harms the integrity of the NDS database. It also is unlikely that many users will experience the mysteries of this interval because most real-world updates happen beyond the narrow borders of the get caught interval, and are always resolved correctly by NDS.

In addition to establishing the order of events, NDS uses timestamps to do the following:

❖ Record the time of update/creation with every NDS update

❖ Set expiration times on temporary NDS entries

Understanding Time-Server Hierarchy

Time-synchronized NetWare servers are classfied into two groups: primary servers and secondary servers. *Primary servers* poll each other to determine a common network time, and then adjust their individual clocks to report that common time. A special kind of primary server, called a *reference server*, provides a stable time source to the network by using the time-synchronization algorithms without actually adjusting its own clock. Secondary servers poll only one primary server, and adjust their clocks to agree with the reported time. Figure 10.2 illustrates the layout of a network with primary, secondary, and reference servers.

Understanding the Synchronization Process

Synchronization is accomplished by a module of the NetWare 4.0 operating system called TIMESYNC.NLM. This NLM is bound to the standard SERVER.EXE, which is invoked by the system administrator when installing NetWare on a server, and is installed by default. This NLM can be uninstalled, although dire warnings display on the server console. Novell made this NLM unloadable to supply alternate time-synchronization NLMs in the future. They will provide more accurate network time by tying into a reliable external time source, such as the NTP time (Network Time Protocol under UNIX), which is very accurate.

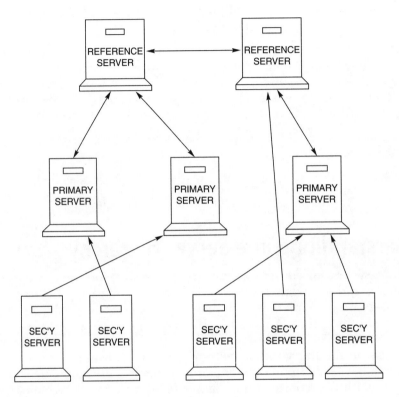

Figure 10.2:

Time-server hierarchy.

The four basic modes of time synchronization are as follows:

❖ **Single Reference Time Server.** A *single reference time server* is the sole source of time on the network—it always claims to be synchronized. In other words, to be designated as a single reference time server, a server's clock must be deemed absolutely and totally trustworthy. No primary servers can be in a network in which a single reference server exists; all other servers are secondary time servers (see fig. 10.3). The secondary servers, in turn, provide time to their clients.

SOAPBOX

What is a *get caught interval?* (Please read the main text, in which it is referred to a bewildering number of times.) Novell NDS super architect, Kevin Kingdon, explains it here in terms that a layperson can understand.

Suppose that you change the phone number property for your user account to reflect your new phone number. Meanwhile, the network administrator across the building changes the same property for your user account, but—alas!—with a wrong phone number. As it happens, your workstation is operating off of a different partition replica than hers. For now, the two NDS replicas of the same partition have accepted two updates of different values to the same phone number property. Which entry will win?

If you made your change at 4 p.m., and the administrator made hers at 4:30 p.m., you might expect that your administrator's entry will win. This means that when you come in the next morning and look at your phone number property, you find it showing the incorrect phone number entered by your network administrator.

Now, suppose that you have just about finished changing the entry when your administrator telephones you to inform you that she just changed your entry (to the wrong phone number). She thinks that she made this change a few seconds after you did, but she's not sure. Which entry will win? In this event, neither one of you are sure. In other words, an interval of a few seconds is so miniscule for both of you in real-world time that you are willing to accept a result that might go either way.

These few seconds, in which an element of doubt exists, is what Kevin calls the get caught interval. He believes that such aberrations in the behavior of a "loosely consistent" database are acceptable in the real world, as long as they don't make people stop and wonder if things are going screwy on their corporate LAN. He used this reasoning, in essence, to design the time-accuracy requirement into the NDS time-synchronization feature in NetWare 4.0.

NetWare 4.0 may misorder updates occasionally, but it is definitely within the get caught interval, wherein you won't think that something is wrong with your corporate LAN.

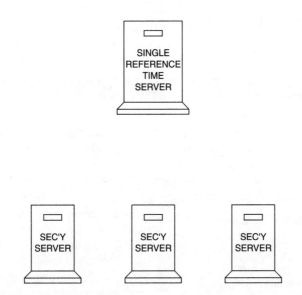

Figure 10.3:

Network with a single reference time server.

❖ **Primary Time Server.** A *primary time server* synchronizes the time with at least one other primary or reference time server to compute the correct network time. This computation can take several polling cycles between the primary time server and other primary and/or reference time servers.

Multiple primary time servers are used on larger networks to increase fault tolerance by providing more than one time source for secondary time servers. If a primary server goes down, the secondary server can get the time from an alternate primary time server. Novell recommends the use of a primary time server at each WAN link to decrease network traffic. This is because secondary servers at a given WAN site need to talk only to their local primary time server to query the time, and only the primary server talks over the WAN link to other secondary/reference servers to compute the correct time.

A primary server needs at least one other primary or reference server that the primary server can contact. Ideally, all primary and reference servers should be able to communicate with each other to compute the correct network time, but it is a requirement that a given primary server have the capability to contact at least one other primary or reference server to compute time.

Figure 10.4 shows a combination of primary and secondary time servers in a network that has LAN clusters connected by WAN links. Note that at least one primary server is at each site.

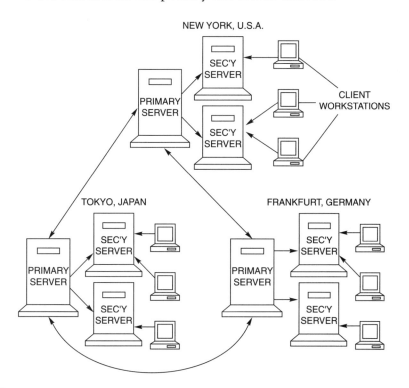

Figure 10.4:

Primary and secondary time servers in a large network.

❖ **Reference Time Server.** A *reference time server* provides a time to which all other time servers synchronize. A reference time server does not adjust its clock, but otherwise acts just like a primary time server. Because a reference time server does not adjust its clock, the primary and secondary time servers must reach a consensus about the time it provides. A reference time server normally has a more reliable clock than the other servers in the network have.

❖ **Secondary Time Server.** A *secondary time server* queries an available primary server for the network time, and adjusts its clock accordingly. As figure 10.4 illustrates, one primary server is picked within a given LAN cluster, and all other servers are secondary servers. This minimizes network traffic, and provides an easier computation of network time.

Configuring Time Servers

For a default installation of NetWare 4.0 on a small LAN, the root server is designated as a single reference time server. All other servers default as secondary time servers.

There are two ways in which a system administrator can intelligently plan and configure the network time-server hierarchy for minimum network time, and for a more accurate and easy computation of network time, between the various time servers. These two methods, defined in the order of their difficulty of configuration, are SAP configuration and custom configuration.

SAP Configuration

SAP (Service Advertising Protocol) configuration is the default mechanism used by primary, reference, and single reference time servers to announce their presence in the network.

Through SAP, primary servers can locate other primary servers to compute the network time. Secondary time servers pick up a SAP to find a primary or reference time server from which to query time.

The use of SAP is the quickest installation method, without regard to the network layout. Reconfiguration is automatic if the network layout is changed through the addition or deletion of time servers.

Custom Configuration

In a *custom configuration*, each time server is configured to contact a specific list of other time servers. A system administrator can specify that a time server not listen to the SAPs from other time servers (in other words, blindly follow the specific list of time servers given), or not advertise its presence to other time servers in the network through a SAP.

Custom configuration uses less network bandwidth for time-server SAPs and time-computation traffic, and is not affected when test servers routinely come up and go down in the network.

The disadvantages of custom configuration are that it takes more time to plan and install, and makes it more difficult to remove primary, reference, or single reference time servers on the network. Approved server lists on each time server might have to be changed manually in such cases.

On smaller networks, Novell recommends the use of the SAP method. On larger networks, in which servers are routinely added to and deleted from the network, custom configuration is appropriate.

Summary

This chapter discussed global time synchronization in NetWare 4.0. You learned about the process of synchronization, the configuration of time servers, and the recommended configuration method.

Chapter 11 discusses communication services that are available with NetWare 4.0.

Communication Services

It is very important that today's computer systems connect and communicate with one another. Two fundamental aspects of computer communication are communication protocols and the network environments in which the protocols are used.

This chapter gives you valuable information about the communication capabilities of the NetWare operating system. It includes descriptions of the communication protocols native to the NetWare environment and some protocols that are typically used in other network environments.

Although you can communicate in a given computer environment by using the communication protocol that is normally used in that environment, it is not required. Because of the expansion of networks to incorporate other dissimilar networks, it is increasingly important to be able to communicate on any network by using any protocol.

The fundamental architecture of NetWare makes communication with other computer systems not only possible but natural. This chapter begins with an overview of the NetWare communications architecture, and explains how and why communications are possible.

You are also introduced to the communication protocols originally used in the NetWare environment. Protocols that are used in other environments are described, along with ways that they operate and function in the NetWare environment.

The technologies that make NetWare communications more efficient are discussed as well. This discussion includes explanations of how these technologies are implemented with NetWare servers and workstations.

The NetWare Operating System Communication Architecture

Understanding the architecture of the NetWare operating system contributes greatly to understanding the value and implementation of the communication protocols. For that reason, this section helps you to consider individual communication protocols.

TIP

An operating system with built-in characteristics can perform certain tasks better than if it did not have those characteristics. NetWare has design characteristics that make it easy to adopt and integrate different communication protocols in its operation.

The NetWare Kernel

The *kernel* of an operating system provides the basic functionality of the operating system. An operating-system kernel should provide fundamental functions, and perform them efficiently.

The developers of NetWare saw the need to expand the operating system to accommodate for new environments and future enhancements. The kernel was designed to expand the functionality of the operating system while maintaining efficiency and integrity.

The developers designed NetWare (beginning with version 3.x) with the capability to add modules of software to interact directly with the kernel—thus expanding the function of the operating system. These modules, which can be programmed and loaded with the operating system, are called *NetWare Loadable Modules*, or *NLMs*. Because of the capability to load multiple modules, many capabilities can be added that increase the functionality of the operating system.

One function of operating-system NLMs is to handle communications on the network for one or more protocols. Figure 11.1 shows the relationship of the NetWare kernel to some of the standard operating system NLMs.

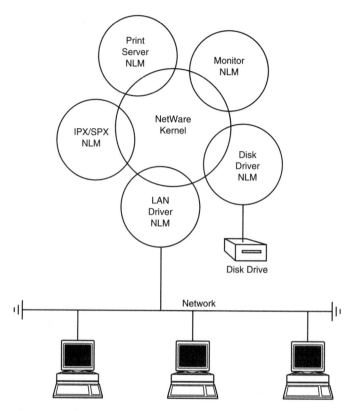

Figure 11.1:

NetWare operating system architecture.

Because of this modular architecture, NLMs are developed that can handle different communication protocols. They can run concurrently, giving the operating system a multiprotocol handling capability.

The NetWare kernel itself performs a set of well-defined functions as efficiently as possible. It receives information and requests from the network through the communication protocol NLMs. Other devices—such as disk drives, the keyboard, and RAM—are monitored and controlled to some degree by the kernel. The kernel maintains the integrity of the operating-system environment. Applications in the form of NLMs often supply the kernel with information or requests.

The type of operating-system architecture that surrounds the kernel affects how flexible and powerful the operating system can be. With the NetWare architecture being modular through the use of NLMs, there are many possibilities. The way that NetWare deals with communication protocols, for example, can be made flexible and powerful.

In order for NetWare to deal with multiple communication protocols, the design must include the capability to keep the messages from each protocol separate from the others. With computers that use different protocols but share the same network cabling, this capability is important. The part of the operating system that separates protocols is called STREAMS.

STREAMS

STREAMS is the name of a device interface, defined by AT&T, for the UNIX operating system. Novell developed a STREAMS module (as an NLM), partly because of the proven value of such a software module. In NetWare's case, STREAMS implements an interface between the operating system and the network (the network is the device being interfaced with).

With STREAMS in place, a stream can be opened to handle communications for a specific communication protocol, and other streams can be opened to handle other protocols. Although STREAMS is not the module that handles the protocol, it provides the capability to concurrently run the modules that handle the protocols and to integrate modules of the communication process.

Each stream is logically separate from the others, enabling communication on two or more streams to take place independently. Each stream also operates in *duplex*, which means that messages can be both sent and received. The communication does not travel just one way, and separate streams are not required for sending, as opposed to receiving.

The communications that come from the network flow to the operating system through streams that are programmed to handle the given protocol. The streams themselves are created when a protocol handler is loaded. It makes a call to STREAMS, requesting that a stream be opened. Processes of the protocol handler, called *modules*, are added to the stream. These processes actually perform the protocol handling. The packets are received from the network, travel up the stream, and are given to the operating system. Messages from the operating system then flow downstream to the network.

TIP
The various modules that can be placed on a stream can meet and match the standards and definitions for the various communication protocols.

Open Data-Link Interface

The *Open Data-Link Interface,* or *ODI*, was developed by Novell to handle multiple communication protocols on a single server. The STREAMS device interface was developed to help implement ODI. The goal was to modularize the component pieces of network communication so that mixing and matching can be done with different hardware interfaces and communication protocols.

The two primary components of communication that ODI deals with are the Network Interface Card (NIC) driver (also called the LAN driver) and the communication protocol handler.

The NIC must be able to interface with the network cabling system on one side and with the operating system on the other side. Figure 11.2 shows the relationship between the communication components. On the network cable side, each type of NIC card detects and emits communications. These communications are based on a defined network protocol. Some examples of network protocols are Token Ring, Ethernet, and FDDI.

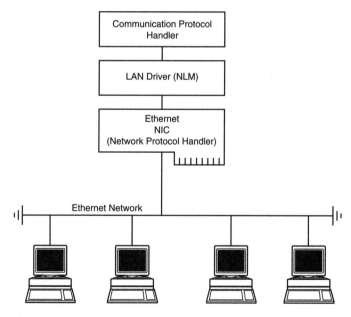

Figure 11.2:

A network interface.

TIP

Many different manufacturers develop NICs for the same network protocol, such as Ethernet, and they all build their NICs to the chosen Ethernet specification. To communicate with the operating system, the manufacturers define their own interface (there is no standard operating system to NIC-interface specification). Thus, you find many different LAN drivers for Ethernet NICs. The LAN driver for one manufacturer's NIC usually does not work for another manufacturer's NIC, even though both NICs use the Ethernet network protocol.

On NetWare servers, the LAN drivers are NLMs. With the LAN driver loaded, the server can receive information from the NIC. When information is received from the NIC, it remains to be determined what form and meaning the information has. The role of a *communication protocol handler* is to identify the information from a LAN driver as a packet of a specific communication protocol type. It also must take appropriate action for handling the packet and its content. In actual implementation, the LAN driver and the protocol handler must be bound to each other and to the operating system before any communication can take place.

Figure 11.3 shows how an NIC receives packets of different types and passes them to the protocol handlers for evaluation.

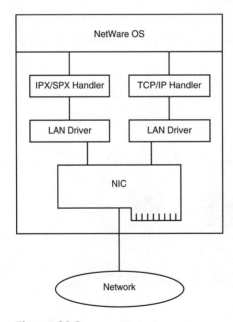

Figure 11.3:

An NIC interface to the operating system.

To understand the origin of Open Data-Link Interface and the ODI architecture, you must look at the OSI model of network communication. The International Standards Organization (ISO) has defined the components of network communication. It calls these components the *Open Systems Interconnection (OSI)* model. This model has seven layers, each identifying a definable component of any network communication. Figure 11.4 shows the Data-Link layer as the second layer of the model.

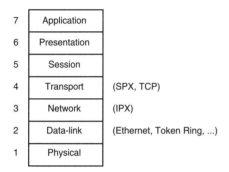

7	Application	
6	Presentation	
5	Session	
4	Transport	(SPX, TCP)
3	Network	(IPX)
2	Data-link	(Ethernet, Token Ring, ...)
1	Physical	

Figure 11.4:

The Open Systems Interconnection (OSI) model.

The communication needs that are defined at the Data-Link layer are handled by the network protocols mentioned earlier (Ethernet, Token Ring, and so on). The Network and higher layers define ways to recognize, identify, and interpret the contents of the information. Because an Ethernet card (or any other card) can receive information in the form of IPX packets as well as TCP packets, the operating system should be able to deal with both types of packets.

By binding a communication protocol handler (such as IPX or TCP) to the Ethernet LAN driver, the operating system can communicate by using the given communication protocol. If both communication protocol handlers are bound to the same LAN driver and NIC, then both types of communication can take place through that single NIC.

TIP

Because this architecture enables communication protocol handlers to bind freely to the LAN driver (which is at the Data-Link layer), the term *Open Data-Link Interface* originated. With this open architecture, it is possible to mix and match LAN drivers with communication protocol handlers as needed, thus accomplishing the objective of multiprotocol communication capabilities.

After the information is received off the network wire by the LAN driver, the protocol handler identifies whether it is a valid packet. The information then is passed to the operating system for processing. The following sections describe how some of the communication protocols work.

Understanding Fundamental NetWare Communications

As LANs were developed, the standards for LANs also were established. The NetWare developers chose to pattern their communication protocol after Xerox's network protocol. This protocol became known as *Internetwork Packet Exchange*, or *IPX*. As the industry matured, the need to improve IPX became more important. *Sequenced Packet Exchange*, or *SPX*, was developed, followed by SPX II. This section explains some of the details, functions, and capabilities of these native NetWare communication protocols.

Internetwork Packet Exchange (IPX)

IPX is the simplest and most fundamental of the NetWare communication protocols. The speed and efficiency of NetWare communications is based on IPX, and it has proved to be a reliable protocol for communicating on NetWare LANs. Because IPX is the foundation on which other protocols are built, it is important to understand the concepts of IPX operation. It also helps to explain why other protocols are necessary.

IPX implements communication by using *sockets*, which are identified by number. These sockets are used as part of the address for sending and receiving packets of information. The other parts of an IPX network address are the network number and the node number. The *network number* is established when a NetWare server is installed, and is based on physical network connections. The *node number* is the physical address of the NIC.

TIP

Primarily for routing purposes, each NetWare server must be given a unique Internal IPX Address. The network number that is part of the IPX address for IPX communication is distinctly different from the Internal IPX Address.

The structure of the data in a packet helps to identify it as an IPX packet. The IPX protocol handler identifies IPX packets by examining the packet data.

The following are IPX functions:

- ❖ Opens socket
- ❖ Closes socket
- ❖ Sends packet
- ❖ Listens for packet
- ❖ Schedules asynchronous event
- ❖ Cancels event

A few other IPX functions are used for address identification and timing. The preceding functions give an idea of the general function and purpose of IPX. Sockets are first opened, then used to send packets and listen for incoming packets. IPX also can be used to initiate an action upon completion of an event or after a specified lapsed amount of time.

IPX does not perform any function relative to the content or purpose of the packets. It is not concerned with whether a packet of information is a login request, a file-transfer request, or anything else. IPX just identifies and stores IPX packets. It does not monitor the communication as a whole, but simply makes sure that packets are sent and received. IPX does not even check to see if the packets it sends ever make it to their intended destination. For that reason, it is sometimes referred to as a *datagram service*, or *non-guaranteed delivery service*.

TIP

The acknowledgment of packet delivery, sequencing of packets received, and other communication concerns must be taken care of by other parts of the program or NLM that is using the IPX protocol. These other aspects of the communication process are defined in the OSI model, and some of them are handled if you use SPX.

Sequenced Packet Exchange (SPX)

SPX is based on IPX, but it is a *guaranteed delivery protocol*. This term means that if a packet is not delivered, you are guaranteed to be informed about it. In guaranteeing delivery, SPX also implements some retries if the first delivery attempt is not successful.

The major difference between implementing IPX and SPX is that with SPX you establish a connection with the partner with which you want to communicate. After the IPX socket is opened and the connection is established, you use the connection number rather than the socket number when delivering and receiving packets. The IPX address (including the socket number) is used by SPX when delivering the packets, but the programmer typically does not refer to that address during SPX communications.

TIP

Using SPX reduces the amount of programming that needs to be done to create reliable and complete communication. Programmers using SPX do not need to write code that will guarantee the delivery of their packets.

Sequenced Packet Exchange II (SPX II)

SPX II is the next generation of SPX. It introduces more intelligent performance by maximizing packet size and windowing packets. It also introduces an interface called the *Transport Layer Interface*, or *TLI*, to the NetWare environment.

Some networks can handle larger packets of information than others. This is a performance advantage when exchanging large amounts of information because one large packet (instead of many small packets) can be sent. Because every packet also includes header and control information, more data congests the network when smaller packets are sent than when larger packets are sent. Because reply packets are also used to verify delivery of each packet sent, more congestion occurs when many small packets are sent.

Windowing protocols assume that most packets will be delivered successfully. *Non-windowing protocols* wait for acknowledgment of successful delivery of each packet before sending the next packet. Windowing protocols send a number of packets, one right after the other, then wait for one acknowledgment that all the packets successfully arrived. The number of packets sent without acknowledgment determines the size of the window. This windowing technique reduces the number of replies required and improves overall network performance.

TLI is a standard interface developed by AT&T. Because of its widespread use on different platforms and ease of programming, it is thought by some to be the interface of choice for peer-to-peer communications.

Peer-to-peer communication is communication that takes place between separate computers using a communication protocol. Some communications are between two workstations. Most NetWare communications occur between a NetWare server and a workstation, or between two NetWare servers or routers.

TIP

If developers use TLI, and their applications need to be ported to another environment or platform, it is easy to do if TLI is supported on that platform.

NetWare Core Protocol

The *NetWare Core Protocol (NCP)* is the set of rules and specifications for submitting requests to the NetWare kernel. The NCP is more of a request or service protocol than a communication protocol. The NetWare core operating system (kernel) is programmed to accept and process specific requests. The specifications for those requests make up the NCP.

Applications that submit NCP requests to the NetWare operating system kernel do so according to the NCP specifications. IPX packets are used to send and receive NCP requests and responses. The application submitting the NCP request fills in the data portion of the IPX packet, according to the NCP specification for the request being submitted.

The NetWare workstation shell uses NCP requests when communicating with the kernel. NetWare servers communicate with each other by using NCP requests. In essence, all requests submitted to the operating system are in the form of NCP requests.

If a workstation application makes a request to a NetWare server, it is usually through the use of an *API library*. These libraries have been programmed to perform certain functions that may involve more than one NCP request. The workstation shell receives these API function requests, and completes them by using the appropriate NCP requests. This process is transparent to the application that made the API request.

By the same token, most third-party NLMs submit requests to the NetWare operating system by using an NLM function library called *CLIB*, which performs the requested function by submitting NCP requests to the kernel. Again, the application NLM is not aware of exactly which NCP requests are being submitted.

NetWare's service protocol, NCP (NetWare Core Protocol), is a proprietary protocol based on IPX. SPX is another high-level protocol based on IPX. Are you wondering why NetWare uses IPX rather than SPX to implement the NCP?

The reason goes back to Drew Major's assertion that NetWare has to provide the fastest core services, especially filing. Given that over 70 percent or so of network traffic is filing, Drew's point is well taken. NCP was designed to be "superfast" (as Drew refers to it) and to satisfy high-performance core services requirements for NetWare. So NCP has been built to be much faster than SPX or SPX II.

At the onset of NetWare 4.0 development, I commissioned the NDS (NetWare Directory Services) team to build a directory protocol on top of SPX. The reason was that I felt SPX needed to be more robust and "featureful." After all, other extended services of NetWare, such as print and backup, use SPX, not NCP. Problems soon surfaced. NDS, many people felt, was a fundamental core service and should be based on NCP.

NDS also included an authentication service that opened up more services to the user after the user signed on to the network. These other services, such as filing, were based on NCP. So it was decided to build the NDS protocol as an extension to NCP. *Application Programming Interfaces,* or *APIs,* were designed and developed in such a way that even

third parties could plug in and use the NCP protocol rather than SPX, SPX II, or TLI. This technology was christened *Extended NCP.*

Novell, however, has not chosen to tout Extended NCPs as the protocol for third-party developers. Using Extended NCPs gives the advantage that a third-party developer's application can be seen as an extension of NetWare core services. In addition, third-party developers can take advantage of RSA-based global authentication services that are provided in NetWare 4.0 for NCP-based sessions. The disadvantage, on the other hand, is that NCP is a very weak protocol, not offering asynchronous request capability or bi-directional request capability, and cannot handle messages greater than 512 bytes.

What is the future direction? For third-party developers, I speculate that Novell will tout SPX II as the preferred choice. It also is likely that SPX II will be supported on a growing number of diverse hardware platforms to which NetWare is being ported (Sun SPARC, HP PA RISC, and so on), before any other protocol. Moreover, SPX II has a TLI interface that is non-proprietary and standards-based, and makes applications written to this interface portable across different operating systems.

For NetWare core functions, it is likely that NCP will remain the main staple. It is likely to be made "featureful" to suit the growing needs of NetWare for the enterprise arena.

Expanding NetWare Communications

Some developers are using NetWare's native protocols to develop applications that are not in the traditional NetWare environment. This IPX technology is now available for purchase.

Rather than develop applications on non-NetWare platforms using IPX, many developers prefer to use a communication protocol that is native to their own environment. These applications can be integrated more easily into the NetWare environment because of NetWare's capability to handle multiple protocols.

Some of the protocols supported in the NetWare environment that are not native to NetWare are listed in table 11.1.

Table 11.1
Network Protocols

Platform	Protocol
UNIX	TCP/IP
SNA	LU6.2
Apple	DDP, ATP and ADSP

Because of the ODI architecture, protocol handlers for these protocols are readily operable in the NetWare environment. NLMs for these and any other protocols, once developed, can be loaded and bound to LAN drivers, thus enabling the protocol. With the protocol enabled on a NetWare server, applications programmed as NLMs can be developed that emulate devices or provide services found in non-NetWare environments. NetWare workstations also can be loaded with special software to communicate by using other protocols.

NetWare for UNIX

The UNIX environment has long had a communication protocol for networking—it is often referred to as TCP/IP, or simply TCP. The *Transmission Control Protocol (TCP)* and *Internet Protocol (IP)* are parts of a suite of protocols that make up an entire protocol specification for network communication. TCP/IP is often used when referring to the entire UNIX communication protocol suite, perhaps because of the widespread use of these protocols on the Internet.

The *Internet* is a large, well-established network used by colleges, universities, and businesses. Because of the number of network applications written to operate on the Internet, it is important that NetWare be capable of using TCP/IP.

TIP

NetWare provides the TCP protocol handler that enables NetWare servers to communicate by using TCP/IP. Applications can be programmed to make a NetWare server look like a UNIX host to a UNIX workstation. Existing UNIX applications that use TCP/IP can communicate with NetWare NLMs that use TCP/IP.

The UNIX file system is implemented in the NetWare environment through the use of this communication capability. NetWare NFS (Network File System) uses TCP/IP to enable the UNIX network file system on a NetWare server. NetWare workstations can access UNIX host computers through a TCP-enabled NetWare server.

NetWare for SAA

The IBM mainframe environment has a defined architecture for growth, expansion, and integration of its systems—*Systems Application Architecture,* or *SAA.* Part of that definition is the *Systems Network Architecture,* or *SNA.*

Within the SNA specification are a number of definitions, one of which defines the protocol used to communicate between certain types of devices. This communication protocol, *Application Program to Program Communication,* or *APPC,* is also called *LU6.2* because logical units (LUs) that meet the 6.2 specification are by definition capable of performing peer-to-peer communication.

NetWare products that provide connectivity to the SAA environment often use LU6.2. NetWare for SAA is implemented by using NLMs that provide the LU6.2 functionality. With NetWare for SAA, a NetWare server can be connected directly to an SNA network. Workstations on the network running LAN Workstation for DOS, for Macintosh, or for OS/2 can obtain sessions on the SNA network through the NetWare for SAA NLM. These workstations can do host (mainframe) printing and file access through these sessions. Figure 11.5 shows the software that must be in place on the LAN to accomplish this.

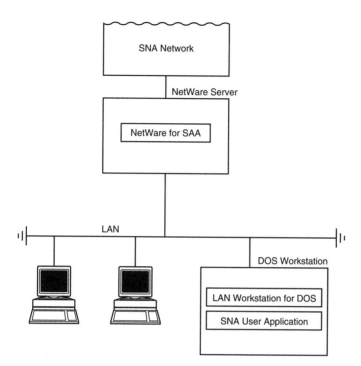

Figure 11.5:

SNA access, using NetWare for SAA.

In the preceding scenario, NetWare workstations communicate with the NetWare server by using IPX/SPX packets. These packets contain encapsulated LU6.2 packets. At the NetWare server, the IPX/SPX packet information is stripped off, and the LU6.2 packet is delivered to the host system on the SNA network.

NetWare for Macintosh

The Apple Macintosh (Mac) environment is very popular and has been integrated with NetWare quite successfully. In addition to enabling the AppleTalk Filing Protocol (AFP) on a NetWare server, the Printer Access Protocol (PAP) has been implemented. These are examples of programming that not only handle the communication protocol, but also the applications that use those protocols as well.

Apple developed a communication protocol similar to IPX called the *Datagram Deliver Protocol*, or *DDP*. Two protocols were developed by Apple to provide for transaction and guaranteed delivery needs: *AppleTalk Transaction Protocol (ATP)* and *AppleTalk Datastream Protocol (ADSP)*. They meet the needs defined at the transport layer of the OSI model.

The two higher-level protocol implementations mentioned earlier (PAP and AFP) use these communication protocols. Because of the tight integration of the printing and file applications with the Mac communication protocols, and because of the nature of Mac networks, the distinct separation of the communication protocol from the application protocol is not often necessary. In the same sense that applications are written to provide services in other environments, PAP and AFP have been written in the Mac environment to provide for printing and file access.

Programmers who want to use the Macintosh communication protocols to provide special applications for the Mac platform can do so. These two applications that use the communication protocols are mentioned because of their successful and popular implementation in the NetWare environment.

Other Protocols

Digital Equipment Corporation has a communication protocol for its Digital Network Architecture called the *Network Services Protocol (NSP)*. OSI also has similar protocols: *TP0*, *TP2*, and *TP4*. These protocols and others can be implemented in the NetWare environment as developers make NLMs that can be loaded to LAN drivers.

TIP

The future of communication protocol development and implementation may include other protocols as well. The NetWare architecture should integrate existing and future protocols through the use and application of NLMs in the NetWare environment.

Exploring Other Communication Technologies

Besides the direct protocol-handling capabilities, other features of NetWare further enhance and improve communication performance.

Packet burst technology and large internetwork packets provide significant performance improvements. Tunneling provides the capability to expand a NetWare network that uses IPX by using a network that uses another protocol. These features are implemented both at the server and at workstations that use NetWare 4.0 Virtual Loadable Modules (VLMs).

These performance technologies are discussed in detail in the following sections.

SPX II uses these technologies to improve performance. They are available to any programmer, and API libraries are available for this purpose.

Packet Burst Technology

Packet burst technology is implemented in the SPX II, as well as between NetWare servers and client workstations. NetWare servers implement windowing through a *packet burst*. This feature is activated only when large amounts of information need to be transferred (thus, it is called a burst technology). This packet burst technology is implemented by using standard IPX packets and protocol, but improves on the efficiency of communication by reducing the overhead required to guarantee the delivery of the packets it sends.

Packet burst technology is similar to SPX because it works on a connection-oriented basis, and it provides guaranteed delivery of packets by using the acknowledgment of multiple packets instead of the acknowledgment of one packet at a time.

Typical IPX applications receive one reply for each packet of information sent. This means that for every packet of data, two packets must be transmitted on the network. The sender formats the data packet and sends it; the recipient of that packet sends a reply packet back to the sender, indicating receipt of the data. If the data packet is corrupt or never arrives, more packets must be sent to indicate a need to send the data again.

With packet burst technology, many packets are sent, one at a time, before the sender expects or receives a reply. The packets that are sent before a reply is returned are called a *block* of packets. The last packet is sent with an indication that a reply is desired. The recipient then sends a single reply, indicating which packets need to be sent again, if any. The sender then sends only those packets requested. Because, under normal operating conditions, a large percentage of packets will arrive without error, this significantly reduces the number of reply packets sent. With fewer packets on the network, more people can get more work done.

Not only can more people work on the network because there is less traffic, but they can work faster. To send ten packets and receive ten replies takes longer than sending ten packets and receiving one reply.

The packet burst technology is built into NetWare 4.0, but it is used through an NLM with NetWare 3.x. If a NetWare 3.x server is not running the packet burst NLM, packet bursts will not occur with that server. Only servers running this NLM can use the packet burst protocol. Workstations automatically attempt to establish packet burst capability when they connect with each NetWare server. A workstation can therefore communicate with one NetWare server using packet burst, and it can communicate with another by using standard SPX protocol.

Large Internetwork Packets

Another performance technology takes advantage of larger packet sizes. Different networks allow different maximum packet sizes. If you can send larger packets of information, you have less overhead because fewer replies need to be sent. Typically, each packet has at most one reply.

Not only does larger packet size reduce the number of replies required, but it also reduces the total number of bytes you need to send on the network. A specific portion of each packet is used for addressing and monitoring that packet. This is called the *header information*, and it must be sent with the data.

If you have 2000 bytes of data to send, and your largest packet size is 512 bytes, you must create and send multiple packets. If your header size is 42 bytes, then you can only put 470 (512-42=470) bytes of data in each packet. That means you have to send five packets, which totals 2000 bytes of data, and five times 42 bytes of header information, or 2210 bytes of information. If you can fit all of the data into one packet, you only have to transfer 2042 bytes of information, which is nearly a ten percent improvement. With less traffic and smaller amounts of information on the network, the performance improves.

Tunneling

The Internet that uses TCP/IP is vast and far-reaching; many SNA networks are installed that also reach far and wide. It has occurred to some that it would be beneficial if two NetWare networks could be connected together through one of those networks. To send packets from a NetWare network through a non-NetWare network to another NetWare network is called *tunneling*.

Tunneling involves the following steps:

1. Originating an IPX/SPX packet

2. Encapsulating the packet

3. Routing the packet

4. Stripping the packet

5. Delivering the packet

Figure 11.6 shows how this concept works when an intermediary network (B) is used to connect two NetWare networks (A and C).

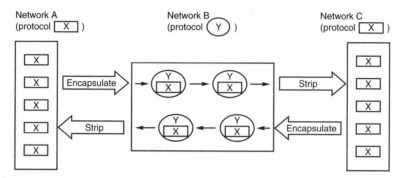

Figure 11.6:
Tunneling of IPX/SPX packets.

If the intermediary network uses TCP/IP, it is called *IP tunneling*. To networks A and C, the only purpose of network B is for tunneling.

Because NetWare can use different communication protocols, it is possible to tunnel through different types of networks. Two good examples of this capability are IP tunneling for TCP/IP networks and SNA link for SNA networks.

TIP

A server is capable of tunneling if it can handle both communication protocols. IP tunneling of IPX packets requires a server that can handle both TCP/IP and IPX packets. There must also be a program (an NLM for NetWare) that can encapsulate and strip the packets that are being tunneled. The intermediary network must have two servers with this capability.

Tunneling can be done by using NLMs on the NetWare servers connected to the intermediary network. The NetWare workstations do not even need to be aware that the tunneling is taking place.

VLM Implementations

The side of NetWare that runs at individual DOS workstations has drastically changed with NetWare 4.0. The NetWare shell is now implemented through a number of Virtual Loadable Modules (VLMs). These VLMs are loadable and configurable at the workstation in a way similar to the way NLMs are loadable at the server.

Because of the modularity of the VLM design, developers can provide protocol handlers that communicate by using any of the communication protocols discussed in this chapter. They are loadable and unloadable, depending on the applications to be run. Most applications should work fine with the SPX II protocol loaded by default, but applications using other protocols can be run by loading the appropriate protocol VLM. The packet burst and large packet technologies are implemented with VLMs.

VLMs make the NetWare workstation shell architecture similar to the NetWare operating system architecture. It is modular, can handle multiple communication protocols, and can be expanded by adding other modules as needed and developed.

Part of the VLM software is a group of modules referred to as the *redirector*. These modules together provide for network communication, printing, file-access requests, and so on. The controlling program of a VLM client is VLM.EXE. Figure 11.7 shows the relationship of some of the modules, and gives an idea of the design of the redirector.

The VLM manager directs (or redirects) the requests to the proper VLM. Each VLM in the redirector prepares the necessary request, then those requests are directed to the communication VLMs that send the requests onto the network.

To maintain backward-compatibility, a special VLM was developed. NETX.VLM emulates the presence of the former NETX.EXE shell functions. The interface to the older shell is different from the interface to the newer NetWare redirector. NETX.VLM provides the front-end interface so that all workstation applications that use the older shell interface still work. The actual execution of the shell-requested function is carried out by the redirector VLMs, but the application that made the request is not aware of that fact. Figure 11.8 shows the structure and interface possibilities that are provided with VLM client implementation.

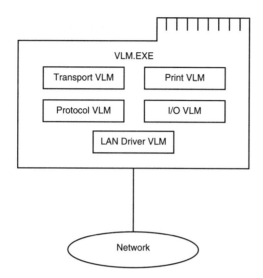

Figure 11.7:

The NetWare redirector VLMs.

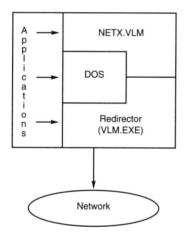

Figure 11.8:

VLM workstation interface.

The VLM interface to NetWare provides application developers three methods of making requests: NETX calls, DOS calls, and VLM (redirector) calls. Because these methods are available, all DOS applications work, older

NetWare applications that used NETX calls work, and new applications that use redirector calls work. The compatibility and flexibility of the redirector make NetWare clients ready for integration today and for expansion in the future.

Summary

The NetWare operating system has seen some design implementations that give it openness, and the capability to adopt and integrate current and future technologies. This is particularly true for communication protocols through the ODI design and implementation.

The enhancements to the NetWare native communication protocol that come with SPX II add growth and performance value to NetWare. Windowing of packets improves performance, as does the use of large packet sizes. The addition of the TLI programming interface makes programming peer-to-peer applications easier and more portable.

Current implementations of enabling NetWare with non-NetWare communication protocols are valuable. The capability to connect networks of different operating system platforms is very functional and manageable.

The future of the NetWare operating system looks good for expansion and integration due to the capability to communicate by using various communication protocols.

PART 4

Upgrading to NetWare 4.0

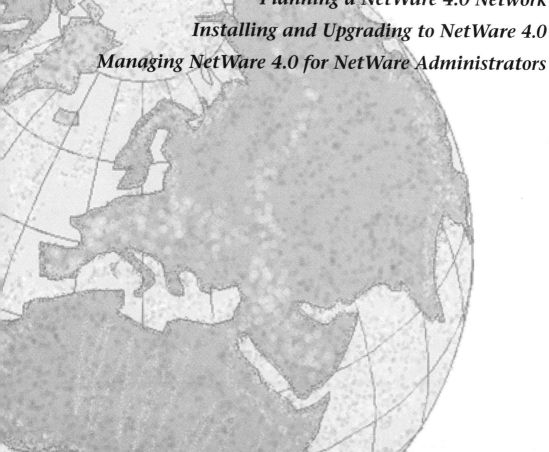

Planning a NetWare 4.0 Network

Installing and Upgrading to NetWare 4.0

Managing NetWare 4.0 for NetWare Administrators

Planning a NetWare 4.0 Network

This chapter gives you an overview of how to plan for a network by using Dorado, Inc., a "fantasy" company, as an example.

In effect, this chapter can be the basis for a planning guide or training document, which can teach information-management or information-services professionals how to plan, implement, and administer a NetWare 4.0 network. It outlines the steps you need to follow to plan and build a NetWare 4.0 Directory Services (NDS) tree, and it can be expanded upon and adapted for your own use.

Introducing a Hypothetical Enterprise-Wide Organization

Dorado, Inc., located in Toronto, Canada, is an imaginary international producer and distributor of sporting equipment. It has factories in Toronto, Mexico, and Spain; and it has a dozen sales and distribution offices in North and South America, Europe, Asia, and the Far East. The company employs 4,000 people worldwide: 1,500 people work in the main office and factory in Toronto; another 2,500 are employed in two other factories and in the sales and distribution offices.

The Central Information Services (IS) department at Dorado Inc.'s corporate headquarters in Toronto organized the company-wide NetWare 4.0 Directory Services tree (NDS tree).This NDS tree was built from the organizational chart that shows the major divisional and department organizations in the company (see fig. 12.1).

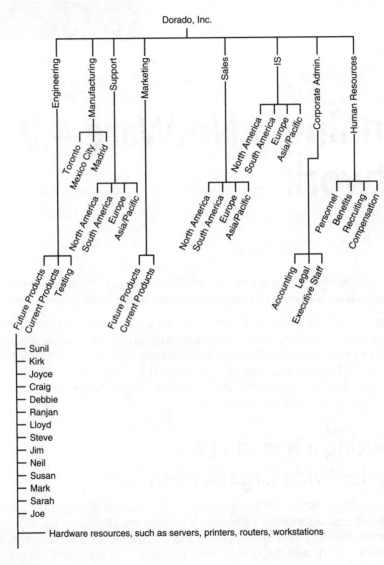

Figure 12.1:

Organizational chart for Dorado, Inc.

TIP
Figure 12.1 illustrates only the major divisions and departments in this organization. The NDS tree built from this chart, displayed later in this chapter, shows the way these departments within the company become objects in the NDS tree.

As part of the process of planning and building the NDS tree, the IS department for Dorado, Inc. conducted a series of training sessions that included both central and local IS employees. *Central* IS employees are those at corporate headquarters who are responsible for planning the entire corporate tree. *Local* IS employees are those at corporate headquarters, and at other offices world-wide, who are responsible for implementing and administering portions of the corporate tree for divisions or departments within the company.

The purpose of the training sessions was to teach and train local IS groups about the importance of planning the NDS tree, and how to plan and implement the NDS tree. The concepts and topics in these sessions included the following:

❖ Planning the NDS tree

❖ Introducing major NDS concepts

❖ Meeting the major objectives of planning

❖ Defining the role of central IS in the planning process

❖ Defining the role of local IS in the planning process

Planning the NDS Tree

Before you implement NetWare 4.0 in your organization, it is critical to plan the NDS tree. This section explains who should plan and why. It discusses two important variables that affect this planning process for any organization: size and complexity.

This section also introduces NDS concepts that are directly related to planning—in particular, emphasizing container objects, partitions, and replicas. Finally, this section discusses the scalability of NetWare 4.0 and the following four major goals you can achieve through careful planning: high performance, fault tolerance and security, backward-compatibility, and the integration and distribution of third-party applications.

SOAPBOX

Careful planning and implementation of NetWare 4.0 in an organization leads to a highly manageable and easily usable network that both administrators and users will come to love. I hope you noticed the accent on *careful planning* in the previous sentence.

What does careful planning mean? This chapter explains that. In fact, this chapter carries a warning somewhere in the middle (not to be taken lightly) that the administration and partition-management tools provided with NetWare 4.0 are not intended to allow the administrator to redesign a poorly constructed tree. The emphasis is then on carefully planning the tree.

Under previous versions of NetWare, each department in an organization built its own network, and plugged and operated with NetWare LANs in other departments when necessary. True, this led to increased administrative expenses and maintenance overhead, but this was like taking medicine in small doses. NetWare 4.0, however, recommends taking the medicine in one dose (one massive, carefully planned spree), and living the rest of your life quite happily.

In my opinion, larger organizations have the manpower and the capacity to plan and implement NetWare 4.0, and should see no big hurdles. NetWare 4.0 will appeal especially to those organizations that are downsizing from

mainframes to LANs because it gives them the same computing model that they had before. If you think about it, the NetWare 4.0 NDS makes the whole network look like one mammoth computer as far as the administration is concerned. From one console, you administer the whole network, which is exactly how people administer mainframe computers.

Note that NetWare 4.0 does not allow for a bottoms-up implementation without enough top-down planning. In other words, if each department in an organization builds its own NetWare 4.0 NDS tree, and some day it decides that it wants to merge all of them into one tree, there are big problems!

I expect that technology will advance enough in the coming years, when merging multiple trees should be an easy process and provided for by Novell. NetWare 4.0 can then be made to work well, even when there was not enough top-down planning and only bottoms-up implementation.

I expect also that NetWare 4.0 may have provided a shot in the arm to the consulting services industry. There are entrepreneurs out there, I am sure, that will provide consultation services to large and medium organizations in this process of top-down planning and bottoms-up implementation.

Who Should Plan and Why

Everyone who implements a NetWare 4.0 NDS tree should make a plan, regardless of the company size. The reason is simple: by planning, you make management of the tree easier, and you increase productivity for those who use the tree. If your company is small, planning lays the foundation for future growth without complications.

WARNING

Although planning includes many tasks and requires an investment of time, without that time investment you may build an NDS tree that does not function efficiently.

Almost all planning tasks are common to both small and large companies. For example, you must plan for porting the NetWare 2.x and 3.x bindery objects to become Directory objects in the NDS tree. Other tasks are important too, such as planning for bindery emulation, planning the implementation of time synchronization, and planning ways to distribute and support network applications. These tasks are extremely important for building a successful, efficient NDS tree.

Planning in a Large Organization

Except for the default NDS tree configuration that the INSTALL utility provides for very small setups, the planning steps are basically the same for small and large organizations. Planning is easier in a small company, however.

If you compare the small organizational chart of Dan's Sporting Supplies, shown in figure 12.2, with the large one of Dorado, Inc., shown in figure 12.1, you see that an NDS tree built from a smaller organization has fewer physical and human resources such as servers, printers, and users. A small company also has less specialization among employees and minimal separation between groups of employees. Therefore, management is also simpler—with few layers separating the upper echelons from the employees in the stockroom.

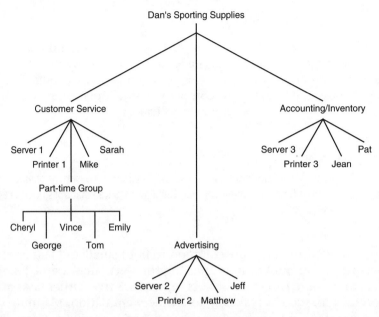

Figure 12.2:

The organizational chart of a small business.

When you build an NDS tree that is based on a small organizational chart, the replication and synchronization of information becomes a much less important issue.

TIP

Note that in the corporate structure of Dorado, Inc., many lower-level components are missing. For example, figure 12.1 shows only a few physical and human resources under the Engineering organization. When detailed illustrations of the NDS tree for Dorado, Inc. are shown later, more of these will be included. You can also imagine the additional departments and units that exist below the major departments shown, thus making the NDS tree for Dorado, Inc. very large.

Planning in a large company is more complex and more critical, primarily because of additional variables that affect planning. For example, you must not only deal with many more resources, but also with more layers within the organization. You must also port many more bindery objects. The difficulty is not the number of objects; rather it is in porting multiple objects at multiple directory contexts.

As you move from one department to another in a large organization, users require different kinds of applications and work with different hardware platforms. As the corporate tree for Dorado, Inc. illustrates, you must consider more layers of management, more and bigger departments and groups, more users, more servers, more directories and files, and more printers working together in one global, distributed database.

Of all the planning tasks, partitioning and replicating the resources in the NDS tree are the most complex. You must not only plan for and implement many resources in the tree, you must also consider how and where these resources are distributed as more users in various departments interact with one another and share resources across department boundaries.

TIP

Later in this chapter, you learn how effective partitioning and replicating can enhance performance and fault tolerance.

Sometimes, a larger organization requires you to implement different geographical locations into the tree. When this is the case, you must consider even more carefully how resources are distributed across the WAN. Distance, bandwidth, and traffic across the wire become major factors that affect performance. These variables make planning and implementing the NDS tree in a large organization more time-consuming, more complex, and more critical.

Introducing Major NDS Concepts

The NDS tree is a global, distributed database that is often referred to as the *Directory*. Because the distribution of resources throughout the directory is inherent in its design and offers tremendous advantages, it is not usually stored on one server (although it can be).

The distributed database is made up of Directory *objects*, as shown in figure 12.3. These objects represent resources such as users, servers, printers, organizations, organizational units, and so on.

Objects in the Directory are classified and known by their type. For example, user, server, and printer objects are of type *common name (CN)*; an organization, such as Dorado, Inc., is an object of type *organization (O)*; and departments within an organization are objects of the type *organizational unit (OU)*.

Figure 12.3 shows the Dorado, Inc. organizational chart converted into an NDS tree design. The respective objects are labeled as CN=Server1, CN=Printer1, O=Dorado, OU=Engineering, OU=Future Products, and so on.

Container Objects

Of the many types of objects in the Directory, only a few are referred to as *container objects*, or *containers*. A container object organizes and contains other related objects within a group in the NDS tree. Objects in the directory that cannot contain other objects are called *leaf objects* because they are located at the end of an NDS tree branch. The two types of container objects shown in figure 12.4 are particularly important to this discussion: the organization object (O) and the organizational unit object (OU).

As the figure illustrates, an organization object, such as O=Dorado, contains a number of organizational units (OUs), which can contain objects such as servers, users, printers, and other organizational units. These organizational units within organizational units can in turn contain other servers, users, printers, organizational units, and so forth.

Partitioning and Replicating

Except for understanding NDS objects (specifically, the container objects mentioned previously), the two most important NetWare 4.0 concepts that affect planning the NDS tree are partitioning and replicating.

Partitioning is the process of mapping a particular subtree of the logical directory onto a physical storage space (a NetWare 4.0 server). The mapping itself is called a *partition*. *Replicating* is the process of copying a partition and placing that copy, or *replica*, onto a server in another partition in the NDS tree.

It is important to emphasize that partitioning is not a method of grouping objects. You group objects logically before you partition, when you plan and design your NDS tree on paper. The design of the NDS tree, therefore, is logical. It is produced as you equate logical names with physical resources, placing them into containers that are usually based on departments within the organization itself (as shown in figs. 12.3 and 12.4).

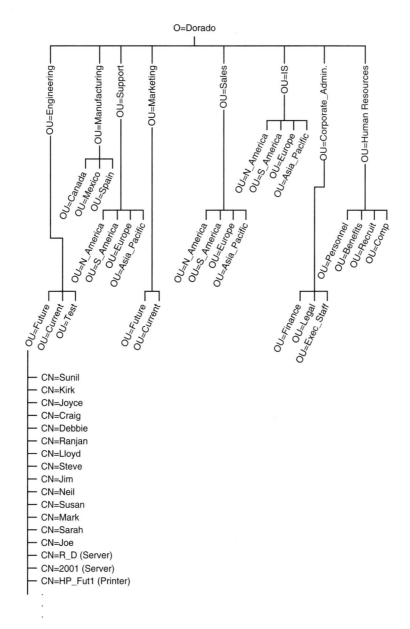

Figure 12.3:

The Dorado, Inc. NDS tree is made up of objects.

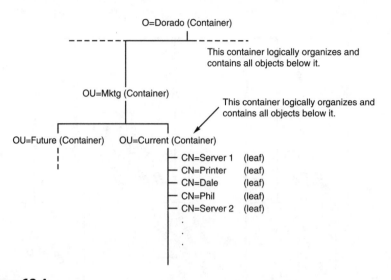

Figure 12.4:

Containers logically organize and distribute resources throughout the NDS tree.

When you run the installation utility as a part of installing a NetWare 4.0 server, you partition by physically storing sections of this logical NDS tree—this directory—onto a server, as shown in figure 12.5. The name of a partition is the OU of the root-most node in the partition; therefore, the name of the engineering partition shown in figure 12.5 is OU=Eng.O=Dorado. The name of the marketing partition is OU=Mktg.O=Dorado.

A partition can be stored on any server in the tree. In figure 12.5, a master replica of Eng is stored on the server 2001, and 2001 is an object in the Eng partition. A secondary replica of Eng is stored on R_D. The partition Eng can be stored on any server in the tree, however.

Strictly speaking, any instance of a partition is called a *replica*. Therefore, if you create a partition, and only one exists, it is called either a partition or a replica. There are three kinds of partitions or replicas, as follows:

❖ **Master replica.** By default, this replica is the initial instance of a partition. Any replica can be designated a master, however, regardless of its initial type. Only a master replica can exist by itself, and only a master replica can be used to create and delete subordinate partitions.

❖ **Read/write replica.** This replica, also called a *secondary replica,* can only exist if a master replica already exists. A read/write replica (and a master replica) can be used to create, modify, and delete NDS objects such as users, servers, printers, OUs, and so on.

❖ **Read-only replica**. This replica can only exist if a master replica
already exists. A read-only replica can be used to read information in
the partition.

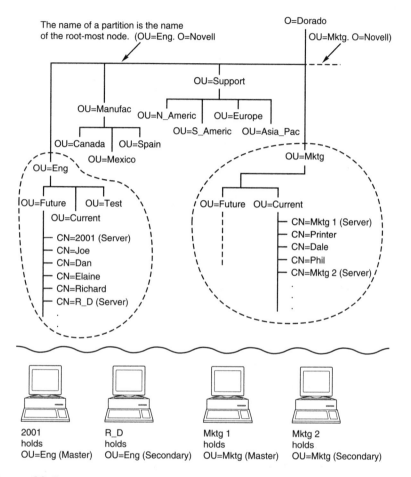

Figure 12.5:

Partitions and replicas of partitions are mappings of the logical directory placed onto a physical storage space.

Most of your planning involves partitioning and replicating on paper
before you ever install a single server. Although you can create and manage partitions in an existing NDS tree by using the INSTALL and PartMgr
utilities (or the Windows-based Browser utility), these tools are not intended to redesign a poorly constructed tree.

Partitions that you create with these two utilities should be part of your overall tree design. The PartMgr utility also enables you to split and join existing partitions as a matter of housekeeping. Partitioning and replicating, in other words, are not afterthoughts.

Meeting the Major Objectives of Planning

One of the major objectives of planning is to carefully partition and replicate your company's resources on paper before you install. This results in easier management of the NDS tree and increased productivity for users in the tree. Administrators often speak of networks and network performance in terms of *scalability*, meaning high performance and fault tolerance, regardless of network size.

NetWare 4.0 scales very well, enabling you to carefully design and implement a small to medium-sized network that can grow while providing high performance and fault tolerance. Scalability does not mean that you can build your NDS tree and let growth take its course, however. During any network expansion, you should consider how your network meets the following objectives:

❖ Performance and ease of use

❖ Fault tolerance

❖ Security

❖ Backward-compatibility

❖ Integration and distribution of third-party applications

These objectives are discussed in the following sections.

Performance and Ease of Use

The major objective that carefully planning the NDS tree brings is the high performance that NetWare is traditionally known for. In general, high performance means fast and reliable server response: reads and writes to disk, execution of third-party applications, use of NetWare utilities and services. These provide a user response that is equal to or better than the response from the local disk, with the advantage of shared resources and information on the network. NetWare 4.0 performance in these areas is as good or better than in previous versions of NetWare.

In addition to high performance in the conventional sense, NetWare 4.0 also gives enhanced performance to users and network administrators by enabling fast global network use and administration.

Although it is possible to designate a *global administrator* for the NDS tree (an individual who has rights to every container in the entire tree), it is typically not done. As shown in figure 12.6, an administrator in the NDS tree is usually responsible for a designated area of the tree. This designated area can have an OU (or container) that can include a number of other OU objects (and within those OUs are many other server, user, and printer objects).

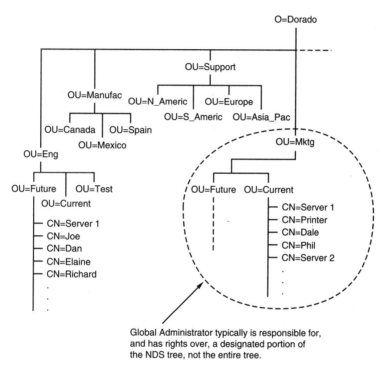

Global Administrator typically is responsible for, and has rights over, a designated portion of the NDS tree, not the entire tree.

Figure 12.6:

Administrators usually have rights over a portion of the NDS tree.

The tools that NetWare 4.0 provides for administrators are key components of efficient administration. The following list includes a few of the DOS- and Windows-based tools that administrators can use to manage particular containers or designated areas:

❖ **INSTALL utility.** This utility enables you to install and partition as you add new servers to the NDS tree.

❖ **DOS NetAdmin and Windows utilities**. Administrators use these utilities to manage objects in the tree and file system (compare it to SYSCON).

❖ **DOS PartMgr and Windows browser utilities**. Administrators use these utilities to manage partitions in the tree.

❖ **Auditcon utilities**. Administrators use these utiliites to administer the security-auditing feature of NetWare.

Despite the tools and other enhancements that NetWare 4.0 offers users and administrators, however, it is still important to emphasize that performance is an objective you achieve through careful planning. Users notice fast network response and take advantage of easy, global access to resources only if you carefully plan the distribution and replication of those resources, while also considering other factors such as bindery emulation and consistent naming of objects in the tree.

For users and administrators, performance is closely linked to ways that you can take advantage of what the directory offers in terms of naming objects. You should plan for consistency of object names from one portion of the NDS tree to another by setting up naming standards for objects in the tree, and by using those standards to rename bindery objects before porting them to the NDS database.

TIP

Names should describe the way people view themselves in the organization. For example, if you think of yourself as an employee in engineering who works on future products, you can easily find yourself in the NDS tree if the names of OU objects in the tree reflect the structure of the organization.

In figure 12.6, the names of OUs and partitions—such as Eng, Test, Future, and Manufac—in the Dorado tree are either short names or abbreviated. There are two performance-related reasons for this: to simplify use as users move about in the NDS tree, and to ensure that the distinguished name does not exceed the number of allowable characters.

A *distinguished name* is a complete specification of an object, with each of its direct ancestor objects all the way back to the root of the tree. For example, the following distinguished name of the server object 2001 is the name of the object itself, the name of its parent, its grandparent, and so on, back to the root of the tree:

```
CN-2001.OU=Future.OU=Eng.O=Dorado
```

Although distinguished names need no further information to uniquely identify them in the directory, a relative distinguished name always is used in conjunction with a context to uniquely identify it in the directory. (The *relative distinguished name* is relative to a specific context.)

The *context* is simply a path in the directory or NDS tree. Therefore, relative to a particular object, the context is the path that provides you with the distinguished name of the object. For example, the context of the object named 2001—that is, the path that specifies the object 2001—can be the following:

```
OU=Future.OU=Eng.O=Dorado
```

The purpose of a context is to allow specification of the majority of the path between a group of objects and the root so that the user does not have to continually type in the entire distinguished name. Context is merely a timesaver, nothing more.

Suppose, for example, that your user object is located in the engineering department of Dorado, Inc. If you type out the distinguished name in the tree, it looks something like the following:

```
CN=user1.OU=Future.OU=Eng.O=Dorado
```

If longer names were used for user objects, server objects, or organizational unit objects, you would have to type many more characters for the complete name. Although the maximum number of allowable characters for a complete name is sufficient for most situations, you can exceed that maximum if you use long names and have many levels in your NDS tree.

The factors that affect performance, such as bindery-emulation and naming conventions, although important, are subordinate to the way that you partition and replicate resources in the NDS tree. Typically, replicas offer an advantage when you must go across a WAN link to access information.

For example, notice the Eng partition (in Toronto) and the Manufac partition (in Mexico City), in figure 12.7. Because manufacturing engineers in Mexico City often need access to design resources in Toronto (such as original plans and drawings, design specifications, or statistics), a replica of the Eng partition is placed on a server in the Mexico City Manufac partition.

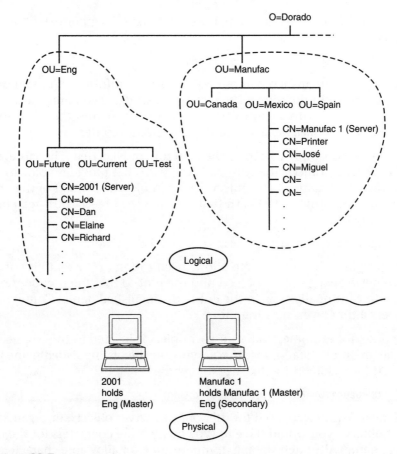

Figure 12.7:

The Dorado Manufac partition can access the Engineering partition.

This replica improves performance by making it easier and faster for manufacturing to access information from engineering. Although information in the replica in Mexico City must be synchronized across the WAN link with the partition in Toronto, there is a considerable performance benefit in the design because the amount of information synchronized across wire is reduced.

Note that the replica also provides increased fault tolerance because the engineering information now exists in two partitions, on two servers. If one server goes down, the information in that engineering partition is still available. Furthermore, if one server is destroyed, the replica provides a backup of the objects in the engineering partition. (Fault tolerance is discussed in more detail later in the chapter.)

The tree in figure 12.7 represents the logical organization of logical (OUs) and physical (employees, servers) resources. The computers in the drawing represent the actual physical resources (servers), on which the logical tree is stored. The logical tree, or any portion of the logical tree (a partition), can be stored on any physical server.

Depending on other factors—such as router speed, bandwidth on the wire, and frequency of access—replicas can also offer some advantage if users in one local geographical area have to go frequently from their own partition to another partition to access information.

Despite the advantages of replicas, you must carefully evaluate the resources and needs in the NDS tree before you replicate any partition. The overall performance of the network decreases if you create too many partitions and replicas, or if you place too many objects (user, server, printer, OU, and so on) in a given partition. Although NetWare 4.0 can handle more, in general, one partition should have no more than half a dozen replicas. Within any one replica, you can have a large number of objects, but a recommended limit is approximately 1000 objects.

Because each organization is different, and each will want to design its own NDS tree, it is difficult to specify exactly how many partitions and replicas should exist in a given NDS tree. NetWare 4.0 and the DIB is a robust and flexible platform, which can handle the needs of large, complex organizations.

Plan the NDS tree so that there is a balance. In other words, you do not generally want a very small number of replicas, each containing huge numbers of objects. Nor do you want huge numbers of replicas, each containing a very small number of objects. In most cases, the ideal way to achieve balance is to create partitions according to the departments that already exist in the company or organization.

WARNING

If you have a *test server* in your NDS tree (a server that is brought up and taken down frequently), do not place a replica on it. A server can exist in the NDS tree without any replica at all—this is recommended for a test server. If the test server holds a replica, and it is continually being brought up and taken down, other servers in the network will have difficulty synchronizing with that replica (with that portion of the database that might or might not be in the NDS tree).

Fault Tolerance

Fault tolerance is the protection you get by duplicating information in the tree through multiple replicas. The degree of fault tolerance that you achieve depends primarily on the way you plan and build the NDS tree—specifically, how you partition and replicate resources in the tree. As you design your NDS tree, you must decide how and where to partition resources, and you must also decide where replicas of partitions will reside. Well-planned replicas provide fault tolerance and enhance security.

The INSTALL utility is particularly helpful because it enforces some degree of fault tolerance. When you install servers in the NDS tree, whether it be the initial server or an additional server being added into an existing tree, the INSTALL utility handles some partitioning automatically.

When you install NetWare 4.0 on the first server in the NDS tree, the INSTALL utility automatically creates the root partition and places a master replica of the root partition on the server.

When you install NetWare 4.0 on each additional server in the NDS tree, the INSTALL NLM does the following:

❖ INSTALL asks for the directory context of the new server.

❖ If you install the new server in a context that currently exists, IN-STALL asks whether it should place a copy of the partition (in which the current context is an object) onto the new server.

❖ If you install the new server in a different context from that of a previously installed server, INSTALL automatically creates a new partition. It also stores a master replica of this new partition on this new server, and a read/write replica of this new partition on the previous server, where the parent partition resides.

For example, suppose you are building the Dorado, Inc. corporate tree, and you are installing the first engineering server, 2001 (as shown in fig. 12.8). You have already installed two servers at the root partition, Dorado_Mst and Dorado_Mst2. When you install 2001, and respond that you want to install it in a new context, INSTALL automatically creates a new partition. The new partition is OU=Eng.O=Dorado because OU=Eng is the root-most container in the new partition. INSTALL stores a master replica of this new partition (Eng) on the new server 2001. It also stores a read/write replica of the new partition on the server Dorado_Mst.

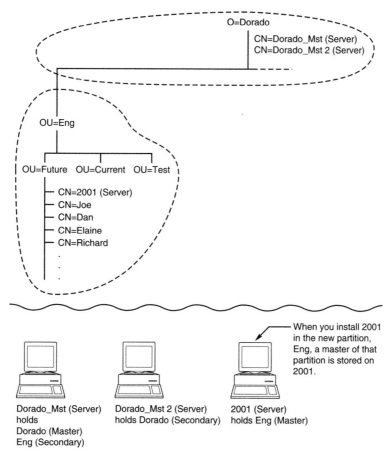

When you install 2001 in the new partition, Eng, a master of that partition is stored on 2001.

Dorado_Mst (Server) holds Dorado (Master) Eng (Secondary)

Dorado_Mst 2 (Server) holds Dorado (Secondary)

2001 (Server) holds Eng (Master)

Figure 12.8:

The INSTALL utility enables you to create a new partition when you install a new server.

Although the INSTALL utility enforces some degree of fault tolerance, remember to replicate each partition, regardless of the number of server objects that exist in the subtree represented in the partition.

WARNING

Fault tolerance, however, can be taken too far. Although replicas provide fault tolerance, and in some strategic cases can boost performance, you can have too many of them. A large number of replicas without regard to location is overkill.

Although replicas in the NDS tree provide fault tolerance for NDS database objects, they do not protect or back up file-system information. You must continue to provide file-system fault tolerance through disk mirroring and regular tape backups.

Security

To ensure tighter security, keep in mind that security should be administered on a group or container basis. Rather than give explicit rights to specific user objects, you should create a group object within a container, make user objects members of the group, and grant the group rights.

Consider, for example, an application of this principle as you implement new servers in an NDS tree. Figure 12.9 shows a partition in an NDS tree, and several separate containers in that partition. You want to administer security for each container separately by creating a group in the container called CONTAINER_ADMIN. The CONTAINER_ADMIN group has supervisor rights at the container.

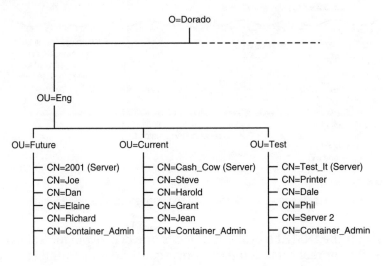

Figure 12.9:

The group CONTAINER_ADMIN is a group of administrators for a specific container.

Local IS individuals or administrators for each container belong to the CONTAINER_ADMIN group. When individuals in this group log in, they have Supervisor rights, and can perform administrative tasks. If an individual moves to another department and another container, she can be taken out of the CONTAINER_ADMIN group. By creating group objects within a container, making user objects members of one of these groups, and granting group rights rather than giving explicit rights to specific user objects, you can easily track users throughout the directory.

In any case, you should not designate a general user name (such as Admin), which anyone knowing the password can use as a login name instead of his own name. This makes it more difficult to know who the administrator is, thereby neutralizing the security benefits you otherwise have when auditing the container/network. (The security auditing capability is discussed briefly later in the chapter.)

Backward-Compatibility

Another major objective of carefully planning your NDS tree is backward-compatibility with NetWare 2.x or 3.x servers. You might want to upgrade your network to 4.0 incrementally, selecting certain servers or certain departments to upgrade while continuing to run 2.x or 3.x versions on other servers. Again, the manner in which you partition and replicate resources in the NDS tree can make a difference in performance.

NetWare 2.x and 3.x users can access NetWare 4.x resources by means of NetWare 4.0 bindery emulation. Although workstations running 2.x or 3.x shells can log in to NetWare 4.0 and use resources in bindery-emulation mode, they cannot take advantage of NetWare 4.0 Directory Services.

If you want to log in under bindery emulation, you must log in to a NetWare 4.0 server on which the administrator has set the bindery context to the immediate container just above where your user object resides. Before the administrator can set the bindery context on a server, that server must hold a writable replica of the partition in which the immediate container of your user object exists.

For example, as shown in figure 12.10, if Grant wants to log in to 2001 under bindery emulation, the bindery context on 2001 must be set to the following:

```
set bindery context = OU=Current.OU=Eng.O=Dorado
```

The bindery context on 2001 cannot be set unless 2001 holds a writable replica of the partition OU=Eng. Therefore, as shown in the figure, the administrator can set the bindery context on 2001, after which Grant can log in. Because the adminstrator cannot set the bindery context on server Test_It (which holds no replica), however, Grant cannot log in to Test_It under bindery emulation.

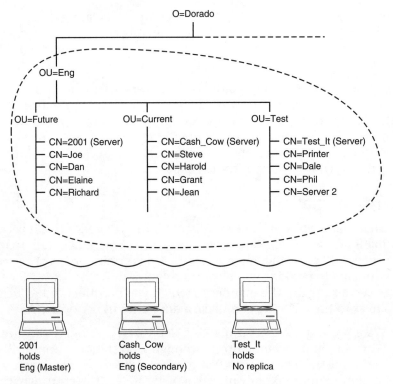

Figure 12.10:

Bindery-emulation logins carry certain restrictions.

Therefore, if the user Grant in the container OU=Current wants to log in under bindery emulation, he must log in to server 2001. This is the only server that holds a writable replica of the partition in which user Grant resides, and the only server on which the bindery context is set.

To take advantage of the NetWare 4.0 Directory Services, workstations must run the NetWare 4.0 VLM (Virtual Loadable Module) shells. The VLM shells can also log in to bindery-based NetWare 2.x or 3.x servers in the network.

You can see the disadvantage if you do not make specific plans to support bindery emulation. If a lot of users throughout the NDS tree attempt to log in to the network under bindery emulation, they cannot do so unless the previously mentioned conditions exist. If many users throughout the network want to log in under bindery emulation, you might end up with many replicas, simply to support their logins. Inherently, there is no performance price to run bindery emulation; however, the need for additional replicas to support bindery emulation can adversely affect performance.

You must carefully evaluate the need for bindery emulation and plan accordingly, rather than implementing it as an afterthought. If you run without bindery emulation, you can get a performance boost in the network, a boost that can be further enhanced as you partition and replicate resources to take advantage of the 4.0 database.

Integration and Distribution of Multiple Applications

As you plan and implement the NDS tree, you move completely away from the 2.x or 3.x server-centric environment to a global, enterprise-wide environment. In such an environment, the integration, distribution, and support of third-party applications must be carefully planned.

In the 2.x or 3.x environment, although specialized servers exist, and users throughout the network share information and resources from one server to another, it is not unusual for one server to contain and provide all services a user needs. For example, one 3.x server holds a word processing application, a database application, a text editor, and all the user directories and files for those who access those applications.

The server is used for research and development, holding directories and files that contain research-related information. It is also used for management tasks, holding information about product schedules, timelines, and employee-performance information. It also holds directories and files for documentation.

In a NetWare 4.0 network, however, the directory lends itself to distributing users and applications in the tree, according to the organization they belong to or the functions they perform. In this environment, you create a partitioner container that is designated for research and development, another for testing, and another for documentation.

Ironically, this move toward distributing resources in the network also makes it easier for one group to interact with another and for services to be shared among different users. Servers can be designated to contain certain kinds of information or perform specialized tasks, but the global nature of the directory makes it easier to access these servers from anywhere in the NDS tree. For example, you can designate one server for word processing, another for database applications, and another for user directories and files.

There is one precaution you must keep in mind, however, as you designate servers to contain particular applications and provide particular services: the proverbial "Don't put your eggs in one basket." You must make sure that your NDS database is protected from hardware problems by carefully implementing fault tolerance, placing applications in multiple locations and on multiple volumes.

As you plan the NDS tree, moving toward the distribution of resources according to organization and function, you should be aware of physical and logical layout of the tree and user needs. Users who require word processing should be able to access the designated server easily, and they should have appropriate licenses. Therefore, applications should be distributed to meet the needs of users, and also to ensure that network performance remains high because many users who access one server for a particular application can degrade network performance.

Defining the Role of Central IS

Planning is the general responsibility of the corporate Information Management, or Information Services (IS) department. The assumption here is a large, enterprise-wide organization with an IS department distributed over a wide geographical area; therefore, planning tasks are divided or shared between a central IS and a local IS.

Typically, central IS is located at an organization's corporate headquarters. Its responsibilities include organizing and directing the planning process; however, individuals in central IS work closely with local IS, doing many of the same kinds of tasks. For example, they both do things such as clean up old 2.x or 3.x binderies, upgrade hardware, run BINDFIX, and so on. The distinction, however, is that central IS must plan or closely direct the planning of the entire corporate tree.

Suppose, for example, that local IS individuals in the Marketing division or department of an organization want to add their department into the corporate tree as its own partition. Local IS provides central IS with information about users, servers, printers, and other resources in the department. Central IS uses this information and its map of the corporate tree, and works with local IS to determine how to partition and replicate marketing resources. This process ensures consistency, and makes it possible for marketing and every other part of the entire corporate tree to function efficiently. In this process, central IS is a facilitator, providing the means and infrastructure for planning and implementing the NDS tree. The specific responsibilities of central IS are listed as follows:

❖ Plans and partitions the corporate tree

❖ Provides standards, guidelines, and concepts

❖ Conducts training

❖ Coordinates server-addressing schemes

❖ Coordinates WAN links and routers

❖ Plans time synchronization

❖ Administers security auditing

❖ Establishes corporate timelines for implementing portions of the NDS tree

These responsibilities are discussed in detail in the following sections.

Planning and Partitioning the Corporate Tree

Central IS plans the corporate tree, deciding how to partition and replicate resources in the tree. One individual is chosen to design the corporate tree by taking information and suggestions from other members of the central IS group and designated local IS representatives.

For the lower, departmental portions of the tree, central IS works closely with local IS to plan the tree. Local IS individuals in various departments throughout the organization provide input for planning their portions of the tree; central IS gives close direction and final approval for the major pieces of the tree (see fig. 12.11).

To carry out the planning process, central IS uses divisions and departments within the organization itself as the primary bases for creating partitions and organizational units. (In some situations, partitions are created on the basis of geography.)

For example, suppose that the Dorado IS department is distributed across wide geographical boundaries, with North American offices in Toronto and Quebec, Canada; Chicago, USA; and Mexico City, Mexico. There are other IS people in Madrid, Spain; Paris, France; London, England; and in various other offices in Asia and the Far East.

With such wide geographical distribution, it is advantageous to create partitions for Dorado's IS department on the basis of geography. IS groups in Canada, USA, and Mexico can be in one partition; Europe can be in one partition; and other smaller, more widely dispersed offices can be independent partitions.

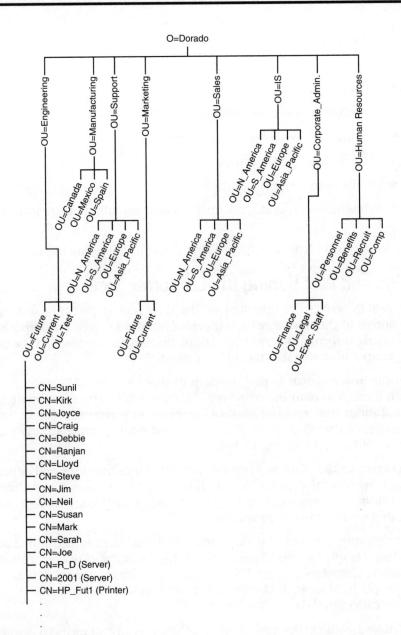

Figure 12.11:

Dorado, Inc.'s corporate NDS tree.

The reason for separate partitions is to decrease traffic across WAN links. Although IS groups in the separate areas need to communicate and share information, it is more effective to create separate partitions based on geography, rather than to create a partition that encompasses wide geographical areas. To ensure communication among the the widespread IS group, replicas can be placed on servers in the various IS offices.

The IS department works closely with HR (Human Resources) to compile a list of the major sites within the company, the major divisions and departments (see figure 12.11), and all employees, as follows:

Major Sites
Toronto
Quebec
Chicago
Mexico City
Madrid
Paris
London
Munich
Milan
Hong Kong
Sydney

This information from HR is combined with information from the various departments, including the number and location of servers, printers, and workstations, as follows:

Servers	1250
Printers	300
DOS workstations	10,000
Macintosh workstations	450
UNIX workstations	1500
OS/2 workstations	400

This information can be used to create both logical and physical maps of the corporate tree. A *logical map*, as shown in figure 12.11, is the logical-tree design. A *physical map* includes information about where these company resources in the tree—users, servers, printers, the offices of departments represented by OUs, and so on—are actually located.

The information in both the logical and physical maps is important in the planning process as a way of examining the extent of a company's resources, as well as how those resources are organized and distributed. As central IS works with local IS to plan and implement each department's part of the tree, this information can also be used as a checklist against information provided by the department itself.

With the backbone planned, and with physical and logical maps of the entire company, central IS can work closely with local IS to plan and implement specific portions of the tree for each department beneath the backbone. Central IS can provide resources for much of the hands-on work, and can assist in handling support issues once a department's portion of the tree is installed.

For example, central IS may have designated individuals who specialize in different aspects of the upgrade or installation. One person can be responsible for time synchronization, another for workstation upgrades, and another for specific questions on security issues.

For organizations or companies whose geographical boundaries are not widespread, individuals in central IS can be present when local IS individuals in various departments install servers into the tree. (Much of this falls under the category of training, which is discussed later in this chapter.) Central IS involvement in this process ensures consistency in the corporate tree, and prevents what can otherwise be planning and implementation mistakes in one department from hurting the corporate tree.

Providing Standards, Guidelines, and Concepts

Another important responsibility of central IS is to provide documents that explain standards, guidelines, and concepts. *Standards* apply to naming objects in the NDS tree. Because the tree is a composite of many different departments that, before NetWare 4.0, were somewhat autonomous, it is critical that a naming standard be established, and a document defining these standards distributed, to all central and local IS individuals.

The *standards document* includes conventions for naming objects in the NDS tree, thus ensuring that various departments in an organization use consistent names for objects in the NDS tree. For example, the standard for electronic-mail names is as follows: they can be up to eight characters long, the first letter is the user's first initial, and succeeding letters are seven characters of the last name. Where identical user names exist, the middle initial distinguishes users.

The standards document also specifies what kind of, and how much other information about, objects must be included. Therefore, it specifies that other information be included about a user object, such as the user's full name, job title, phone number, electronic-mail address, and so on.

The *guidelines document* includes steps or procedures that central and local IS individuals follow in planning and implementing the NDS tree. Most of these steps are beyond the planning stage in which central IS maps out the entire corporate tree. Therefore, they include more hands-on preparatory tasks, such as porting bindery objects, ensuring that bindery objects of different types—but with identical names—are resolved, ensuring that time synchronization is correctly set up, and so on.

This guidelines document can be a kind of checklist that either central or local IS people can use, primarily during the implementation stage.

The *concepts document* goes hand-in-hand with the guidelines and standards documents. It includes definitions and explanations of NetWare 4.0, and NDS terms and concepts. For example, this document defines such things as container objects, partitions, replicas, and so on. Although the on-line documentation that ships with NetWare 4.0 includes much of this kind of information, central IS should ensure that this information is known and made available to all IS personnel involved in planning and implementing the NetWare 4.0 NDS tree as part of its role in giving direction to the planning process.

Conducting Training

Central IS is responsible for seeing that local groups in a large organization know how to plan and implement the NDS tree in their departments or groups. In large, national, or world-wide organizations, IS people from other satellite locations may need to meet at the company's main corporate office. Central IS can organize training sessions, in which IS trainees receive the documentation, and then have the chance to practice planning and installing NetWare 4.0.

Labs can be set up to simulate portions of the company, and the trainees can gain valuable experience by partitioning and replicating resources that are exactly like those in their own departments. Although central IS plans the corporate tree, it is essential that local IS provide input about its particular department.

During training, central IS can make available (from HR) much of the information about each department's resources. Again, the physical and logical map of the NDS tree that central IS builds can be invaluable for training and giving direction to local IS people about partitioning, replicating, providing backward-compatibility through bindery emulation, and so on.

Coordinating Server-Addressing Schemes

Because determining and administering server addressing in the NDS tree is an organization-wide issue, central IS needs to plan and implement it. Each cable segment and server in the NDS tree must have a unique address. Although the INSTALL NLM automatically generates unique random addresses, in a large organization, the administration and assignment of addresses is more efficient if handled by central IS. Central IS can assign a range of addresses to each department or division. In this way, each department can handle and administer its own addresses locally, but central IS still has control over the addressing scheme for the company as a whole.

Coordinating WAN Links and Routers

Central IS is responsible for the performance of the NDS tree as a whole. It should be closely involved in setting up WAN links and routing servers in the NDS tree. Assuming that central IS is located at or near corporate headquarters, this responsbility is typical because corporate headquarters is likely the de facto communication hub.

Because central IS works with corporate offices, and because offices and departments are spread throughout the company, it should determine communication needs, and plan accordingly. This planning not only includes the overall picture, but minor details as well, such as the kind of machine needed in a particular communication path. At critical communication points or possible single points of failure, it is essential to have high-performance, reliable hardware. Distance, bandwidth, and traffic are also vital considerations as IS sets up WAN links and routing.

Central IS should collect information on traffic between various physical points in the NDS tree, and on directory-access patterns by users and applications. It can then plan for necessary hardware upgrades or alternate routes to handle high volumes of traffic. This kind of information is useful as IS plans partitions and makes decisions about creating replicas. In these matters, planning on the basis of departments or groups can be combined with planning on the basis of geography.

Planning and Administering Time Synchronization

Central IS plans and administers time synchronization in the NDS tree. The primary purpose of *time synchronization* is to generate consistent timestamps to maintain the distributed NDS database files. In other words, time synchronization ensures a consistent network time so that information in partitions distributed across the network can be accurately updated and synchronized.

Time synchronization is not responsible for ensuring reliable time, according to Universal Time Coordinated (UTC) time. Therefore, without an external, reliable time source, all NetWare 4.0 servers may drift from UTC time yet still maintain consistent time among themselves. By doing this, the servers can accurately synchronize partition information that is shared among themselves, thereby meeting the goal of time synchronization.

Ideally, NetWare 4.0 network time will also be accurate, according to UTC time. This accuracy requires that a server, designated as either the Single Reference or Reference Time Synchronization server, synchronize itself with an external, reliable time source. For example, an NLM running in the Time Synchronization server on the 4.0 network can periodically call and check UTC time so that the network can be updated accordingly.

TIP

For more information on time synchronization, see Chapter 10.

As shown in figure 12.12, for large organizations, you should implement one—or at most two—reference servers, with two only for backup. If you use two, however, it is critical that they stay exactly synchronized, using an identical external source to ensure UTC time.

For a large organization, you should implement one or two primary servers at each site. All the other servers can be secondary servers. You must also ensure that the reference server can see all primary servers and be seen by all primary servers. An e-mail server as a primary server, for instance, serves this purpose well.

For smaller organizations, you can use a single reference server—all other servers can be secondary (see fig. 12.13).

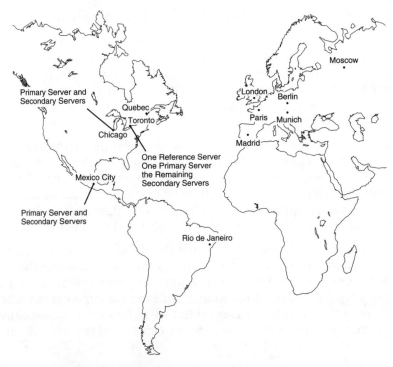

There is one reference server at corporate headquarters in Toronto.
There is one primary server at each site.
The remaining servers are secondary.

Figure 12.12:

The time-synchronziation configuration at Dorado, Inc.

Administering Security Auditing

NetWare's auditing feature enables designated individuals, acting independently of supervisors or users on the network, to monitor transactions that take place in specific server-volumes or in specific containers in the network's NDS tree. By limiting an auditor to a certain area of the directory tree or to a certain volume on a server, you can create auditors within groups or departments. This is an advantage, especially in organizations in which the confidentiality of information can vary from department to department.

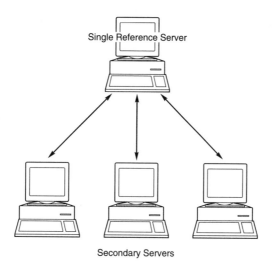

Figure 12.13:

The single reference server configuration.

The capability to designate auditors over portions of the tree gives you flexibility as you decide how to manage security auditing. For example, you might have a security division in a large organization that is responsible for auditing the company as a whole. This division can maintain tight centralized control, handling all auditing itself. Or it can designate auditors in departments throughout the company, but work closely with those auditors and their activities. If it chooses, a security division in a large organization can delegate auditing completely, allowing each department to handle its own auditing.

TIP
For more information on security auditing, see Chapter 9.

Establishing a Schedule for Upgrading the Corporate Tree

The corporate tree must be built, piece-by-piece, on a department basis. Thus, a critical responsibility of central IS in the planning process is to establish a corporate schedule for planning and to implement each piece of the corporate tree.

As soon as several servers are installed in the NDS tree, and user workstations are upgraded to take advantage of the directory, central IS may be busy with support issues as users and administrators adapt to the 4.0 environment. These support issues include upgrading workstation shells, handling questions about NetWare 4.0 utilities, and finetuning the NDS tree so that performance meets expectations. Because this takes time, it is important to establish a timeline and schedule for implementing the NDS tree.

TIP

Servers at the root partition should be installed first, followed by servers in the IS department. Other departments can be added to the NDS tree as soon as the local IS individuals are ready.

An important consideration for the upgrading order should be the experience and skill of the local IS people who will do the work.

Defining the Role of Local IS in Planning

Individuals who help plan and later administer departmental portions of the NDS tree make up local IS, whether they are actually in the IS department or not. The specific responsibilities of local IS are as follows:

❖ Provides information for planning departmental portions of the NDS tree

❖ Cleans up, prepares, backs up

❖ Upgrades hardware

❖ Installs servers

These responsibilities are discussed in the following sections.

Providing Information

The first responsibility of local IS people is to provide information to central IS about the department. This includes general information: the number of servers, their locations, their purposes, the applications running on them, and so on. It also includes server-specific information, such as network and node addresses, name-space support, LAN and disk drivers, I/O ports, memory addresses, interrupts, frame types, mirrored disks, disk size, and so on.

Central IS uses this information, along with information from HR (each department's name; and its managers, supervisors, and employees). It works closely with local IS to detemine how a department's portion of the NDS tree should be set up.

Local IS does the real hands-on work of upgrading to NetWare 4.0, building the NDS tree, and administering the department subtree once the tree is built. This work consists of tasks such as cleaning up old 2.x or 3.x binderies, porting bindery objects to the NDS, running BINDFIX, installing necessary server hardware enhancements, and so on, up to running the INSTALL NLM and bringing up NetWare 4.0 on the servers.

Cleaning Up, Preparing, Backing Up

As a local IS individual, you must do some preparatory work before you install NetWare 4.0 on a server and bring it into the NDS tree. First, back up the server or servers that are to be upgraded. Using the standards document, you should do some cleanup work on the bindery, including deleting unused or old bindery objects, checking for bindery objects of the same name but of different type, and changing the names of bindery objects to adhere to the naming standards established in the standards document. You should also run the BINDFIX utility to repair any problems with the bindery, and then back up your server again.

Other preparatory work includes cleaning up the file system by looking for and deleting file-system directory structures that are outdated or that existed with a deleted bindery object.

Although much of this cleanup work is routine, it is important. Whatever is not cleaned up before the upgrade will need to be done later. The following is a quick checklist of the critical tasks that must be done:

1. Back up.

2. Clean up names and delete unused bindery objects (old users, temporary or test user names, printer objects) by running BINDFIX.

3. Change bindery user names and other object names (for example, print servers, queues) to be consistent with the naming standards contained in the standards document.

TIP
One recommended standard to follow is the use of e-mail names. These names ensure consistency, prevent user-name conflicts within containers, eliminate the use of two names for one user, and simplify the naming process.

4. Clean up file-system directory structures that are outdated or that existed with a deleted bindery object.

5. Run BINDFIX.

6. Back up again.

Hardware Requirements

The following are the hardware requirements you must consider when planning to install NetWare 4.0 and add a server to the NDS tree:

❖ **Disk space.** Ensure that you have 50M of free disk space on volume SYS.

❖ **RAM.** Ensure that you have enough RAM. NetWare 4.0 can run with 8M of RAM; however, 16M is recommended.

❖ **CPU.** A 386 or 486 CPU is required to run NetWare 4.0. Beyond that, the most important factor when planning the NDS tree is the CPU speed. If your server contains a large number of partitions, or if it handles a lot of traffic between two points (as routing or WAN link servers do), it should have a CPU speed of at least 25Mhz. A faster CPU, of course, increases performance and ensures that the network works more smoothly and efficiently.

❖ **CMOS.** The CMOS clock on a server is important, particularly for a designated time-sychronization server. Ensure that the CMOS clocks on reference and primary servers keep accurate time.

Installing Servers

As you plan to upgrade servers in a 2.x or 3.x network, or install new servers in the NDS tree, there are some important installation issues to consider.

First, you should carefully choose the first server you install in any new partition in the NDS tree. The first server you upgrade should be one that most users in your group/department log in to. The reason for this is the manner in which NetWare 4.0 handles upgrades when multiple user accounts are involved.

If a user has accounts on two servers, for example, and both servers are to be upgraded into the same context in the NDS database, these accounts are merged. When the two are merged, the login script from the first user account upgraded is retained; the login script from the second account for the same user is discarded. Therefore, if the first server you upgrade has the accounts of most of your users, the cleanup work is less.

Because the first server you upgrade contains the largest number of user objects with their login scripts, password properties, and so on, it is simpler to upgrade it first. Later, when you upgrade additional servers, you can bring in other users.

Although fault tolerance was discussed earlier, there are some special fault-tolerance considerations regarding single-server installations. If your organization has a number of small, single-server sites, for example, and a single server is installed in the NDS tree and exists in a new partition, you must ensure that the new partition is replicated.

TIP

This replication happens automatically as you run the INSTALL NLM, adding the new server, and creating a new partition. Be aware of partitions at single-server sites, lest replicas of them are inadvertently deleted.

Another consideration for installing the first server in the NDS tree is time synchronization. The upgrade process is simpler if the server you upgrade initially acts as the primary time server.

WARNING

Finally, it is important to give a strong word of caution regarding the order and process of server installs. Once you upgrade one server with its directory-tree infrastructure in place (containers, user objects, server objects, and so on), you might be tempted to add to that existing tree the infrastructure for other 3.x servers before you actually upgrade those servers.

Do not do this, however. If you do, information (such as passwords, rights, and login scripts) that resides with the objects in those 3.x servers will be lost when you upgrade the 3.x servers and merge their objects into the infrastructure you created.

Summary

This planning chapter has given some general suggestions about how to plan and implement an NDS tree. You learned the importance of planning for building an efficient NDS tree. Although planning does require time, it is absolutely essential to prevent the long-term problems that a poorly constructed tree can cause.

The second topic was a discussion of some Directory Services concepts that are important for planning. This section introduced the concept of objects in the NDS tree, emphasizing container objects because they are important as a means of logically organizing other objects in the tree.

The concepts of partitioning and replicating were also discussed. Of all the planning tasks, partitioning and replicating the resources in the NDS tree is perhaps the most complex. You must not only plan for and implement many resources in the tree, you must also consider how and where these resources are distributed as more users in various departments interact with one another and share resources across department boundaries.

The next section discussed how careful planning enables you to build the most efficient NDS tree. You learned that, although NetWare 4.0 performs as well or better than previous versions of NetWare, you must carefully plan to achieve the performance benefits.

Finally, the different roles that central and local IS groups play in the planning process was discussed. Important to this discussion is the idea that the NDS tree must be centrally planned so that it is consistent from one department to another.

This chapter can be the basis for a planning guide or training document. Although this chapter cannot begin to explain in detail the many different ways of implementing an NDS tree, it provides some basic, essential information. With this information as a foundation or template, the IS department in any organization can begin to build a more detailed, workable guide to train its IS people how to plan and implement a NetWare 4.0 Directory Services tree.

13

Installing and Upgrading to NetWare 4.0

This chapter takes you step-by-step through installation and upgrading to NetWare 4.0, giving helpful hints and things to watch for and beware of as you go.

The basic installation process is covered first, followed by some variations to the basic installation. The process of upgrading from previous versions of NetWare is then covered.

Installing NetWare 4.0

The NetWare 4.0 installation process is straightforward, particularly if you are already familiar with installing previous versions of NetWare. It can be tricky to install NetWare 4.0 on many servers—particularly if you are upgrading from previous versions of NetWare.

TIP

The first thing that will make your upgrade to NetWare 4.0 smoother is proper planning. Be sure to read Chapter 12 before you install any NetWare 4.0 servers.

If you are installing a network from scratch, your primary concerns will be the following.

- ❖ Selecting your first server machine

- ❖ Your tree structure

- ❖ Workstation installations

If you are upgrading an existing network, you need to be concerned with the following:

- ❖ Sequence of server upgrades

- ❖ Sequence of workstation upgrades

- ❖ Data backups

- ❖ Network bindery and database cleanup

- ❖ Backward compatibility

TIP

For networks that are being upgraded, this is a good time to clean up and organize users, groups, login scripts, data files, application files, directory structures, and so forth.

Installing a Single 4.0 Server

Installing your first NetWare 4.0 server may take longer than subsequent server installations if you install by using floppy disks. The three methods that can be used to install are:

- ❖ Floppy disks

- ❖ CD-ROMs

- ❖ Network drive

Regardless of which method you use, you must start with the intended NetWare server machine set up as a DOS machine. If you use the CD-ROM method, you must have a CD-ROM drive and the appropriate drivers installed for that drive.

To use a network drive, you must already have a server on the network. You must copy the operating system and installation files from the floppies or CD-ROM to the directory on the server from which you want to install. You must install your NIC (Network Interface Card) on the intended NetWare 4.0 server machine, load the NetWare shell or requester, then attach and log in to the source server. Next, you must map a drive to the directory that contains the operating system files.

The installation procedure that follows is the same for all three methods. The only difference is speed: network drives and CD-ROMs work faster than floppy disks.

Hardware Recommendations

The first server you install should be fast and powerful. It holds the master copy of the Directory, and is involved in certain synchronization procedures. It is also important that this server have a reliable and accurate time clock because all other servers synchronize their time with this master server.

The minimum hardware configuration requirements include:

❖ 50M of hard disk space for the NetWare system volume

❖ 5M of hard disk space for a DOS partition

❖ 8M of RAM

❖ 386 CPU

TIP
Check the NetWare installation manuals for further recommendations on calculating memory requirements.

Server Installation

There are a few preliminary steps to perform as part of your NetWare 4.0 installation. These installation instructions assume that the computer being used is the first NetWare 4.0 server to be installed. It is also assumed that a 5M DOS partition has already been created on the hard drive. When reference is made to the source of the NetWare installation files, one of the following is assumed:

❖ If installing from floppy disks, the source is the A drive.

❖ If installing from a network drive, a connection to a server with the NetWare installation files has been made, and a drive has been mapped to access them.

❖ If installing from a CD-ROM, the CD-ROM drive is properly installed, is accessible, and has the NetWare installation CD in it.

One of these sources of access must be established prior to initiating the INSTALL program. Once the intended server machine has been set up as described, the installation is begun by typing **INSTALL** from the source drive (the A drive, the network drive, or the CD-ROM drive).

Before you begin the installation, you should have the following items:

❖ A licensing disk

❖ Your IPX internal network number

❖ Your external IPX network address(es)

❖ Your Directory Services design

❖ The settings for your LAN board(s)

❖ The settings for your hard disk drive(s)

To complete a NetWare 4.0 installation, follow these steps (many of them are automated by the installation program, but they are initiated by you as you reply to the prompts):

1. Initiate the installation program.

2. Select the type of installation (new or upgrade).

3. Prepare partitions.

4. Give the server a name and IPX internal network number.

5. Copy system startup files to the local DOS hard drive.

6. Load the SERVER.EXE program.

7. Load the disk driver.

8. Create NetWare partitions.

9. Create and mount NetWare volumes.

10. License the server software.

11. Copy NetWare utilities and files to the newly created NetWare volumes.

12. Load the LAN driver(s).

13. Install Directory Services.

14. Edit the system NCF files.

15. Perform other installation options (create a registration disk, copy on-line documentation to the server, create client disks, and so on).

The following sections give details and recommendations for each step. As you complete an installation, press Enter or F10 to continue. Rather than explain this for each of the following screens, you are expected to read the instructions and use the appropriate key. The instructions are either within a dialog box or in the instruction portion at the bottom of the screen. You also see the current function keys at the bottom of the screen.

With the disk inserted into the A drive, begin the installation by typing **A:\INSTALL.** If you are operating from a CD-ROM or network drive, use the appropriate drive letter instead of A. Figure 13.1 shows the first screen display you see.

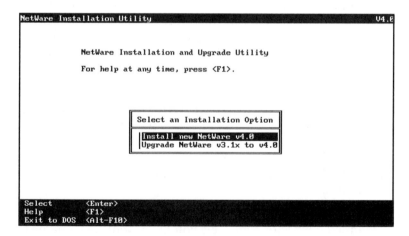

Figure 13.1:

Starting screen of a NetWare 4.0 installation.

Select the Install new NetWare v4.0 option. A disk partition screen appears, as shown in figure 13.2.

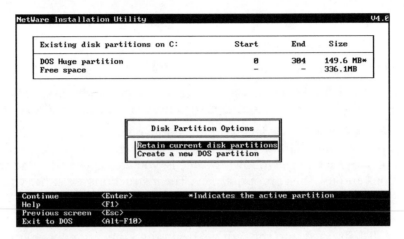

```
NetWare Installation Utility                                         V4.0

┌────────────────────────────────────────────────────────────────────┐
│  Existing disk partitions on C:          Start     End     Size      │
│                                                                      │
│  DOS Huge partition                        0        304    149.6 MB* │
│  Free space                                -         -     336.1MB   │
└────────────────────────────────────────────────────────────────────┘




              ┌─────────────────────────────────────┐
              │      Disk Partition Options          │
              │  ┌────────────────────────────────┐  │
              │  │Retain current disk partitions  │  │
              │  │Create a new DOS partition      │  │
              │  └────────────────────────────────┘  │
              └─────────────────────────────────────┘


  Continue          <Enter>        *Indicates the active partition
  Help              <F1>
  Previous screen   <Esc>
  Exit to DOS       <Alt-F10>
```

Figure 13.2:

The disk-partition screen.

For this installation, the assumption is that a DOS partition has already been created. The 149.6M partition shown here may be larger than you would use (typically, 5M is ample for the DOS partition). If you have large NLMs that you want to store in the DOS partition, you may need more space than that (the NetWare startup files alone take 2M to 3M of disk space).

If you used a boot disk and installed from floppy disks, you may not have created a DOS partition on the hard drive. You have the option of creating a DOS partition at this point (Novell DOS is used to create the DOS partition). A DOS partition must exist on the hard drive in order to continue. Because your hard drive should already have a DOS partition, you should retain the current disk partitions.

The next screen, shown in figure 13.3, asks for the server name. Having previously planned your Directory Tree, you have identified a name that is unique for the context of this server.

TIP

If you need help to determine the legal characters, press F1.

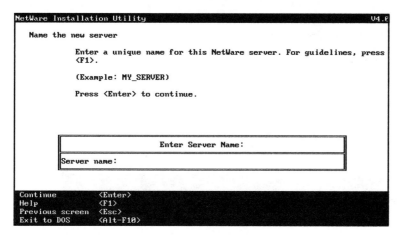

Figure 13.3:

The server name entry screen.

You may have planned to assign IPX internal network numbers according to certain numbering conventions. If not, you can use the randomly generated unique number given to you by the installation program. That number appears by default when the next screen appears. The number must be unique for your network; the number supplied by INSTALL is checked for uniqueness before it is given to you. If you are not connected to an existing network, the number cannot be guaranteed to be unique for the network to which you will be connecting.

After the DOS partition is created, the server boot files are copied to it. Figure 13.4 shows an example of copying these files from an existing server on the network. Prior to initiating the installation utility, this computer had attached to an existing server, and mapped the X drive to a directory on that server, which contained the NetWare 4.0 operating system files.

Note the use of the F2 and F4 keys to change the paths. If a CD-ROM is used, the drive and path of the CD-ROM should be used as the source path.

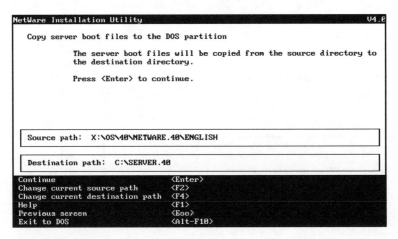

```
NetWare Installation Utility                                    V4.0

   Copy server boot files to the DOS partition

              The server boot files will be copied from the source directory to
              the destination directory.

              Press <Enter> to continue.




   ┌─────────────────────────────────────────────────────────────────┐
   │ Source path:   X:\OS\40\NETWARE.40\ENGLISH                        │
   └─────────────────────────────────────────────────────────────────┘

   ┌─────────────────────────────────────────────────────────────────┐
   │ Destination path:  C:\SERVER.40                                   │
   └─────────────────────────────────────────────────────────────────┘
Continue                              <Enter>
Change current source path            <F2>
Change current destination path       <F4>
Help                                  <F1>
Previous screen                       <Esc>
Exit to DOS                           <Alt-F10>
```

Figure 13.4:

Source and destination paths for server boot files.

When you press Enter to begin, a new screen appears to show the progress of the copying process. This copy should take less than a minute. When it is done, the following question displays:

Do you want AUTOEXEC.BAT to load SERVER.EXE?

If you answer **Yes**, the AUTOEXEC.BAT file on your DOS drive is changed to include an instruction to start SERVER.EXE.

The next step of the installation process is to load SERVER.EXE. The server is automatically loaded by the installation program, and the system is operating as a NetWare server. The heading at the top of the screen changes from NetWare Installation Utility to NetWare Server Installation V4.00 (see fig. 13.5). If you are installing from a network drive, and you do not proceed with the installation promptly to completion, your connection to the source server can be lost, and you may have to start again. (If you are installing from floppy disks or CD-ROM, losing a connection to a server is not a factor.)

TIP

From here, the installation is very similar to using the INSTALL NLM. The difference between them is that the installation program prompts you and guides you from one menu item to the next. If you install by using the INSTALL NLM, you have to select the menu items you want to perform, one at a time. Figure 13.5 shows the main menu of the INSTALL NLM.

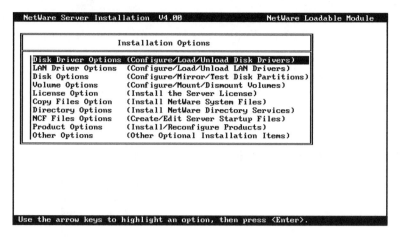

Figure 13.5:

The INSTALL NLM main menu.

The rest of the installation involves Disk Driver Options, LAN Driver Options, and so on. The screen displays shown were taken from the INSTALL NLM—they do not match exactly what you see when using the installation program.

At this point, the installation program needs to know where it can find NetWare files that it will copy onto the SYS: volume. Figure 13.6 shows the screen you see.

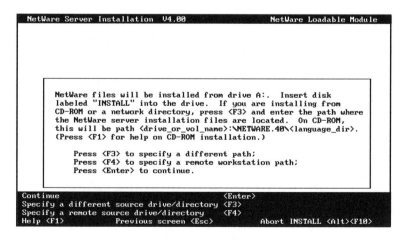

Figure 13.6:

Selecting the source path for NetWare files.

This example assumes that you are using floppy disks, so you are asked to insert a disk into the A drive. You can use the appropriate keys to specify otherwise.

Before copying to the NetWare volume, however, the capability to communicate with the drive must be established. Figure 13.7 shows the screen used to select a disk driver that enables NetWare to communicate with the disk.

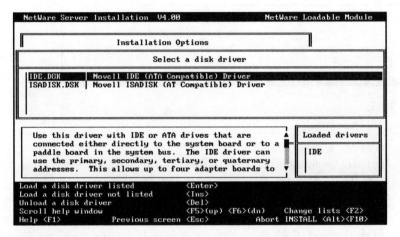

Figure 13.7:
Loading a disk driver screen.

Up to this point, disk access has been with the DOS partition through DOS. Now, however, you want to communicate through NetWare, so a driver that works with NetWare must be loaded.

TIP
Although this figure only shows two drivers, you will probably see many more on your system.

When you select a driver, you are asked to fill in some necessary driver settings, such as Interrupt, port, and scatter/gather. Simply fill them in and proceed. When the driver is loaded, you will be informed and asked to proceed.

With the driver loaded, you then must create the NetWare disk partitions and set up NetWare volumes. You can have this done automatically, or you can do it manually (all available space is used if you choose the automatic option).

Next, you have the option of specifying the volumes that will be on this server: SYS:, VOL1:, and so on. You first must specify the size of each volume, and you can then set certain options, as shown in figure 13.8.

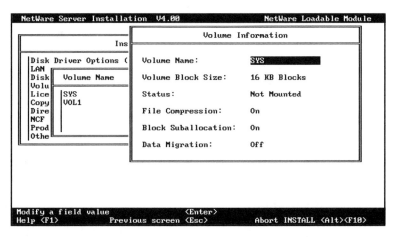

Figure 13.8:
The volume information screen.

WARNING
Once the Volume Block Size is set, File Compression is turned on, or Block Suballocation is turned on, they cannot be changed without deleting and reinitializing the volume.

At this point in the installation, the volumes status is not mounted. When you proceed, the volumes are automatically mounted in preparation for copying the NetWare files.

The next step is to license your copy of NetWare. Just follow the instructions, and you will be informed when licensing is completed. Proceed to the Copy NetWare Files step when requested. Prior to copying the NetWare files, you are asked to select the source drive for the NetWare files. After you choose the drive, the screen seen in figure 13.9 appears.

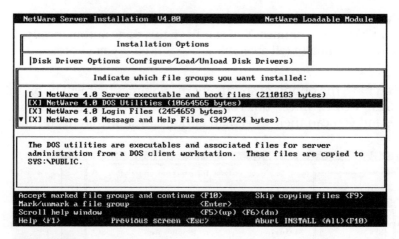

```
NetWare Server Installation  V4.00              NetWare Loadable Module
┌──────────────────────────────────────────────────────────────────────┐
│                        Installation Options                            │
├──────────────────────────────────────────────────────────────────────┤
│ Disk Driver Options (Configure/Load/Unload Disk Drivers)               │
├──────────────────────────────────────────────────────────────────────┤
│               Indicate which file groups you want installed:           │
├──────────────────────────────────────────────────────────────────────┤
│  [ ] NetWare 4.0 Server executable and boot files (2110183 bytes)      │
│  [X] NetWare 4.0 DOS Utilities (10664565 bytes)                        │
│  [X] NetWare 4.0 Login Files (2454659 bytes)                           │
│▼ [X] NetWare 4.0 Message and Help Files (3494724 bytes)                │
├──────────────────────────────────────────────────────────────────────┤
│  The DOS utilities are executables and associated files for server     │
│  administration from a DOS client workstation.  These files are copied to│
│  SYS:\PUBLIC.                                                          │
│                                                                        │
├──────────────────────────────────────────────────────────────────────┤
│ Accept marked file groups and continue <F10>      Skip copying files <F9>│
│ Mark/unmark a file group                  <Enter>                       │
│ Scroll help window                        <F5>(up) <F6>(dn)             │
│ Help <F1>            Previous screen <Esc>        Abort INSTALL <Alt><F10>│
└──────────────────────────────────────────────────────────────────────┘
```

Figure 13.9:

Copying NetWare files.

This figure shows that server executable and boot files will not be copied. (You will probably want to copy everything if you have room on your volume.)

When you begin the copying, a progress screen displays, which shows the percentage of completion as the copy process proceeds. If you are copying from a network drive, and have lost your connection, you cannot complete this step without starting over.

When the copy completes, you are informed, and you can proceed to loading the LAN driver(s). Figure 13.10 shows the screen for selecting LAN drivers. You probably see more than two LAN drivers listed. Select the one for the LAN board you have installed.

When you choose the LAN driver, you need to supply the LAN board settings. A screen similar to the one shown in figure 13.11 is presented for this purpose.

The interrupt and port must be specified for the NE2000 board, but the node address is read directly from the board—you do not have to supply it. It is important to specify the frame type—no communication can take place without it.

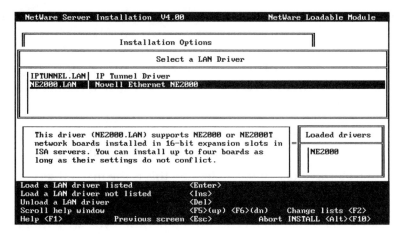

Figure 13.10:

LAN board driver selection.

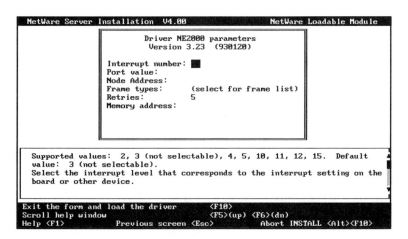

Figure 13.11:

LAN driver settings for the NE2000 LAN board.

WARNING

If you have two LAN boards installed, be sure to specify the settings of the correct LAN board. You may be using one of the LAN boards to connect to a server that is the source of your installation files (instead of a floppy drive or CD-ROM drive). If so, specify the other board, or the new server will compete with your DOS workstation connection for the use of the LAN board, resulting in problems with the remainder of this installation.

You are told when the LAN driver has been successfully installed. A summary screen reminds you of the settings you have specified before binding to a communication protocol. Be sure that the binding is done.

If you want to use a protocol other than IPX/SPX, indicate that you do not want to bind at this time (you will have to install and configure the desired communication protocol yourself). With the communication protocol installed, you then need to bind that protocol to the LAN driver you are using. The AUTOEXEC.NCF file should include these loading and binding instructions, so add them to that file, and save the file.

Next, you install Directory Services. Because this is the first 4.0 server you are installing, you need to create the Directory tree you will be using. When the screen shown in figure 13.12 appears, press Ins, and give your tree a name. If you install on an existing 4.0 network, you see a list of trees, and you can add this server to an existing tree.

TIP

When planning the network you have chosen a specific tree name. Use that name here. Once the tree is named, you cannot change it. The objects that you add to the tree later have name changes, but the tree name always stays the same.

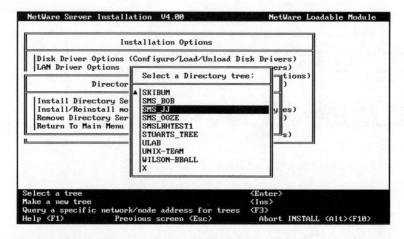

Figure 13.12:

Choosing a Directory tree.

After the tree is named, you are required to select a time zone for this server. Because the time-zone parameters are already set up, you should not need to edit the configuration parameters after you select the zone by name. This is true as long as your system date and time are current. Figure 13.13 shows the screen in which you select the time zone; figure 13.14 displays the time configuration parameters screen.

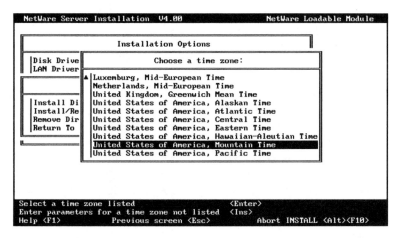

Figure 13.13:

Selecting the time zone.

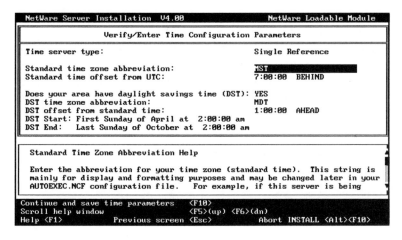

Figure 13.14:

Time configuration parameters screen.

291

SOAPBOX

Selecting a time zone (you figure) should be pretty easy. There is the mountain time zone, central, eastern ... Go around the world and you may find a few more. Right? No!

Trying to make the selection of time zone and parameters an easy part of installation turned out to be a big headache. First, we found that there were quite a few named and unnamed time zones in this world. Daylight savings time and other such adjustments were regional and not followed as a norm everywhere. People in many parts of the world (including our own Novell sales people in some locations) were grossly ignorant of time zones and their implications. Amazingly enough, I could not find one authoritative manuscript that detailed all the different time zones of the world.

In the middle of all this hullabaloo, I found out that the state legislature of Arizona abolished daylight savings time adjustment a few months back. Yet, no map that I saw conveyed this accurately. I also heard from someone that all clocks in China are set to Beijing. If it is daytime in some part of China and the time in Beijing is 10 p.m., the clocks in that region of China must also show 10 p.m... I do not know if this is true.

Anyway, in the end I had to go by the fairly obvious rule. In countries where NetWare sold fairly well, we collected definitions of all time zones and adjustment practices and incorporated them into the v4.0 product. If v4.0 lacks any time zones, be sure to write a note to those brave Novell engineers. The next version of NetWare v4.0 will surely find your favorite time zone.

The next step is to establish in which context in the tree the server will reside. In your planning, you should have identified the containers that will be in the tree and their relationships. Depending on where in the tree this server will be placed, enter the appropriate Organization and Organizational Unit names. Figure 13.15 shows that the server being installed will be placed in the container object Documentation, which is in the Novell organization.

The Admin object is created by default directly under the organization object. If you do not give it a password, you will be reminded before objects are created.

TIP

The *Admin object* is the user object that creates and manages all other objects in this context of the tree. It has all rights and privileges at this context, and it is the only user object created by the installation program.

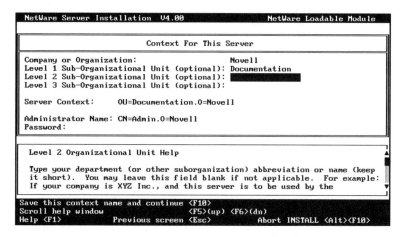

```
NetWare Server Installation  V4.00            NetWare Loadable Module

                        Context For This Server

Company or Organization:                     Novell
Level 1 Sub-Organizational Unit (optional): Documentation
Level 2 Sub-Organizational Unit (optional): ████████████████
Level 3 Sub-Organizational Unit (optional):

Server Context:        OU=Documentation.O=Novell

Administrator Name: CN=Admin.O=Novell
Password:

   Level 2 Organizational Unit Help                                   ▲

   Type your department (or other suborganization) abbreviation or name (keep
   it short).  You may leave this field blank if not applicable.  For example:
   If your company is XYZ Inc., and this server is to be used by the        ▼

Save this context name and continue <F10>
Scroll help window                 <F5>(up) <F6>(dn)
Help <F1>           Previous screen <Esc>        Abort INSTALL <Alt><F10>
```

Figure 13.15:

Setting the server context.

The installation program then creates an object for each volume you created earlier in the installation. It also creates the Admin user and the server object, along with the container objects you specified when setting the server context. If you name your server MIKEY, place it in the Documentation organizational unit in the Novell organization, and create SYS: and VOL1: as disk volumes, your tree has the objects shown in figure 13.16.

```
*** Directory Services Mapping ***

[Root]
  └O=Novell
      ├OU=Documentation
      │   ├CN=MIKEY
      │   ├CN=MIKEY_SYS
      │   └CN=MIKEY_VOL1
      └CN=Admin
C:\SCREENS>
```

Figure 13.16:

An initial Directory tree.

Note how the volume object names have been preceded by the server name and an underscore. The physical volume names remain the same (SYS: and VOL1:). The Directory object name is created so that many servers can reside at the same context with a SYS: volume. (Remember: objects at a given context must have a unique name.)

SOAPBOX

NDS is one sophisticated technology. A corporate user can explore this technology to its depth by using partitioning, replication, authentication, access control, schema modifications, and so on. But what about old faithful Joe's Bike Shop that has a couple of NetWare servers, and does not need any of the extended features of NDS? Does Joe have to go through a myriad of complicated questions on NDS before setting up his network?

In trying to simplify Joe's life, yet retaining the flexibility for Mr. Fortune 500 to do his NDS things, Novell engineers had to use every last bit of ingenuity. As is explained Chapter 6, out went the "country" object, which normally starts the definition of the NDS tree. Asking Joe to type in his country name seemed pretty silly. Furthermore, many of our users did not like the idea of the top of the NDS tree having a country name—they thought that their

organization name was more relevant.

Because most software—even extremely user-friendly ones—required the user to type in his/her name and the company name (as part of the authorization scheme), we decided that requiring an organization name wasn't so bad. We kept the depth of the tree limited (to lessen complexity), and provided the capability to deepen the levels of the tree or shrink them through GUI-based tools that ran on the workstation.

In other words, we did not sacrifice flexibility by making the installation simpler, but we made all advanced features optionally exploitable through workstation tools. Overall, we made the NetWare v4.0 NDS installation a million times simpler than any comparable directory installation scheme in the marketplace. Just look at the UNIX-based DNS installation scheme to see what I mean.

The final screen of the Directory Services portion of the installation summarizes the location of your server (see fig. 13.17). This is information that you should remember.

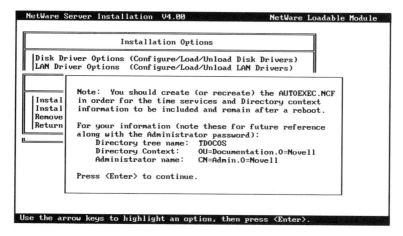

Figure 13.17:

Final summary screen of the Directory Services installation.

The installation program then enables you to edit and save the STARTUP.NCF and AUTOEXEC.NCF startup files.

Last, you are enabled to do other installation options. Figure 13.18 shows the next screen from which you can select these other options.

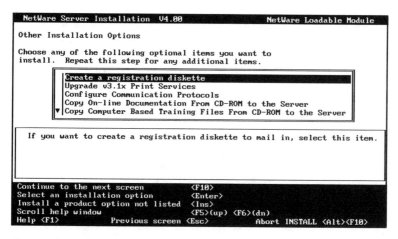

Figure 13.18:

Other options of the installation process.

These installation options include the following:

- ❖ Create a registration disk
- ❖ Upgrade v3.1x Print Services
- ❖ Configure Communication Protocols
- ❖ Copy On-line Documents From CD-ROM to the Server
- ❖ Copy Computer Based Training Files From CD-ROM to the Server
- ❖ Create DOS/Windows Client Install Disks From CD-ROM Files
- ❖ Create OS/2 Client Install Disks From CD-ROM Files
- ❖ Create Upgrade/Migration Disks
- ❖ Install an Additional Server Language
- ❖ Install NetWare for Macintosh
- ❖ Install NetWare for NFS
- ❖ Install NetWare for SAA

This is the point at which you can also install TCP/IP, other languages, and so on. When you continue beyond this menu, the final screen of the installation displays (see fig. 13.19).

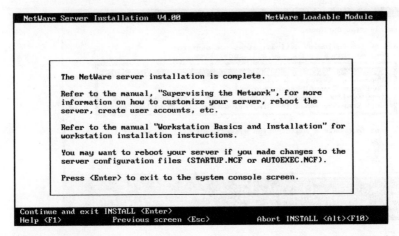

Figure 13.19:

The final installation screen.

The server installation is now complete, and you can continue your network installation by installing other servers and workstations.

You can perform the other tasks at any time by using the INSTALL NLM at the server. Enter **LOAD INSTALL** at the server, select Maintenance/Selective Install, choose Other Options, then select the option you want.

Installing Workstations

The DOS and Windows workstation environments have changed with NetWare 4.0. NetWare 3.x clients can still access NetWare 4.0 servers, but NetWare 4.0 bindery emulation is used. Directory Services access is not performed unless the new DOS requester Virtual Loadable Modules (VLMs) are used. A NetWare 4.0 client is a client running the VLMs instead of the NETX shell.

Client files can be installed on workstations from floppy disks or from a server directory. If this is a new network, and you are installing from CD-ROM, create the client-install disks by using the Other Options menu selection of the server-installation program. Format and label four high-density disks before you run this option, then simply follow the instructions.

If you are installing from disks, use the workstation-installation disks that came with the package (or make copies of them to use). You may decide to copy the installation-disk files into a directory on a NetWare server. Your existing client workstations can then attach to that server, map a drive to that directory, and run the workstation upgrade without using the floppy disks.

Figure 13.20 shows the initial screen of the client INSTALL program. The default setup is to copy the NetWare 4.0 client-shell files to a NWCLIENT directory on the C drive.

If you press **Y** in step 2, the CONFIG.SYS and AUTOEXEC.BAT files are saved with a BNW extension before the specified changes are made. The CONFIG.SYS file gets the line LASTDRIVE=Z added to it.

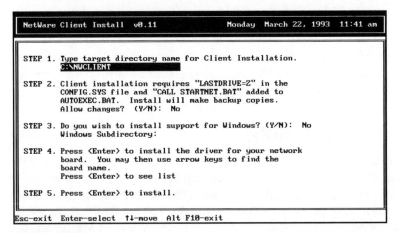

```
NetWare Client Install   v0.11              Monday  March 22, 1993  11:41 am

   STEP 1. Type target directory name for Client Installation.
           C:\NWCLIENT

   STEP 2. Client installation requires "LASTDRIVE=Z" in the
           CONFIG.SYS file and "CALL STARTNET.BAT" added to
           AUTOEXEC.BAT.  Install will make backup copies.
           Allow changes?  (Y/N):  No

   STEP 3. Do you wish to install support for Windows? (Y/N):  No
           Windows Subdirectory:

   STEP 4. Press <Enter> to install the driver for your network
           board.  You may then use arrow keys to find the
           board name.
           Press <Enter> to see list

   STEP 5. Press <Enter> to install.

Esc-exit  Enter-select  ↑↓-move  Alt F10-exit
```

Figure 13.20:

Default setup screen for DOS/Windows workstation installation.

The STARTNET.BAT file created by INSTALL contains instructions such as the following:

```
C:
CD \NWCLIENT
SET NWLANGUAGE=ENGLISH
LSL
NE2000.COM
IPXODI
VLM
CD\
```

If you press **Y** in step 3, you must specify a valid Windows directory. The NET.CFG file is updated, according to what you specify in step 4. The following shows the contents of a NET.CFG file:

```
LINK DRIVER NE2000
     PORT 300
     INT 3
     FRAME Ethernet_802.3
     MEM D0000
NetWare DOS Requester
     FIRST NETWORK DRIVE = F
```

If you want the NET.CFG files to have other information automatically added to them, edit the INSTALL.CFG file found on the installation disk. For example, add **PREFERRED TREE** and **NAME CONTEXT** lines to the INSTALL.CFG file, as follows:

```
[NETCFG]
     NetWare DOS Requester
     FIRST NETWORK DRIVE = F
     PREFERRED TREE = NOVELL_INC
     NAME CONTEXT = "OU= .O=NOVELL"
  .
  .
  .
```

The NetWare DOS Requester section of the NET.CFG file now contains the FIRST NETWORK DRIVE specification, the PREFERRED TREE specification, and the NAME CONTEXT specification. The NAME CONTEXT specification of the resulting NET.CFG files for given workstations still needs to be edited to specify the OU in which they are contained. You enter the **NAME CONTEXT** line in anticipation of updating many clients from the same network drive.

You are ready to install the client when the installation screen looks similar to that shown in figure 13.21.

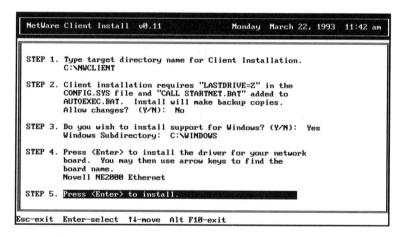

Figure 13.21:

Completed client-installation screen.

When you press Enter at step 5, the necessary files are copied and updated, as specified on the client workstation. The screen shown in figure 13.22 displays.

299

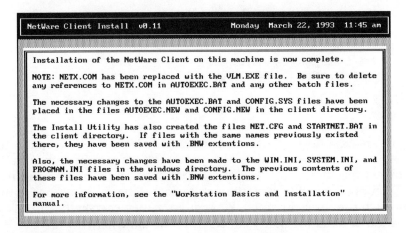

```
NetWare Client Install  v0.11                Monday  March 22, 1993  11:45 am

  Installation of the NetWare Client on this machine is now complete.

  NOTE: NETX.COM has been replaced with the VLM.EXE file.  Be sure to delete
  any references to NETX.COM in AUTOEXEC.BAT and any other batch files.

  The necessary changes to the AUTOEXEC.BAT and CONFIG.SYS files have been
  placed in the files AUTOEXEC.NEW and CONFIG.NEW in the client directory.

  The Install Utility has also created the files NET.CFG and STARTNET.BAT in
  the client directory.  If files with the same names previously existed
  there, they have been saved with .BNW extentions.

  Also, the necessary changes have been made to the WIN.INI, SYSTEM.INI, and
  PROGMAN.INI files in the windows directory.  The previous contents of
  these files have been saved with .BNW extentions.

  For more information, see the "Workstation Basics and Installation"
  manual.
```

Figure 13.22:

Final client-installation screen.

The next time the client boots and logs in, it uses VLMs and is a NetWare 4.0 client. Depending on the original content of the AUTOEXEC.BAT file, you may need to change the use of STARTNET.BAT so that the order of loading the DOS requester VLMs occurs properly.

Installing a Server from Another Server

With a 4.0 server up and running, you may want to install other NetWare servers by using your first server as the source for the operating system files. To do this, set up a workstation as a client of that server (you can create a client boot disk for this purpose by performing the client workstation installation process described previously).

Using the client boot disk, attach your intended server machine to the existing NetWare 4.0 server. Once attached, you can install the new server from the existing 4.0 server (the only disk you need, other than the boot disk, is the license disk for the new server).

Using Other Installation Options

Depending on the kinds of services and clients on the network, you can install other options on some of your servers. The following sections discuss some of these installations.

Macintosh, NFS, and SAA Installation

By purchasing additional NetWare products, you can enhance the functionality of your server. For example, you can install NetWare for Macintosh to make your server accessible to Macintosh client workstations. To enable UNIX clients to access the server's file system, you can install NetWare for NFS. Your server can be a link to the IBM SNA (Systems Network Architecture) environment with NetWare for SAA.

These products are implemented as NetWare Loadable Modules (NLMs), and each has its own installation procedure, which is performed from a workstation onto an existing NetWare server. Loading the service is typically done through the AUTOEXEC.NCF server boot file. Appropriate commands to load the NLMs that provide the given service are placed in the AUTOEXEC.NCF file. The service is loaded and made available automatically when the server is brought up.

TCP/IP Installation

You can install other communication protocols, in addition to the IPX/SPX protocol. For example, the TCP/IP protocol is included with your purchase of NetWare 4.0. It is implemented by using NLMs.

The TCP/IP protocol is actually installed and ready for loading when you have completed the NetWare server installation. To implement it, you must load it and bind it to a LAN driver. The following commands can be entered at the server console, resulting in TCP/IP being enabled:

```
LOAD NE2000
LOAD TCPIP
BIND IP TO NE2000
```

After you enter these commands, you are prompted for certain information that is necessary to initialize the LAN board and TCP/IP protocol.

Loading the LAN driver with LOAD NE2000 requires an interrupt, port, frame type, and name. BIND IP TO NE2000 requires an IP address and a name of a board being bound to, as specified when the LAN driver was loaded. The following commands do not prompt you for any parameters:

```
LOAD NE2000 INT=3 PORT=300 FRAME=ETHERNET_II NAME=IP_LAN
LOAD TCPIP
BIND IP TO IP_LAN ADDR=137.3.7.254
```

In the BIND command, ADDR is the IP address that is assigned to the NE2000 LAN board named IP_LAN. With this communication protocol loaded, other applications and products can be run on a NetWare LAN that uses the TCP/IP protocol.

Some examples include Novell's LAN workplace products, which enable DOS, OS/2, and Macintosh workstations to communicate by using TCP/IP. A NetWare server with TCP/IP can route packets to a TCP/IP network or send IPX packets through a TCP/IP network.

Upgrading 2.1x and 3.1x Servers to NetWare 4.0

The following three methods can be used to upgrade your 2.1x or 3.1x servers to NetWare 4.0:

- ❖ Across-the-wire upgrade
- ❖ In-place upgrade
- ❖ Same-server upgrade

The in-place and same-server upgrades do not require an additional server machine, but they may require a workstation. Upgrading across-the-wire requires an additional machine for the new server. The following steps should be taken, regardless of the method you use when upgrading:

- ❖ Install the operating system
- ❖ Migrate the file system
- ❖ Migrate bindery objects to Directory Services
- ❖ Upgrade print queues and job configurations
- ❖ Transfer login scripts
- ❖ Upgrade client workstations

An *across-the-wire upgrade* is the safest method of upgrading. This upgrade involves buying a new machine, installing NetWare 4.0 on it, and then copying and migrating information to it from the old server. It is not only safer but easier and faster to upgrade to a new machine instead of using the same machine. You can keep the original server machine up, running, and intact even after you install your new 4.0 server. If there is a problem with the upgrade, you can immediately go back to the original server machine. Even if your clients have been upgraded to NetWare 4.0, they can still access and log in to the old machine as needed. You can also copy your files over the LAN wire instead of using a backup and restore technique.

The *in-place upgrade* modifies the existing system without copying files. With this method, the operating system, Directory services, and file system are upgraded in place on the machine.

The *same-server upgrade* involves backing up the data files to tape, restoring them from tape onto a newly installed upgrade of the operating system, then migrating bindery information to Directory Services.

Regardless of the upgrade method being used (and whether you are upgrading from NetWare 2.x or 3.x), the operating system must be installed; and the files, directories, trustee assignments, bindery information, and login scripts must be migrated.

TIP

Think of an upgrade in three parts: the operating system upgrade (or installation), the file system information upgrade, and the bindery (Directory Services) information upgrade.

With an in-place upgrade, the three parts are combined into one process—everything is left in place and converted as needed. If you do not change the disk-block size, upgrade your server operating system by using the in-place method.

The sections that follow cover each of these methods in more detail. Before you upgrade, however, you must prepare for it. The next section covers this preparation process.

Preupgrade Preparation

The following processes should be complete before upgrading to NetWare 4.0:

- ❖ Verify the server name and addresses to be used
- ❖ Prepare the hardware
- ❖ Back up the server
- ❖ Communicate plans to managers and users
- ❖ Clean up the file system
- ❖ Consolidate bindery objects and login scripts

If your NetWare 4.0 installation planning includes specific naming and numbering conventions for network addresses, be sure to have the assigned server names and addresses. Familiarize yourself with the general plan, and become familiar with the Directory Services design that has been planned. This is also a good time to locate and have at hand your NetWare 4.0 server license disk.

The server must have 50M of disk space available on volume SYS: to hold the new 4.0 server files and data. If that space is not available, install new hardware, or move some data off of SYS:. There must be a minimum or 8M of RAM (more is better).

WARNING

When you back up the server, be sure that it is a good backup by restoring a file or two from the backup taken. This is very important when using a single machine—once the NetWare 4.0 operating system is installed, your pre-4.0 volumes and data are gone. The only way to retrieve that data is from a backup. Make a backup, even if you are upgrading to a new machine, because you will be deleting files, cleaning up the files and directories, and purging the deleted files later. If you make a mistake in that process, you can recover by restoring from the backup.

To ensure a smooth upgrade, print the contents of, or list, all the NCF files, users, groups, login scripts, applications, printers, FAX servers, and so on that are installed.

TIP

Before this process begins, you should communicate your plans and schedules to any individuals who will be affected by this upgrade. With large organizations, communicate plans at least five days in advance of the day of the upgrade.

You can also ask people to clean up their directories and files. Let them know what your plans are for purging and deleting files, and for consolidating or deleting directories so that they can notify you of any problems they may have with your plans. They can also take precautions and responsibility for their data. Any other changes should be explained to them prior to the upgrade.

As the backup is done just prior to the upgrade, it is also a good time to shape up the files and directories yourself. You may want to purge all deleted files and delete files that have not been accessed for 90 days or so.

One of the most important areas of concern is the consolidation of user accounts, which is done before the first server is upgraded. Subsequent server upgrades will not require as much effort.

If a user has accounts on multiple servers, a primary server should be selected for consolidating his login scripts. That server should be the first one upgraded because the login scripts of duplicate user names in subsequent upgrades do not overwrite the existing login script of that user.

Other properties, values, and assignments will be merged if possible, but login scripts are not merged. Having consolidated the login scripts for a user from all servers, edit them by eliminating any duplications (such as multiple attachments to a server).

The system login script of the first server installed at a given context is used as the container login script at that context.

You may want to delete accounts, queues, or groups from the bindery that are not in use any more. Because Directory Services requires unique names for objects within a given context, you may need to rename some objects. If a server has the name MIKE and there is a user named MIKE, one of those names needs to be changed. Some companies use electronic mail names to ensure uniqueness.

Once the bindery has been prepared, you should run BINDFIX before the upgrade. (BINDFIX cleans up associations between objects' properties and values in the bindery.) Just prior to the upgrade, you may elect to take another backup to avoid repeating your cleanup if something goes wrong during the installation.

TIP

You may not be concerned with all these issues. It is a good idea to take these suggestions and make a checkoff sheet, adding others as appropriate for your site. With these preliminary steps taken care of, proceed with the server installation.

In-Place Upgrades

In-place upgrades are performed differently for NetWare 2.1x servers than for NetWare 3.1x servers. NetWare 2.1x is upgraded in-place by using an UPGRADE disk. On that disk is a copy of a NetWare 3.11 server operating system and a special upgrade NLM (2XUPGRDE.NLM). After upgrading from 2.1x, the NetWare 3.1x server is upgraded in-place by using the upgrade option of the NetWare 4.0 installation program.

WARNING

If you have a 286 machine, you cannot run 3.x or 4.x versions of the NetWare operating system on it.

In this discussion, references to 2.1x NetWare includes 2.1x, 2.2, and 3.0x because these versions of NetWare cannot be upgraded directly to NetWare 4.0 by using the in-place method. Therefore, if you choose the in-place method, and you have a NetWare 2.1x, 2.2, or 3.0x server, you need to perform two in-place upgrades to make your machine a NetWare 4.0 server. Figure 13.23 shows the migration process flow for an in-place upgrade from NetWare 2.1x to 4.0.

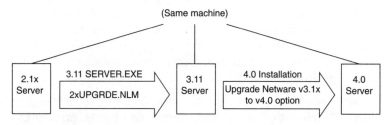

Figure 13.23:

The flow of the in-place upgrade process.

To perform a 2.1x upgrade, you must use the 3.11 operating system (SERVER.EXE) and a special upgrade NLM (2XUPGRDE.NLM), which comes with NetWare 4.0. You can perform this upgrade from CD-ROM or from floppy disks.

To create the floppies from CD-ROM, run a batch file (MAKEDISK.BAT) that is found on your CD-ROM in a directory named \CLIENT\UPGRADE. Two disks are created: a bootable system disk (used for the 2.1x upgrade) and a disk for migrations that use methods other than the in-place method. The 2.1x upgrade files on the disk you create can also be found on the CD-ROM in the \CLIENT_____\UPGRADE subdirectory.

The steps in the 2.1x in-place upgrade are listed here. It is assumed that you are upgrading by using the UPGRADE floppy disk (created by using MAKEDISK.BAT) and that the disk is in the A drive:

1. Back up your 2.1x server.

2. Make sure that 10% of your disk space is free (3.11 takes more disk space). It is recommended that a 5M DOS partition also be created on the hard drive. It is also recommended that you have 12M of RAM to run the upgrade program.

3. Load the 3.11 operating system with NetWare 3.11-compatible versions of the LAN and disk drivers (once the machine has been booted with DOS) by typing A:\SERVER.EXE.

4. Load the 2.1x upgrade NLM (at the server console, type **LOAD A:\2XUPGRDE.NLM**).

5. Complete the upgrade by carefully following instructions.

In completing the upgrade, the 2XUPGRDE NLM analyzes the disk and converts it to 3.11. It then converts the 2.1x bindery to a 3.11 bindery.

TIP

These steps discuss the major parts of the installation. An experienced NetWare installer should be able to perform them with little or no instructions. For less-experienced installers, there is plenty of help for this installation process in the NetWare installation manual.

Once the server has been upgraded to a NetWare 3.11 server, the in-place upgrade is similar to a new NetWare 4.0 server installation. Run the same INSTALL.EXE program that is described in the instructions for installing a new NetWare 4.0 server. Figure 13.24 shows the opening screen of this program.

Figure 13.24:

Initial in-place 3.1x to 4.0 upgrade screen.

Select the Upgrade NetWare v3.1x to v4.0 option and proceed. The differences between this upgrade and a new installation of NetWare 4.0 are few. Watch for the following during this in-place upgrade:

1. Before starting the upgrade, copy the existing NetWare operating system startup files to another directory to keep them from getting written over.

2. Be sure to specify a frame type for your LAN drivers in the new AUTOEXEC.NCF file.

3. Examine closely and execute the new AUTOEXEC.NCF file when prompted.

Same-Server Upgrades

A 2.x server can be upgraded directly to NetWare 4.0 by using the same-server upgrade method. A NetWare 3.1x server can be upgraded to 4.0 by using the in-place upgrade method or the same-server method.

Figure 13.25 shows the process and the steps of upgrading by using the same-server method.

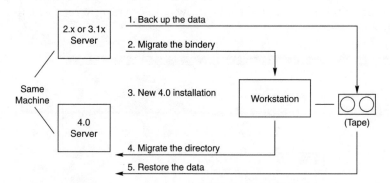

Figure 13.25:

Same-server upgrade process.

The data backup and restore steps can be done by using any third-party backup utility. It is a good idea to restore a file or two from the backup to make sure that you have a good backup. Once NetWare 4.0 is installed on the machine, the only copy of your data is on the backup you took.

Once the backup is taken, you then migrate the bindery to a hard disk on a workstation. The migration program (MIGRATE.EXE) is found on the migration disk you created using MAKEDISK.BAT. MIGRATE.EXE can also be found on the CD-ROM in the \CLIENT_____\MIGRATION subdirectory.

The migration program is run from a workstation that is attached to the 2.x or 3.x server being upgraded. It reads the bindery of that server, and copies the information onto its local drive. Once the target NetWare 4.0 server is installed, the migration utility adds the previously collected bindery information into the Directory Services database.

The opening screen of the MIGRATE program is shown in figure 13.26. For this type of upgrade, select the Custom migration option.

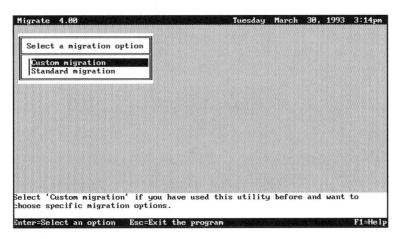

Figure 13.26:

Same-server migration beginning screen.

The MIGRATE program is also used for across-the-wire upgrades. Select the Same-Server migration option, as shown in figure 13.27.

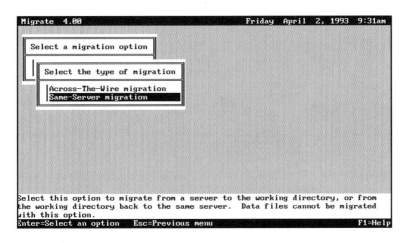

Figure 13.27:

Same-server migration option selection.

To migrate the bindery from the server, specify the Migrate to the Working Directory option. Once the bindery has been migrated to a workstation hard drive (the working directory), install NetWare 4.0 on the machine. This is done the same way a new installation is done. Be sure to follow the steps necessary to make the workstation you have been using into a NetWare 4.0 client.

With the NetWare 4.0 operating system installed on your machine, you again use the MIGRATE program (be sure you have logged in to the server as a NetWare 4.0 client before running it). You are migrating the Directory Services data stored on the workstation hard drive (working directory) to the newly installed 4.0 server machine.

Follow the migration program instructions, restore your data from the tape backup, and the installation is complete.

Across-the-Wire Upgrades

Across-the-wire upgrades are similar to same-server upgrades. You use the same MIGRATE.EXE program and the same NetWare 4.0 installation program. You also need a workstation for similar purposes. One difference, however, is that you install NetWare 4.0 before you run the migration program.

Although a backup should be taken, it is not critical because you will not be destroying the data or bindery on the original server machine (across-the-wire upgrades go from one machine directly to another). Figure 13.28 shows the upgrade process.

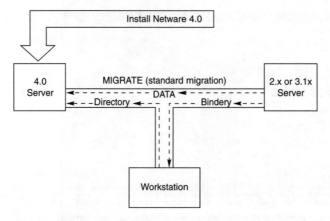

Figure 13.28:

Across-the-wire upgrade process.

You must be attached to both servers before running the migration utility, and your workstation must be running the 4.0 workstation software (VLMs). Figure 13.29 shows the screen you see after choosing the Standard migration option of the migration utility. From there, follow the prompts and instructions, and your upgrade is completed.

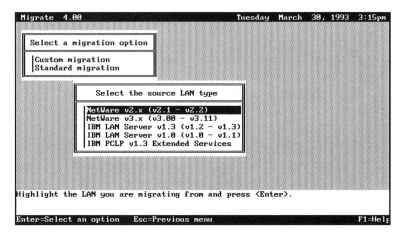

Figure 13.29:

Standard across-the-wire migration.

You can also select the Custom migration option, and choose the Across-The-Wire migration option, as shown in figure 13.30.

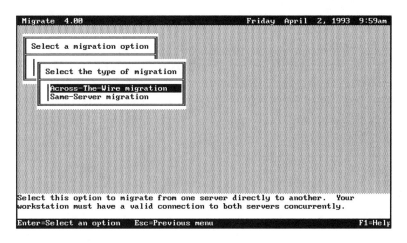

Figure 13.30:

Custom across-the-wire migration.

TIP

The *custom across-the-wire migration* is only used if you return to the upgrade for some reason. If you previously upgraded your server by using the standard method, and you need to repeat all or part of the migration, use this custom option.

Network Migration Considerations

Installing one NetWare 4.0 server does not necessarily complete your network upgrade or installation. Total network migration also involves upgrading clients, printers, and other servers. Plan your progress carefully because of the effect of each server upgrade on network clients.

Having installed or upgraded your NetWare 4.0 server, make sure that login scripts and applications are functioning properly. You may need to modify login scripts, adjust Directory Services privileges, or adjust file-system privileges if applications are not functioning normally.

Look at the network upgrade from a user's point of view. If a user accesses data and/or applications on more than one server, but you only upgrade one of those servers to NetWare 4.0, the user's tasks will be affected. If a user's name needs to be changed to establish uniqueness in the Directory, that user's accounts on other servers will be affected. (Specifying which server the user should log in to, and adjusting the user login script for that user on that server resolves these problems.)

Printers can be upgraded by using PUPGRADE, which is a relatively simple process. You may need to adjust login scripts, however, because of printer or queue name changes resulting from bindery migration to the Directory.

The sequence of server upgrades is another consideration. (Chapter 14 discusses this topic in more detail.) The decision about the order in which to upgrade servers is based on which users and groups use the servers, and where you are going to store replicas of the Directory.

You must also decide which servers connect to dissimilar networks requiring special NLMs, and what kind of impact upgrading those servers will have.

Having considered these issues prior to upgrading, your installation should go smoothly.

Summary

This chapter gave you a step-by-step introduction to the installation of NetWare 4.0. If you experience difficulty during the installation, you can start over without worry. The suggested points for backing up the system provide you with the ability to recover from any problem. You learned ways to install a single 4.0 server, to install workstations, and to install a server from another server.

Methods for upgrading NetWare 2.1x and 3.1x servers to 4.0 were covered. These methods include across-the-wire, in-place, and same-server upgrades.

The next chapter deals with managing and maintaining the network after the installation.

Managing NetWare 4.0 for NetWare Administrators

The addition of NetWare Directory Services (NDS) changes the scope and philosophy of managing a NetWare network. Under previous versions of NetWare, managing the network essentially involved managing the bindery database on NetWare servers.

The bindery contained information on user accounts, printers, queues, and other objects that were either resources based on that server or objects that had access to resources based on that server. Under NetWare 4.0, the paradigm shifts to managing a directory database that holds objects of interest to the entire network—that is, objects recognized by all servers and workstations connected in the network.

Another interesting aspect of network administration under NetWare 4.0 is the addition of new Graphical User Interface (GUI) tools that make network administration simpler.

Although NDS changes much about the administration of networks, other aspects continue to be the same or are changed very little under 4.0. For example, file system and printing administration is similar to that under previous versions of NetWare. NetWare Loadable Modules (NLMs) operate the same, but new capabilities are available that can be utilized by new NLMs.

Some standard NetWare utilities have been replaced or changed, including command-line utilities and menu utilities. The utilities that pertain to managing the network are discussed in detail in this chapter.

The first part of this chapter introduces the tools available for managing a NetWare 4.0 network. Ways to use these tools, what they look like, and what they can be used for are discussed.

This chapter also discusses management concerns that NetWare administrators face, and offers some suggestions on how to deal with those concerns.

Using NetWare Management Tools

NetWare 4.0 introduces new utilities to help administrators better manage their networks. Network-administration programs were developed as menu utilities and as GUI utilities so that administrators can use either or both, depending on their preference and need.

The management tools provided with NetWare 4.0 probably are the only tools you need to manage your network.

NetWare Administrator

Often referred to as the NetWare Administrator, the NWADMIN.EXE program is a GUI utility that runs under Microsoft Windows. It includes almost every capability you need for managing the network. This section covers some of the things you can do with this utility, but it is not intended to be comprehensive in scope.

Figure 14.1 shows the main screen of the NetWare Administrator. The execution of this utility is based largely on the *browser*, which presents a view of the network directory tree for you to work with. As shown in the figure, the NetWare Administrator utility starts with one browser window opened. In this figure, the browser is browsing the tree, beginning at the O=Novell object context.

Multiple browser windows can be open at the same time so that you can move from one context of the tree to another by making the desired browser window your active window.

Some of the objects in the tree are *container objects*; others are *leaf objects*. It is important to differentiate between the two because you can do things with container objects that cannot be done with leaf objects. The Novell object, for example, is a container object and other objects can be added under it in the tree. Admin is a leaf object, which cannot have objects added under it.

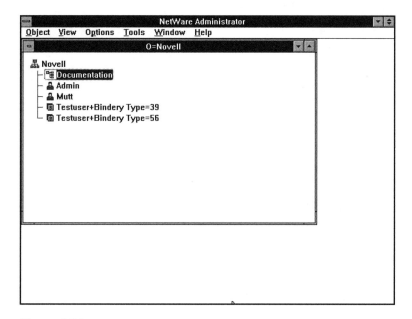

Figure 14.1:

The NetWare Administrator utility main screen.

With at least one browser window open, you can see the objects in the specified portion of the directory tree. Figure 14.2 shows the type of objects you can add. The New Object window was activated from the initial screen (see fig. 14.1) after selecting the Documentation container, then pressing the Insert key. The Documentation container was selected by double-clicking it with the left mouse button.

All printer objects necessary for printing on a NetWare 4.0 network can be set up by using this utility. You can still use the PCONSOLE menu utility to perform printer setup if you want, but you can set up all print queues, printers, and servers for printing in the NetWare Administrator.

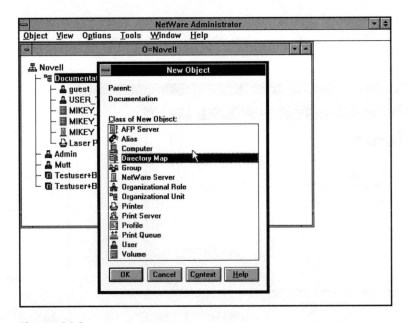

Figure 14.2:

Adding a new object with the NetWare Administrator.

In the New Object window shown in figure 14.2, the Directory Map object type is highlighted. Most of the other objects in the window should be familiar to you. The Directory Map object is noted here because an object of this type can be used to make network administration easier.

A *Directory Map* object is an object that defines a path. The path can be anywhere on the network. You can use a Directory Map object named Apps, for example, to designate the directory in which applications are stored. A user who wants to map a drive to that directory can use the following command in a login script or from the command line:

```
MAP S3:=Apps
```

The APPS (Directory Map) object can be referencing server MIKEY, the SYS: volume, the DATABASE directory, or the APPS subdirectory. The normal map command is as follows:

```
MAP S3:=MIKEY/SYS:DATABASE\APPS
```

You can see that it is easier to remember and enter the first command. An administrator easily can install an upgrade to the database applications into MIKEY/SYS:DATABASE\APPS1 without deleting the original applications and directory. This can be desirable because the original version of the application has been running, and is known to be functional. If the update turns out to have bugs or problems, the administrator can revert to the original version without needing to reinstall it—it is still in the SYS:DATABASE\APPS directory.

If you are using a Directory Map object, you easily can switch from using the APPS subdirectory to the APPS1 subdirectory. Users do not need to know the name of the new directory or even to be aware of the change. The administrator simply needs to change the directory reference found in the Apps object from the APPS subdirectory to the APPS1 subdirectory. After this is done, the MAP S3:=Apps command maps the third search drive to MIKEY/SYS:DATABASE\APPS1 instead of mapping it to MIKEY/SYS:DATABASE\APPS. Login scripts and command-line parameters remain the same.

Each object in the tree can be manipulated from within the browser window. Figure 14.3 shows the user guest being updated. The pages of information listed on the right of the edit window can be selected, and the information can be edited.

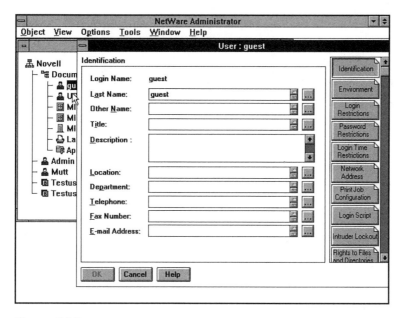

Figure 14.3:
Managing a user object.

In addition to the pages shown in figure 14.3 (Identification, Environment, Login Restrictions, and so on), the following pages also are part of the editable user information:

- ❖ Group Membership

- ❖ Security Equivalences

- ❖ Postal Address

- ❖ Account Balance

- ❖ See Also

For the most part, each page represents a property of the object, and the information found therein is the value of that property. The page information is stored in the Directory Information Base (DIB).

If you highlight a volume object (see fig. 14.4) and press Ins, you are given the option of creating a new directory on the volume.

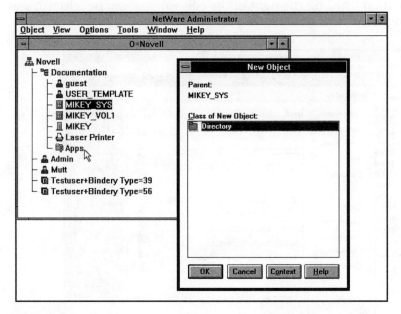

Figure 14.4:

Adding a file system directory to a volume.

The resulting directory is added to the file system (not the NDS Directory Information Base), but it is displayed as subordinate to the volume when using the browser. To view the file-system structure of a given volume, double-click on the volume object (for example, MIKEY_SYS) by using the left mouse button. Figure 14.5 shows a file whose identification information is being viewed.

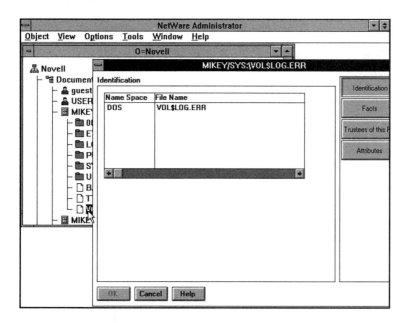

Figure 14.5:
Viewing a file's information.

Double-clicking on the object named MIKEY_SYS expands the browsed view of that object to show the directories and files found on that volume. Next, double-clicking on the file named VOL$LOG.ERR brings up the window titled MIKEY/SYS:\VOL$LOG.ERR. Notice the reference to the true volume name (SYS:) on the server named MIKEY, as opposed to the object name (MIKEY_SYS) of the volume.

So far, you have seen the use of the left mouse button to select objects on which you want to work. Figure 14.6 shows the options available if you select an object by using the left mouse button, and then pressing the right mouse button. If an option is dimmed, that option does not apply to the object you selected.

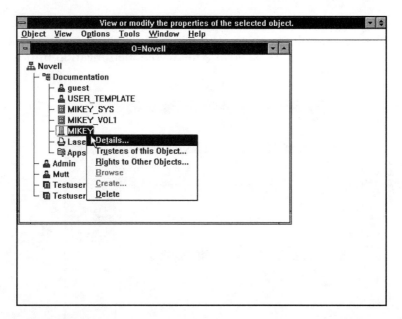

Figure 14.6:

Pressing the left, then right mouse button, gives you quick access to an object's information.

The **B**rowse and **C**reate options do not apply to the MIKEY object because it is a NetWare server. NetWare servers are leaf objects, so nothing is under them to be browsed, and nothing can be created under them.

TIP

When working with objects subordinate to a volume object, browsing, creating, deleting, and so on are performed on the file system, not on information found in the directory itself. This implementation of browsing the file system is added to the NetWare Administrator browser for convenience.

Selecting the De**t**ails option, shown in figure 14.6, is the same as double-clicking on the object itself. Figure 14.7 shows the types of information available for changing and managing a NetWare server object.

The pages of information for a server are not the same as those for a user (see fig. 14.3). Each object type has different information that can be managed.

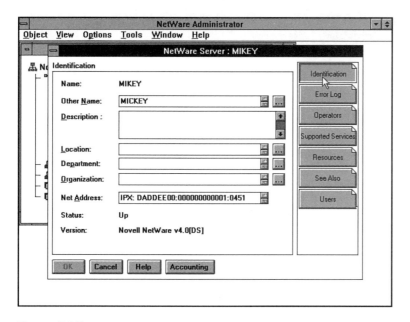

Figure 14.7:

Managing a NetWare server object.

The browser function of the NetWare Administrator is perhaps the key function of this utility. Other functions are built in to the NetWare Administrator that work with the browser (or browsers) you invoke. The Object pull-down menu, shown in figure 14.8, lists the options available for the object you currently are managing.

Some of these options are the same as those shown in the quick-access method (see fig. 14.6). The dimmed options differ, depending on your privileges to the object with which you are working and on the type of object it is.

The View menu has three global settings and two object-applied options. The Show Hints option (checked) instructs the NetWare Administrator to display explanations at the top of the screen. Figure 14.9 shows the option-sensitive description (for example, `Display the View menu`) for the View menu. As the cursor is moved to other options or menus, a descriptive message displays that gives a "hint" about the purpose of that option or menu.

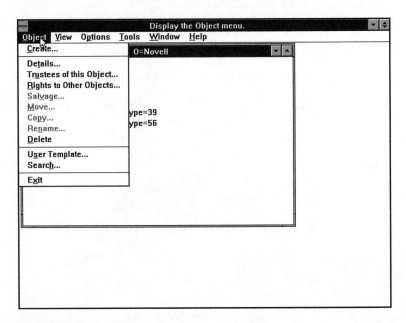

Figure 14.8:

The Object pull-down menu of the NetWare Administrator.

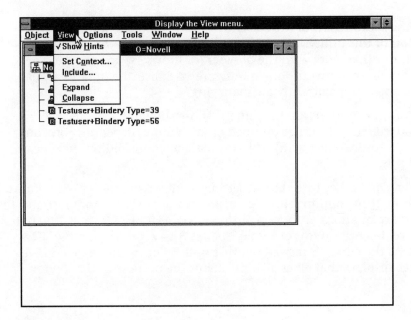

Figure 14.9:

The View menu of the NetWare administration.

The Set Context item applies globally in this utility. The Include item is used to specify the types of objects to include when browsing. If you want to browse only for servers, you can specify this by using the Include menu item.

The other two options of this menu are used to expand or collapse the contents of a container object, volume, or directory for viewing.

The Options menu enables you to designate whether to confirm each deletion when it occurs. It also enables you to select the preferred name space for your file access (DOS, Macintosh, NFS, and so on). The Window and Help menus offer the standard Microsoft Windows functionality.

The Tools menu offers some significant tools for managing your network. If you want to open additional browse windows or operate a remote console for a NetWare server, you can use this menu (see fig. 14.10).

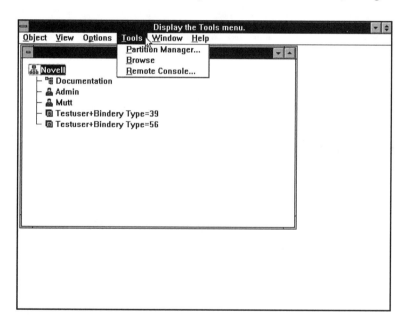

Figure 14.10:

The NetWare Administrator Tools menu.

To perform partition management, select Partition Management from the Tools menu. Figure 14.11 shows the partition-management screen for a small directory tree. The only object that can be selected for creating a new partition is the Documentation container object. As you can see, the partition manager is used to split (create), join (merge), replicate, and view the partitions residing on a server; or to delete servers from a partition.

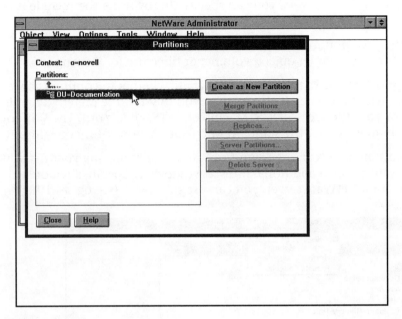

Figure 14.11:
NetWare Administrator Partitions window.

TIP
Use the Partition Manager to delete servers from the tree to avoid deleting servers that hold the only copy of a given partition.

As you have seen, the NetWare Administrator can be used to do the following things:

❖ Add and delete objects from the tree

❖ Manage users

❖ Manage volumes, directories, and files

❖ Manage servers

❖ Manage partitions

❖ Operate remote server consoles

The same tasks can be done from the command line or from text-based menus by using different utilities.

Menu Utilities

The menu utilities are run from the DOS prompt, and can be used to perform network-management functions. If the network manager needs to perform management functions from different locations or workstations on the network, some of those workstations can be running Windows and some can be running DOS.

NETADMIN

The NETADMIN menu utility can perform many of the administrative functions of the NetWare Administrator. Type **NETADMIN** at the DOS prompt, and the initial screen of the NETADMIN.EXE menu utility, as shown in figure 14.12, appears.

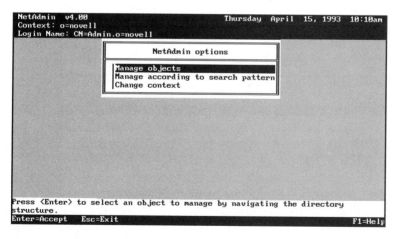

Figure 14.12:
The NETADMIN main menu.

The Manage objects option enables you to manage the directory objects. File-system directories and files are not managed with this utility; they are managed by using FILER. Partitions are managed by using PARTMGR; remote-console access is accomplished by using RCONSOLE; and printer setup and management are done by using PCONSOLE. NETADMIN, FILER, PARTMGR, RCONSOLE, and PCONSOLE, which provide the same capabilities as the NetWare Administrator GUI utility does.

The Manage according to search pattern option enables you to select the type of objects to view and manage. This option is similar to the Include option of the View menu in the NetWare Administrator utility.

The Change context option is self-explanatory. You find the last two options of this main menu in other menus within this utility.

If you select the Manage objects option of the main menu, all objects in your current context are displayed. Note in figure 14.13 the similarity of objects to those shown in figure 14.1.

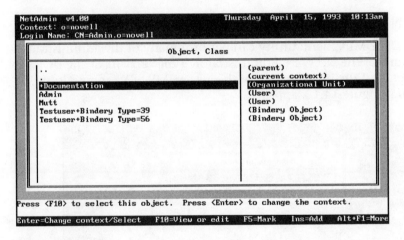

Figure 14.13:
NETADMIN object management.

When you select an organizational unit (such as Documentation), and press Enter, your context is changed, and the objects in the new context are presented. Compare the objects listed in figure 14.14 with those shown in figure 14.4 under the Documentation container.

If you press Insert to add an object, you see the list of objects shown in figure 14.15. Compare this list with the one shown in figure 14.2.

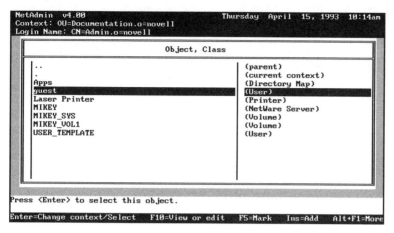

Figure 14.14:

NETADMIN leaf-object management.

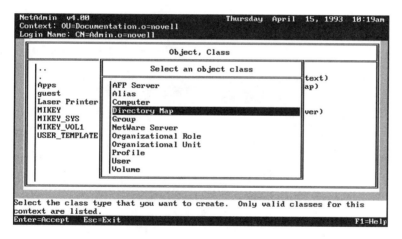

Figure 14.15:

Adding an object by using NETADMIN.

To continue the comparison of NETADMIN with the NetWare Administrator, if you select a user object (such as guest), you are presented with the options shown in figure 14.16.

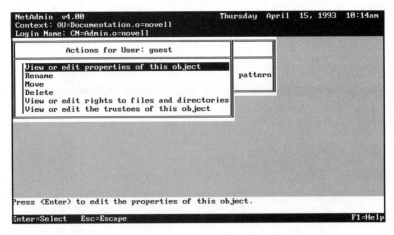

Figure 14.16:

Managing a user object by using NETADMIN.

The View or edit properties of this object item gives you the option of performing the same updates to the object as with the information pages of the NetWare Administrator. Compare figure 14.17 with figure 14.3.

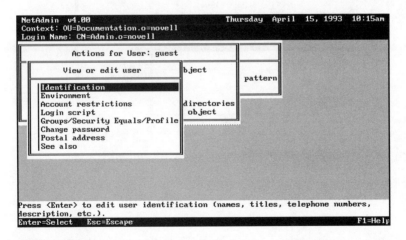

Figure 14.17:

Managing a user's properties by using NETADMIN.

Although the options are not all in the same order, and are sometimes grouped differently, both NETADMIN and the NetWare Administrator can be used to perform the same functions on a user object.

If you select a volume object instead of a user object from the list found in figure 14.14, the options listed in figure 14.18 appear.

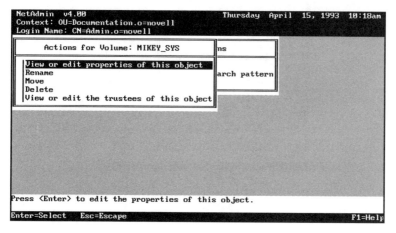

Figure 14.18:

Managing a volume object by using NETADMIN.

Volume objects do not have rights to files and directories. Therefore, the option to view or edit them is missing from the menu.

A user's file-system trustee assignments and other limited file-system functions can be performed within the NETADMIN utility. If you are using menu utilities, most of the file-system management and administration functions must be done by using the FILER utility.

FILER

Figure 14.19 shows the FILER utility main menu screen. This utility can perform all file-management functions, including moving and copying files, granting and restricting access to files, setting volume limits, salvaging and deleting files, and so on.

The Manage files and directories menu item can do most, if not all, file-management functions you need to perform. Figure 14.20 shows the directory contents that are presented when this menu item is selected.

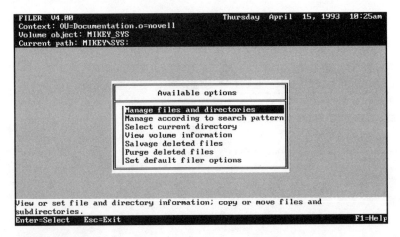

Figure 14.19:

The FILER main menu.

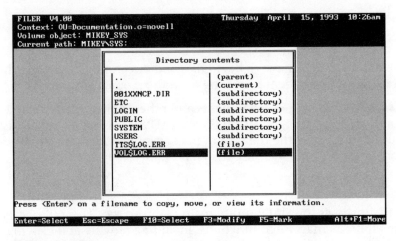

Figure 14.20:

File management using FILER.

The function of managing files in this manner is included as part of the
NetWare Administrator GUI utility (see figure 14.5).

PARTMGR

Partition management is accomplished with the PARTMGR menu utility.
When PARTMGR is executed from the DOS prompt (command line), the
menu shown in figure 14.21 appears.

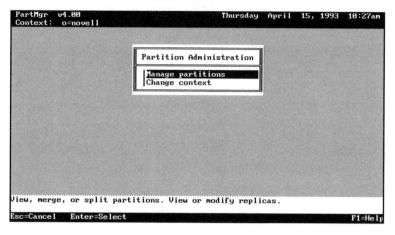

```
PartMgr  v4.00                          Thursday  April  15, 1993  10:27am
Context:  o=novell
```

Partition Administration

Manage partitions
Change context

View, merge, or split partitions. View or modify replicas.

Esc=Cancel   Enter=Select   F1=Help

Figure 14.21:

PARTMGR main menu.

The operation of this utility is fairly straightforward: PARTMGR performs the same functions as the partition manager within the NetWare Administrator utility.

RCONSOLE

Network managers often find it valuable to be able to operate a NetWare server console without going to the NetWare server console itself. Remote-console operation is possible through the use of the RCONSOLE.EXE program or from within the NetWare Administrator utility described earlier.

Whether you are using the NetWare Administrator or RCONSOLE, the NetWare server being remotely accessed must have the RSPX NLM loaded. Without RSPX loaded at the server, no remote-console access or operation can be performed.

PCONSOLE and Printer Utilities

The PCONSOLE utility is used to set up printer, queue, and print-server objects in the directory. Part of that setup includes configuring these objects with each other. Print servers must be assigned queues to service and printers to use.

The network managers must not only set up the objects for printing; they must also install the printers and print servers. (Print servers are NetWare servers running the PSERVER NLM.) Printers for network use must be connected to a workstation or NetWare server running NPRINTER.EXE or NPRINTER.NLM, respectively.

The utilities for setting up printing (PCONSOLE, PRINTDEF, and PRINTCON) remain the same as in previous versions of NetWare, with one significant addition. With the introduction of NDS and directory objects comes the designation of printers as objects.

Under previous versions of NetWare, you designated a queue (for collecting print jobs to be printed) and a print server (for getting print jobs out of the print queues and sending them to a printer). Configuring print servers to service certain print queues and send print jobs to certain printers was necessary and possible. The users needed to route their print jobs to a specific print queue. If the print server that serviced that queue was configured to send print jobs for a given queue to any one of many printers, the user was never certain on which printer the print job would be printed.

With the new print utilities, a user can designate the printer to which a print job goes, and is guaranteed that it will print on that printer. Any one of a number of queues can be used, and the user does not necessarily know which one is being used.

A print job still can be sent to a print queue, but the possibility of that job being printed on one of many printers still exists.

Upgrading print queues and services to NetWare 4.0 is relatively straightforward with the PUPGRADE utility that comes with the NetWare 4.0 installation programs.

The menu and command-line utilities for printing were changed to allow for the designation of a specific destination printer. Additionally, they have been changed to deal with NDS when searching for queues, printers, and print-server objects.

Command-Line Utilities

Some commands and management functions can be more quickly completed directly from the command line without using a menu or GUI utility. This section explains just a few of the new or changed command-line utilities.

CX

The CX utility is similar in function to CD (change directory), but CX is used to change a directory context rather than to change to a different directory.

Sometimes, you want to change the context without performing any other management functions. It is not necessary for you to go into a menu or graphical utility to do so.

All of NetWare's new command-line utilities have help messages. To invoke the help screen from the command line, type /?, along with the command. For example, CX /? entered at the DOS prompt presents the information shown in figure 14.22.

```
CX                          Options Help                              v4.00

Syntax:   CX [new context] [/R] [/[T : CONT] [/ALL]] [/C] [/?]

To:                                          Use:
   view all container objects below the        /T
   current or specified context.

   view container objects at the current       /CONT
   or specified level.

   modify /T or /CONT to view ALL objects      /ALL
   at or below the context

   change context or view objects relative     /R
   to root

For example, to:                             Type:
   view directory tree below the current context   CX /T
   view containers within a specific context       CX .O=Novell /CONT

>>> Enter = More    C = Continuous    Esc = Cancel
```

Figure 14.22:

The CX initial help screen.

You can use this command to change your context to any location in the directory tree.

NLIST

The NLIST command-line utility now combines the functionality of some previous utilities (SLIST and USERLIST) with many options for finding and viewing objects in the directory tree. Not only can you display objects themselves, but you also can search for and display properties and values of objects.

RIGHTS

The RIGHTS utility combines the functions of TLIST (for listing trustees); and REVOKE, GRANT, REMOVE, and ALLOW (for establishing and restricting file system access privileges).

NDIR

The NDIR utility now includes the functionality of the VERSION, CHKVOL, CHKDIR, and LISTDIR utilities. It lists directories and files, and gives information about them. It also now gives volume and version information.

TIP

If a command-line utility that was eliminated is run by a user, a message appears, telling the user which utility to use instead. For example, if VERSION is run, the following message displays:

```
This utility is no longer supported with v4.0.
Use NDIR [path] /Ver
```

Management NLMs

A few utilities are run at the NetWare server itself. These are in the form of NLMs, but they can be loaded and run by using remote-console capabilities.

SERVMAN

You can load the Server Manager NLM from the NetWare server console by typing LOAD SERVMAN. It is used mainly for information purposes, but it also is valuable for setting up server options and IPX/SPX communication configurations. Figure 14.23 shows the main screen of this utility.

One valuable thing about this utility is that it stores the changes you make. This is good for two reasons: your changes are still in effect after you restart the server, and you do not need to modify the AUTOEXEC.NCF and STARTUP.NCF files manually. The Server Manager utility updates those files for you.

The Console Set Commands option can be used to establish server-configuration settings for packet sizes, watchdog limits, memory handling and usage, file-system limits, error-handling procedures, and so on.

The IPX/SPX Configuration option sets the maximum number of IPX sockets possible, the SPX retry and watchdog limits, and the router and service advertising limits.

The other options are for visual checking and monitoring of storage, volume, and network information.

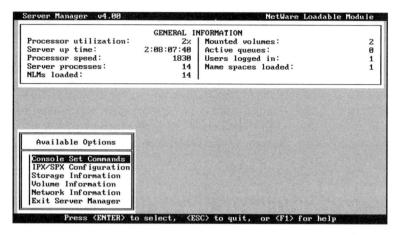

```
Server Manager  v4.00                    NetWare Loadable Module
                        GENERAL INFORMATION
    Processor utilization:        2%   Mounted volumes:          2
    Server up time:          2:08:07:40 Active queues:           0
    Processor speed:            1830    Users logged in:          1
    Server processes:             14    Name spaces loaded:       1
    NLMs loaded:                  14




        Available Options
      Console Set Commands
      IPX/SPX Configuration
      Storage Information
      Volume Information
      Network Information
      Exit Server Manager

        Press <ENTER> to select,  <ESC> to quit,  or <F1> for help
```

Figure 14.23:

The Server Manager console utility.

DSREPAIR

If the directory tree is corrupted or is not functioning properly, the DSREPAIR utility can fix it. The DSREPAIR NLM is an almost totally automated utility that cleans up and repairs any problems with the directory tree.

This utility is run from the NetWare server console by using the LOAD DSREPAIR command. You must first select the execution options, then have DSREPAIR perform the repair.

You can specify that DSREPAIR pause and wait for your response for each error encountered in the directory. You can specify a file for recording all errors. You can check for consistency of replicas, or check only the master replicas. You can check for valid mail directories, trustee IDs, and stream files.

TIP

A *stream file* is separate from the directory information base files, and holds information that is specific to a property of a given object in the directory.

After you have specified the options desired, select the option from the main selection menu to perform the repair.

WARNING

The use of DSREPAIR requires a highly skilled administrator; it should not be used by the novice. The documentation that accompanies DSREPAIR with NetWare 4.0 does not adequately explain its features and uses. Make a backup copy of the NDS partition before you attempt to run DSREPAIR on it.

Understanding Administrative Functions

These new and updated utilities make it easier and more convenient to manage a network. The tools for managing, however, cannot replace or provide the value of good practices and theory of implementation. The best network managers plan their networks well, use good sense, and follow well-thought-out practices of network management.

This section introduces some areas that are worth analyzing. No two networks are alike, and no two organizations are the same. For that reason, this is a general discussion. The best solutions and practices come from analyses of specific installations.

Partition Management

Managing partitions begins with the planning of your directory tree and installation of servers. After the network is up and running, an adequate number of replicas of each partition of the tree should be available to ensure reliable operation of the network. You might want to keep a hard-copy list that shows which replicas are stored on which servers.

As use and operation of your new network proceeds, note the differences in response time. Users are aware of this, and can be asked to make comments on the system performance for the first few days after the upgrade. As the manager, you then can compare trends in performance change with partition configuration to determine whether replicas of partitions should be moved to other servers.

TIP

A general rule-of-thumb is to store a partition (and replicas) on servers used by objects in that partition. If possible, replicas should be stored on servers that are physically distant from one another. If separate power supplies are in place, it is a good idea to store replicas on servers that are connected to different power supplies.

As new servers are installed, the analyses of replica needs should be straightforward. Even for very large networks, replica distribution can be logical and easy to manage.

Object Management

The job of network management is that of managing change. When an employee changes jobs, a department moves and takes its printers and servers to a different location, or any other change in the organization occurs, it becomes the network manager's responsibility to perform needed adjustments. Partitions might need to be changed or replicas relocated. Objects such as printers and users might need to be moved from one portion of the tree to another.

Although using the utilities already discussed makes initiation of these changes rather easy, a network manager must be careful about timing. Because the directory information base is a distributed database, the updates made to it are not immediately in place network-wide. Sometimes it takes time for the replicas stored throughout the network to synchronize or receive the updates submitted.

For example, suppose that user ONE and printer LASER have been moved from OU=Engineering to OU=Marketing in the directory tree. Assume that OU=Engineering is in a partition that has four replicas; OU=Marketing is in a separate partition that has three replicas. When the move is made, the master replicas of the two partitions are updated almost immediately.

Depending on how often partition synchronization is scheduled to take place, it may take awhile for all replicas to receive the update. All replicas must be updated before the update can be considered complete. If some updates are over a WAN, or if one of the servers involved is temporarily down, the impact of these situations must be considered. Before attempting to log the user in or use the printer involved, the update should be complete.

TIP

You cannot move an object a second time until the first move is synchronized on all replicas.

Even when the directory partitions are synchronized for that update, the question of security access remains. If a user changes departments, it can be necessary to grant and/or revoke certain directory and file-system access privileges for that user.

Directory Security

You can assign access privileges to and for objects within the directory in two ways. The first is through *inheritance*, based on the directory-tree structure. The second is through *direct assignments* to specific objects. In the case of direct assignments, certain objects can assume the privileges of other objects because of group membership or security equivalence.

Actually making access assignments is not difficult. It can be done through the use of the utilities already discussed. Any object in the directory tree can be given directory-access privileges to any other object. The user attempting to make the access-control change must be logged in as a user object with access-control privileges for the object to which access will be granted or revoked.

If your approach to implementing access security is not sufficiently straightforward, it can be difficult to manage changes when they are necessary. Limit privileges that are inherited. Critical access privileges should be assigned directly and specifically. The use of groups and security equivalences should be logical.

TIP

As you plan, install, and manage the directory, the access privileges discussed here grant access to other objects in the directory. Under previous versions of NetWare, if you wanted to grant users access to a NetWare server, you had to set up user accounts for them on that server. With the directory, you give them directory privileges to access the server and volume objects. It becomes very easy to manage objects through use of the directory-access utilities.

SOAPBOX

Managing security in a large network can be tricky. You might, for example, grant user John Doe access rights to some part of the tree temporarily, but then forget to remove those rights when such privileges are no longer needed. Over a period of time, certain users can gather privileges that they really should not have, and can misuse those privileges.

As NetWare 4.0 development was coming to an end, this security concern was brought to my attention. It was recommended that Novell provide a utility that an administrator can execute periodically to get a detailed report on all privileges that any NetWare user (from any part of the network) has on a given part of the NDS tree. Another approach proposed was for the NDS software component of the NetWare server itself to "walk" the tree and plug any security loophole detected (at the option of the administrator) after posting a notice to that effect to the system administrator.

Unfortunately, both of these approaches remained just that—ideas. It is expected that Novell will provide such a utility subsequent to the shipment of NetWare 4.0.

Learning To Manage NetWare 4.0

In the final analysis, a network manager's job is easier and more efficient if certain things are done correctly. Even if things are not done perfectly, network management still can be secure and functional. The built-in structure and controls of NDS and the NetWare operating system as a whole help to make a reliable and secure networking environment.

A well-planned directory tree is probably the most critical part of managing a NetWare 4.0 network. Even if the best plan is not known to begin with, the management utilities and flexibility of NetWare 4.0 make it possible to mold, shape, change, update, and improve the security and structure of your network.

TIP

Although it is possible to change the NDS tree any time, the alteration of the NDS tree can cause objects to require new names. For instance, if you overhaul a tree with three levels to have four levels in its hierarchy, the names of objects at the bottom parts of the tree now have four components, as opposed to the previous three.

continues

> This can cause some configuration files on user workstations that contain references to objects in the tree (NET.CFG on DOS and Windows workstations, for example) to become invalid and cause the NetWare-resident NDS software on workstations to operate improperly. Users who are used to navigating the tree in a certain way now must deal with a new tree that requires them to browse differently. Users who are used to typing in their full names when they log in now must remember to type in their new names, caused by changes in the hierarchy of the NDS tree.

It is important for network managers to learn the NetWare Administrator GUI utility and the command-line and menu utilities, particularly if some clients are Windows users and others are DOS clients.

Network managers should monitor the performance of the network by using the server utilities and by getting feedback from the users. Analysis of the network-tree structure and partition replication and distribution can help performance.

Unless it is necessary to make changes, it is probably a good idea not to do so. Changes of convenience or personal preference should be avoided. If it is working, and no future implementations are required, do not do it.

When updates or changes are necessary, plan ahead. Notify all who will be affected by the change well in advance. Schedule the update to allow adequate time for directory synchronization to take place. Perform the changes during noncritical and low usage times. Check and test for desired results after changes are completed.

The NetWare 4.0 operating system offers a significant step forward for network managers. The flexibility and power of NetWare Directory Services and the utilities for management make it functional and amenable for expansion and growth. Network managers should find that NetWare 4.0 improves their control, flexibility, and efficiency in performing their duties and maintaining a smoothly running network.

Summary

This chapter showed you how to manage NetWare 4.0 as a NetWare Administrator. You learned about NetWare management tools, including the NetWare Administrator, menu utilities, and command-line utilities. Administrative functions, such as partition management, object management, and directory security, were also discussed. The chapter also gave you important management advice.

Symbols

1988 CCITT X.500 specifications, 139
1992 CCITT X.500 specifications, 139
80386 microprocessor, 8

A

abbreviations of names, 122
access, global, 151
access control list, *see* ACL
access rights, 150-151, 154
   administering Class F2, 142
   assigning, 340
   objects, NDS, 149
   verifying, 142
access-control schemes, 139
accessing compresses files, 180
account restrictions, 153
ACLs (access control lists), 147-149, 153
   object property, 150
   rights, 150-151
   rights mask, 149-150
across-the-wire upgrades, 302, 310-312
activating TTS, 173-175
Add or Delete Self rights, 150
addressing servers, 268
Admin object, 151, 292

ADMIN user object, 147
administering
   access rights, 142
   networks, 15-17
ADSP (AppleTalk Datastream Protocol), 230
algorithms
   LRU (Least-Recently Used), 166-168
   RSA MD-4 message digest, 159
aliases, 126
allocating
   blocks, TTS, 175
   memory, 93-95
      file-cache buffers, 167-168
   transaction nodes, 175-177
Alpha microprocessor (DEC), 17
APIs (Application Program Interfaces), 87, 135-136
   libraries, 225
   system auditing, 158
   TTS, 177
   TTSBeginTransaction, 176
   TTSEndTransaction, 176-177
   TTSGetApplicationThresholds( ), 174
   TTSGetWorkstationThresholds( ), 174
   TTSSetApplicationThresholds( ), 174
   TTSSetWorkstationThresholds( ), 174
APPC (Application Program to Program Communication) protocol, 228-229

Q-R

S

NetWare 4: Planning and Implementation
REGISTRATION CARD

NRP

Fill out this card to receive information about future NetWare books and other New Riders titles!

Name _____ **Title** _____

Company _____

Address _____

City/State/Zip _____

I bought this book because _____

_____

I purchased this book from:

☐ A bookstore (Name _____)

☐ A software or electronics store (Name _____)

☐ A mail order (Name of Catalog _____)

I purchase this many computer books each year:

☐ 1-5   ☐ 5 or more

I currently use these applications: _____

_____

_____

_____

I found these chapters to be the most informative: _____

_____

I found these chapters to be the least informative: _____

_____

Additional comments: _____

_____

☐ I would like to see my name in print! You may use my name and quote me in future New Riders products and promotions. My daytime phone number is: _____

New Riders Publishing 11711 North College Avenue • P.O. Box 90 • Carmel, Indiana 46032 USA

Fold Here

- -

New Riders Publishing
11711 North College Avenue
P.O. Box 90
Carmel, Indiana 46032
USA